The Death of Rural Engla

The recent foot-and-mouth catastrophe, the BSE outbreak and concerns over environmental pollution and factory farming have forced British townspeople to reform their attitudes to the countryside. Farmers' profits as well as their public image have severely suffered from these crises.

Alun Howkins' thorough survey is the first social history of twentieth-century rural England and Wales. He discusses the impact of the First World War on the countryside, the changing role of agriculture throughout the century and the expectations of the countryside from urban dwellers, offering an analysis of the role of the countryside in today's society. He examines the conflicts and problems associated with the countryside as both workplace and a space for recreation and leisure.

This well-researched survey will be welcomed by all those interested in agricultural and social history, also historical geographers and anyone interested in contemporary rural affairs.

Alun Howkins is Professor of Social History at the University of Sussex. His previous publications include *Poor Labouring Men* (1985) and *Reshaping Rural England* (1992). He wrote and presented a four-part history of agriculture for BBC2, *Fruitful Earth*, in 1999.

The Death of Rural England

A social history of the countryside since 1900

Alun Howkins

Routledge
Taylor & Francis Group

LONDON AND NEW YORK

First published 2003
by Routledge
11 New Fetter Lane, London EC4P 4EE

Simultaneously published in the USA and Canada
by Routledge
29 West 35th Street, New York, NY 10001

Routledge is an imprint of the Taylor & Francis Group

© 2003 Alun Howkins

Typeset in Perpetua by Wearset Ltd, Boldon, Tyne and Wear
Printed and bound in Great Britain by St Edmundsbury Press, Bury St Edmunds,
Suffolk

British Library Cataloguing in Publication Data
A catalogue record for this book is available from the British Library

Library of Congress Cataloging in Publication Data
Howkins, Alun.
   The death of rural England : a social history of the countryside since
1900 / Alun Howkins.
         p.   cm.
Includes bibliographical references and index.
   1. Country life—England—History—20th century. 2. Landscape—
England—History—20th century. 3. England—Social conditions—20th
century. 4. England—Historical geography. 5. England—Rural conditions.
I. Title.
   DA566.4 .H66 2003
   307.72′0941′0904—dc21

                                                            2002152298

ISBN 0-415-13884-1 (hbk)
ISBN 0-415-13885-X (pbk)

In memory of Ben, 1972–93

That is the land of lost content,
I see it shining plain,
The happy highways where I went
And cannot come again.

A.E. Housman

Contents

PART IV
What is the countryside for? Rural society, 1945–2001   161

Plates

Acknowledgements

Anyone who writes a book incurs huge debts – and I am no exception. I would like to thank all those who have given me help and access to materials and records in the past few years. Thanks then to the staffs of the East Sussex Record Office, the Cambridgeshire Record Office, the Northumberland Record Office and the Norwich and Norfolk Record Office. The staff won't remember but I was always treated with great courtesy and helpfulness. Thanks especially to the staff and the Rural History Centre at the University of Reading, the natural home of rural historians and the source of much material in the book, as well as the pictures. At Reading thanks particularly to Jonathan Brown in the archive, Caroline Benson in the photographic collection and the Director, Professor Richard Hoyle. Thanks also to the Trustees of the Mass-Observation Archive at the University of Sussex for allowing me to use materials held by them, and for facilitating the research on modern attitudes to the rural. As with all historians I owe a great deal to our (still) public libraries, especially the British Library and the library and staff of the University of Sussex. I also would like to thank the British Academy for a term's grant, which the University of Sussex made into a year and without which this certainly would not have been written.

There are also different, personal debts to friends, colleagues and students. During the past few years I have taught the history of twentieth century rural England in many different guises to many different levels of students. Thanks to them for listening to me, giving me ideas and, knowingly or unknowingly, shaping a lot of my thoughts. There are also individual colleagues and graduate students who I would like to thank for listening, arguing and giving of their own precious time. Thanks then to Pat Thane, Carol Dyhouse, John Lowerson, Brian Short, Nicola Verdon, Lara Phelan, Anne Meredith, Lucy Robinson, Toby Harrison, Tom Williamson and James O'Brien.

Finally there are personal thanks, which go that bit deeper. Ian Gazeley who has taught, talked and drunk with me while this book was written has been a huge support – even if he disapproves of the idea of the countryside! I owe a great debt to Paul Brassley. His knowledge of late twentieth-century farming and farm policy has been central to this book, as have his comments. Vicky Peters at Rout-ledge has supported the book she took over from an earlier editor with real understanding when things went wrong. Special thanks go to my comrade and friend Selina Todd, who took time from her own work to read mine with great care and sympathy — and correct it. Finally, and as so often before, thanks to Linda Merricks, who deep in a different academic world, always found time to listen about the countryside and to care about the book. In the end, and as always though, the fault is mine.

The author and publishers wish to thank the following for their permission to reproduce copyright material: Extract from *Slough* by John Betjeman from his *Collected Poems*, by permission of John Murray (Publishers) Ltd; XL from *A Shrop-shire Lad* by A.E. Housman, by permission of The Society of Authors as the Liter-ary Representative of the Estate of A.E. Housman.

Abbreviations

AHR	*Agricultural History Review*
CCRO	Cambridgeshire County Record Office
CPRE	Council for the Preservation of Rural England
EcHR	*Economic History Review*
EG	*Estates Gazette*
ESRO	East Sussex Record Office
EWP	*Eastern Weekly Press*
FW	*Farmers Weekly*
HWJ	*History Workshop Journal*
LW	*Land Worker*
MAFF	Ministry of Agriculture and Fisheries
MLE	*Mark Lane Express*
M-O	Mass Observation
NN	*Norfolk News*
NRO	Northumberland Record Office
PP	*Parliamentary Papers*
RH	*Rural History*
RHC	Rural History Centre

Introduction

There can be little doubt that the last 10 years have seen a profound crisis in both the rural areas and the agricultural industry. This crisis has been both material and ideological. The material crisis or, rather, crises are clear enough. Worries about environmental damage and factory farming, followed by a series of food scandals culminating in the horrible and sorry tale of BSE, were followed, in their turn, by the outbreak of foot-and-mouth disease in the spring of 2001. This took place against a background of falling farm profits from the mid-1990s, and a continued decline in rural services. The ideological crises are no less clear and closely related to the material ones. Centrally, public opinion towards the countryside and especially agriculture has changed significantly. Worries about the environment and many modern farm practices, fears about the quality of food, and a growing sense that a subsidised agriculture is simply protecting a rich and privileged group have all contributed to a much harsher public view of agriculture than in the past.

Against this the largely urban population of England and Wales continues to love the countryside, want to spend holidays in it, and ultimately live there. Between 1993 and 2000 the numbers of 'tourist trips' to the countryside increased by 50 per cent, while in 1995 a survey showed that 48 per cent of the population of urban England wanted to live in the countryside. However, what these visitors and 'incomers' want is often seen by the agricultural industry as being in conflict with the demands of farming. Complaints about the destruction of hedgerows and other environmental damage coupled with demands for access or the 'right to roam' cut little ice with farmers and landowners and are seen as evidence that the urban majority does not 'understand' the countryside.

With the exception of BSE few of these problems were new to the 1990s. What was different was the scale of the problem and the level of public debate around them. But there are real changes, many of them hidden behind the spectacular headlines about 'farming crisis', which mean that rural England and Wales changed more in the twentieth century than at any time since the agricultural revolution. However, that change was not apparent for much of the first 40 years of the century. Despite agricultural depression, the Great War and the beginnings of agricultural science and technology rural England and Wales retained many traditional features right up until the outbreak of the Second World War. Indeed, the economic plight of sections of agriculture in the years between the wars kept the countryside 'traditional' but discouraged investment and economic change. This was particularly true of upland areas, which suggests that the profound regional variation in farming and rural social structure, which characterised the nineteenth century, did not simply vanish with the dawn of the twentieth. Even in the 1950s there were areas of Wales and northern England where farming patterns and social and cultural patterns would have been familiar to a nineteenth-century inhabitant of the same region.

On the surface what change there was seemed to be more of the same. The numbers employed in agriculture, especially the numbers of farm workers, continued to fall, as did the contribution of the sector to Britain's economy. The spectre of the 'deserted village' with its cottages tumbled, its shops and pubs gone and its great house closed up and shuttered was as much a picture of the 1920s and 1930s as it had been of the 1880s and 1890s. Similarly, images of unused and wasted land gone to tares and docks occur in writers of the 1930s as they do in those of the 1900s. The market towns were also seen to be in decline, their local papers replaced by national dailies, their shops challenged by the new 'multiples' and their clubs and meeting halls replaced by the new cinema and radio. But again these complaints were old enough and the cause of decay – the attractions of towns and urban cultures – was familiar enough to William Morris or Henry Rider Haggard writing in the 1890s.

Yet there were different changes which, although barely visible in the first 40 years of the century, were there and were beginning to make their presence felt. The decline in population of rural areas began to be reversed as early as the 1900s, when sections of the urban elite began to move into the countryside to live, or at least spend their leisure. As a result, by the 1930s rural counties around London like Surrey had as many, if not more, white-collar workers as they had men and women working on the land. Also by the 1930s holiday making in rural areas had ceased to be simply the preserve of the elite and was spreading down the social scale. As a result the first clashes took place on the moors of northern England between those who sought the right to roam and those who held private property in land to be sacred. Gradually at first the town was coming back to the countryside.

Similarly, although agriculture as a whole was depressed in the inter-war period, there were areas, especially in dairying and even in some arable districts where things were at least reasonable. Here technical change was beginning to have an influence. Indeed, it has been argued that many of the technical and scientific advances, which made such a huge contribution to agricultural success in the 1950s and 1960s, had been available in the 1920s and 1930s.

In the conventional accounts it was the Second World War that changed all this. Wartime demand for food caused both the adoption of technical and scientific advances, and a shift in government attitudes which saw production subsidies as central to agricultural productivity and, indeed, to the very survival of the industry. While there is some truth in this it was really the post-war period, especially the 1950s and 1960s, which brought change, and even here it came unevenly. As important as technical change within agriculture was the rapidly changing nature of rural society in the same period. In the second half of the twentieth century population growth increasingly occurred in rural and semi-rural districts, which changed the character of the countryside forever. Equally important, the years after 1950 saw the erosion of the old tripartite social structure of rural England and Wales. Since at least the eighteenth century rural society had been divided into landowners, farmers and labourers. By the 1990s the farm labourer had all but disappeared. This meant that the few that remained were increasingly strangers in their own land and sought closer alliance with the farmers and even the landowners.

By the 1980s Britain was self-sufficient in temperate foodstuffs, and the post-war policy of subsidy seemed vindicated. Yet increasingly it seemed that the costs had been too high. From the 1960s onwards environmental movements developed a wholesale critique of modern agriculture, which was supported not only in the urban areas but also by those, now the majority of country dwellers, who lived in the rural areas but had nothing to do with farming as an industry.

This historical account goes a long way to showing not only how but also why the crisis, which is so apparent in the rural areas in the 1990s, came about. However, all such accounts, especially in a relatively short book like this, must be partial. The coverage is regionally uneven, although I do not think anywhere is completely lost. The coverage of Wales particularly comes and goes, but again I believe the story is clear. As a social history it perhaps concentrates on some aspects of country life more than others, and on different aspects at different times – but that is in the nature of the beast!

Finally a personal note. I was born in the country just after the Second World War. I remember horses in the fields; my father repaired some of the earliest combines. Like those quoted later in this book I remember when cows weren't all black and white and when corn fields were full of poppies. I literally saw the fields of my childhood turned into a housing estate. But I also remember low wages and houses without toilets or tap water. I have stood with a union banner while a family was turned out of a cottage, which had been their home for the best part of 20 years. So in a way this is the background to my own story – the land of lost content where '. . . I went and cannot come again' is my own past as well as the past of rural England and Wales.

Part I
'Blue remembered hills'
Rural society, 1900–21

1 The countryside in a new century, 1900–14

Rural England and Wales were, in 1900, countries of contrasts and of regional diversity. It was a land which presented a Janus face, with many elements of traditional and even backward agricultural practice and social structure, coexisting with others which were profoundly modern and efficient. This split personality was to continue to be a part of rural society well into the mid-twentieth century. It was only being resolved in the period after 1950 when a 'second agricultural revolution' based on the widespread use of chemicals and machinery finally gained the upper hand.

Conventionally, rural England and Wales has been divided into two great regions following the lines laid down by James Caird in 1852,[1] but long predating his description. Also, since the divisions were based in the first instance on climate, landscape and soil they still dominate the countryside of today.[2] Simply Caird divided England into an area south and east of a line drawn from the Scottish Border in West Northumberland to the Exe, which was lowland and largely arable, and an area north and west of that line which was upland and largely pastoral. In Caird's 'map' Wales is included in the upland zone, although there were areas of cereal production in Anglesey and on the southern coast. Caird also argued that these areas of England and Wales were dominated by different farming types. The north and west were areas of small farms and the south and east of large ones. To this we can add that the upland areas were, and are, areas of scattered homesteads dispersed across the landscape, while the lowland regions are characterised by village settlements.[3]

At the end of the nineteenth century, and even more at the end of the twentieth, we might wish to tinker with Caird's divisions, but they remain essentially the same now as they did in 1852. More importantly Caird's divisions conceal almost endless regional variations. A county as firmly southern as Sussex contains, as Peter Brandon and Brian Short have shown,[4] three or even four landscape types and settlement patterns, and this can be duplicated in many counties of England and Wales.[5] What is important to remember, and we will return to this often, is that these divisions were not purely spatial but also social, cultural and economic. In a very real sense, even in the mid-twentieth century, England and Wales were not only two nations but also many regions.

If the persistence of regional and landscape divisions can be seen as supporting the traditional face of Janus, one of the most distinctively modern aspects of England and Wales in 1900 was its population distribution. The 1901 census revealed that England, and to a lesser extent Wales, was firmly established as the world's first truly urban and industrial nation. In that year 77 per cent of the population of the two countries lived in urban areas and 23 per cent lived in the rural districts. In the 10 years before 1901 the rural population had declined by about 12 per cent. This followed a long-term trend. As the *General Report* of the 1921 census says, '[a]fter 1851, when the proportions were about equal, the urban element gained a definite lead which was rapidly and consistently increased in each decennium up to the year 1901.'[6] The urban nature of this population distribution was also reflected in the occupations of the people. Although there were still over 1.3 million men employed in agriculture in Britain in 1901 this made up only 11.5 per cent of the working population; while for women the figure was less then 1 per cent.[7]

Nevertheless, in most country districts in 1900 agriculture remained the main employer, although there were areas in the north and west of England and parts of Wales where coal mining and quarrying provided a working population that was distinctly non-agricultural. In addition there was a huge diversity of trades in the rural districts and in the county towns, but at the turn of the twentieth century these men and women usually relied on agriculture.

The numbers employed in agriculture in 1900 are a problem since certain categories, especially women, are clearly underestimated. There are two main reasons for this. First, the category of 'farmer's wife or daughter', clearly recognised as a working category in the census of 1851–71, was dropped in 1881 thus causing an apparently huge decline in the number of farmers and the obliteration of a whole working group.[8] While some wives and daughters of farmers did not work most did, a fact recognised by the reintroduction of this category in 1911. Second, the work of Nicola Verdon and Celia Miller has shown that the census constantly underestimated the numbers of women employed on farms in all capacities.[9] Finally, the number of 'landed proprietors' also had women removed in 1871 and then the category as a whole disappeared in 1881. It is however possible to produce some figures (see Table 1.1) which give a sense of the numbers working the land of rural England and Wales in 1901 divided into what Caird had called in 1851 'the three great interests connected with agriculture – the landlord, the tenant and the labourer.'[10]

The industry in which all these worked or drew a profit from was still, in the early 1900s, in a period of mixed fortunes, and nobody felt this mix more than the farmers. The whole idea of the farmer is in some ways a difficult one since it covered such a variety of men, women and holdings. As B.A. Holderness put it:[11]

The census category [of farmer] included capitalists occupying 2,000 acres and small holders with but 5 or 10 acres. . . . [After] 1851 farmers were readily differentiated only by the size of their holdings, but the diversity of agriculture was such that mere acreage was an inadequate indicator of social status.

However, for many farmers, whatever the size of their holding, the great profits and successes of the 'golden age of high farming', which stretched for the best part of 40 years from the late 1840s, came to an end in the 1870s and 1880s with the import of cheap cereals, especially from North America. To contemporaries, like Henry Rider Haggard, who toured rural England in 1901, it was a disaster. He wrote that 'the impression left upon my mind by my extensive wandering is that English agriculture seems to be fighting against the mills of God.'[12] Yet historians have argued since at least the 1960s that the 'Great Depression' in agriculture was essentially a regional phenomenon.[13] It hit most at those counties where cereals were grown in the south and east, and especially those areas, like the heavy clay lands of Essex, where input costs were high.[14] Aubrey Spencer, who visited the Denegie Hundred in northeast Essex for the Royal Commission on Labour in 1894, left a powerful descriptions of the area's decay.[15]

> The heavy clay land . . . is essentially a wheat producing district. . . . This part [of England] has suffered terribly by the agricultural depression – probably as much or more so than any other part of England. . . . A considerable amount of land is altogether out of cultivation. . . . A more melancholy sight from an agricultural point of view can scarcely be imagined than this part of the district presents.

But these farmers were, as Richard Perren points out, 'only a fraction of all British farmers, and even before the depression arrived cereals were only a small part of the total value of British agricultural output.'[16] Where other crops were

Table 1.1 The 'Agricultural Orders', England and Wales 1901–11

Year	Landowners	Farmers	Labourers	Total
1901	25,431*	475,633**	621,068**	1,124,701
1911	25,431*	383,333	656,337**	1,065,101

Notes
*These figures are those given at the last available date (1871). They are crude and clearly do not represent all landowners, only those who described themselves as such. But there is no reason to think they changed substantially during the period 1871–1931 or even later.
**These figures contain an element of adjustment, adding in an estimated number of women in these categories. The basis of the estimation is explained in Alun Howkins, *Reshaping Rural England 1850–1925* (London, 1992) p. 11.

produced, and even in areas, like Norfolk, where large cereal farms and good soils enabled farmers to carry the cost of the fall in price, things could and did look different. Put simply while the price of wheat, the basis of Britain's staple diet fell, wages remained stable. As a result working men and women had more money to spend on other goods including food such as dairy products, meat and even fresh fruit and vegetables, and so the sectors of agriculture producing these showed real expansion in the years after 1880. By 1913 nearly 75 per cent of gross agricultural output was accounted for by livestock products. Of these the most important was meat but the fastest growing was milk.[17] However, even more unlikely elements were beginning to emerge. By 1908 the total value of fruit, flowers, poultry and eggs made up 6 per cent of British agricultural output compared with wool, once a staple product, which made up only 1.7 per cent.[18]

What this meant was that the effect of the depression and indeed the speed of the recovery from it were profoundly regional – a theme we shall come across again and again in this book. Those areas or farmers who were able or willing to adapt weathered the worst of the bad years. In 1895 Mr Wilson Fox visited the Spalding district of Lincolnshire and saw an area of real prosperity.[19]

> In the neighbourhood of Spalding I made a somewhat exhaustive enquiry among some of the market gardeners. A great variety of vegetables, fruit and flowers are grown for the northern and London markets. The following produce is raised in this district: early potatoes, early cabbages, horse radish, carrots, celery, rhubarb asparagus, turnips, mangold and mustard seed, beans, peas, black and red currants, gooseberries, apples, pears, plums, greengages, cherries, bulbs . . . also violets. Strawberries are also grown at Long Sutton, this industry having been started by some Kent growers.

Such spectacular changes were often, as Joan Thirsk has written, 'modest, local efforts, which only the assiduous seeker in out-of-the-way places was likely to uncover'. Yet, as she continues, 'they expanded the frontiers of farming business . . . [and] in a positive frame of mind, their undertakers met and accepted the challenge of a changed situation in a fresh and constructive way.'[20]

The ability to adapt or change clearly affected how those who lived through the depression experienced its outcome, and this in turn depended, in part at least, on what part of England and Wales we are discussing. The north and west, already pastoral economies and often near the cities of the industrial revolution were, as T.W. Fletcher argued many years ago, virtually untouched by the depression.[21] For this reason these areas were able to build on that success and knowledge in the first part of the twentieth century, as were other areas in Yorkshire, Wales and even the English west country. Farmers near big towns in the south, especially around London, were able to switch to dairying or other alternative crops, as were the small holders of Evesham in Gloucestershire, Spalding or

Sandy in Bedfordshire, which had good rail links to the cities and towns of the industrial revolution. The market gardeners and plantsmen (and women) of Surrey and north Sussex benefited from the first waves of middle-class suburban-isation with its demand for garden plants, flowers and vegetables.

On the other side, the cereal farmers and even some who were producing livestock suffered, although this was not universal. The worst hit areas were those of marginal cereal lands, like Essex, which had relied on high prices and high inputs coupled with cheap labour to maintain profits. However, it is also clear from the experiences of the Scots, Welsh and west country migrants who took many of these farms between the 1880s and 1930s, and made a living from them, that the standard of life expected by many an English farmer was way beyond the means of his land, except in very good times.[22]

As the 1900s progressed a new kind of equilibrium began to appear in the agriculture of England and Wales. Some of the worst land went out of produc-tion altogether. 'In 1872', L. Margaret Barnett writes, 'the United Kingdom had 24 million acres under crops, or 51.3 per cent of the cultivated area. By 1913 this had shrunk to $19\frac{1}{2}$ million or 41.6 per cent.'[23] However, this loss of land tended to be piecemeal, in most areas, rather than whole districts reverting to thistles and scrub. Further, despite much press comment at the time, there were relatively few farming bankruptcies since reduced rents in arable areas cushioned many against the worst effects of depression.[24] Also the increase in dairying and other forms of 'alternative husbandry' meant that some at least continued to do well. By the late 1900s farming seems to have adapted well to the new patterns of demand and supply, even if it left the British consumer heavily reliant on imports. In 1911–12, A.D. Hall made three 'farming tours' through England and concluded: 'We must recognise that the industry is at present sound and prosper-ous. . . . To the man who takes the trouble to learn and attend to his business, farming now offers every prospect of a good return on his capital.'[25]

Most farmers in England and Wales in the 1900s were tenants – they rented their land. Landownership still remained firmly the prerogative of a few, for while many thousands held some land the vast majority of the land of England was still the possession of a small number of great territorial magnates. The only figures we have were from the 'New Domesday' of 1876, which listed all owners of land in Britain and revealed that just under a million men and women in England and Wales owned land. However, over 700,000 owned less than an acre. It was the work of the notably non-radical John Batemen that, by analysing this material, produced the clearest picture of the inequality of landownership in England and Wales. His *Great Landowners of Britain and Ireland*[26] analysed the data of the New Domesday and provided radical critics with the clear figure that about 7,000 families owned four-fifths of the British Isles. This group, especially the 'top thousand' who owned more than 10,000 acres and had incomes of more than £10,000 a year, constituted a class apart. As David Cannadine has written:[27]

During their heyday, and also in their century of decline (after 1880), the most important reference group for most notables was that they belonged – or had once belonged – to the British landed establishment. For most of the time, they had much more in common with each other (whatever their occasional and sometimes abiding differences) than with any other social group (whatever their occasional and sometimes abiding similarities).

Despite their power and wealth the agricultural depression affected the landowners more than any other group in rural society. On the highly successful Leicester estates in Norfolk rents fell by 45 per cent between 1878 and 1894. Even so the Earl of Leicester had farms 'in hand', and he believed that eight farms whose leases would be due for renewal in 1895–6 would not be renewed despite rent reductions of between 40 and 60 per cent.[28] In Lincolnshire, where there were more mixed farms, rents had been reduced by between 20 and 60 per cent; however, as Richard Olney points out, here, as elsewhere, 'net income fell even more sharply because landlords were not able to cut back their expenditure in proportion.'[29] It was this decline in rents that provoked Oscar Wilde's Lady Bracknell to quiz the hapless Jack Worthing about the sources of his income.[30]

LADY BRACKNELL: . . . What is your income?
JACK: Between seven and eight thousand a year.
LADY BRACKNELL (makes a note in her book): In land or in investments?
JACK: In investments chiefly.
LADY BRACKNELL: That is satisfactory. What between the duties expected during one's lifetime, and the duties exacted from one after one's death, land has ceased to be either a profit or a pleasure. It gives one position but prevents one from keeping it up. That's all that can be said about land.

Yet we should beware going too far down this line. In the upland regions rents remained stable and even, as on Lord Derby's Fylde estate, actually increased in this period.[31] Nor were the very greatest effected. The incomes of most of the 'top thousand' were derived as much from 'mines and docks, markets and building estates, and some, like the Dukes of Sutherland, also maintained massive investments in the Funds and railway shares.'[32]

Those who suffered worst in every county were those who relied entirely, or mainly, on agricultural rents, and these tended to be drawn from the 'lower' ranks of the aristocracy and from the gentry. As Richard Olney writes of Lincolnshire, rent reductions 'exaggerated the differences that had always been significant in rural society' between those who relied solely on rents and those who had other sources of income.[33] Those who did rely solely on rents, often the minor gentry, suffered badly, or even went to the wall, like F.W. Alix of West Willoughby Hall in Lincolnshire who let his house to a Captain Rennie and retired to the cheaper life of Brussels where he died in 1894.[34] In Norfolk the papers of the Rolfe family show a similar decline. During the eighteenth century they had been improving landlords and enclosers.[35] However a series of family problems in the mid-nineteenth century and a disastrous chancery suit depleted the family fortunes. As a result the family let their house and remaining land and lived in Italy and Germany. Eustace Rolfe, the head of the family, wrote in 1886 from Karlsruhe, 'I look upon my own exile from England as interminable now – At my age it is unlikely that things will ever take such a turn as will enable me to do anything else than vegetate here.'[36] The agricultural depression brought rent reductions of nearly 60 per cent on the Rolfe Estate and, on top of that, some tenants were in arrears with their rent. The final blow was the realisation that the new death duties introduced in 1894 would make the position of any heir untenable and the estate was finally sold in 1899.

The new death duties, although limited, were signs of what many in the aristocracy saw as a radical attack on their position. This seemed to be confirmed when, after the Liberal landslide victory in the General Election of 1906, parliament turned its eyes towards the enormous wealth of the largely Tory landed elite. In 1908 tenants' rights were strengthened and County Councils were given powers to compulsory purchase land for small holdings and allotments – a scheme that was mild enough but which, to some of the elite, seemed like the beginnings of radical land reform on the Irish model. The 1909 Budget augured worse to come with an Increment Value Duty and Undeveloped Land Duty. But worst of all was the rise to power of David Lloyd George. Lloyd George, who had cut his political teeth in struggles against English landlordism in Wales, had a deep and abiding hatred of the English rural elite. In July 1909 he used his key position as Chancellor of the Exchequer to make his famous speech at Limehouse whose language 'chilled' *The Times*, which accused him of launching a class war. 'Who is the landlord?', he asked his largely working class audience:[37]

> The landlord is a gentleman – I have not a word to say about him in his personal capacity – the landlord is a gentleman who does not earn his wealth. He does not even trouble to receive his wealth. He has a host of agents and clerks to receive it for him. He does not even take the trouble to spend his wealth. He has a host of people around him to do the actual spending for him. He never sees it until he comes to enjoy it. His sole function, his chief pride is the stately consumption of wealth produced by others.

Fears of a radical attack may have frightened some, but for most it provided an excuse to do what they wanted to do anyway. As F.M.L. Thompson points out, Lloyd George 'provided self justification for a course which had long seemed wise, the realisation of some of their landed assets so soon as the favourable market should appear.'[38]

From the late 1890s and certainly from the early 1900s that favourable market gradually appeared, and land sales increased dramatically in England and more noticeably in Wales. In Wales, a mainly pastoral economy, demand for land had remained high even during the depression. In addition a powerful movement based on small farmers was turning political attention against non-resident, English landowners. This resulted in the 1880s and 1890s in many of these landowners 'shedding' the Welsh parts of their estate. From 1910–14, as prices continued to rise, 'almost every major Welsh landowner whose territorial identity was mainly within the Principality began to dispose of parts of their estates.'[39]

The English market was slower, but after 1905–6 substantial areas of land began to appear on the English market, and by the summer of 1910, according to the *Estates Gazette*, some 72,000 acres were on offer in thirty-two English counties.[40] Three years later the same journal wrote, 'not for many generations has there been so enormous a dispersal piecemeal of landed estate as in 1911 and 1912, and the supply of ancestral acres in the provinces is apparently unlimited.'[41] Yet again though we need caution. For all the crocodile tears of loss, for all the cries of the 'break-up of the Great Estates', the top end at least of the rural landed elite was, as yet, barely challenged: as the lords of all they surveyed, they owned England. Their life style, with its round of house parties, the London season, shooting in Scotland and, increasingly, time on the French Riviera, at Biarritz or a fashionable German spa continued to be one of unparalleled luxury and ease. Their contacts with their estates and with the land which provided at least part of the income were, in many cases, increasingly symbolic, although it was a system of symbols which retained a huge power, and which would continue to do so for much of the twentieth century.

The landlords owned the land of rural England and Wales; the farmers managed it but men and women who usually had nothing to sell but their labour worked it. As was the case with the farmer the experience of those who worked the land was profoundly regional. Farm workers were divided not only by wages and by skill but also by the very way they lived. The most important divide was between those who hired by the 'term', 6 months or a year, and lived in or near the farmhouse where they worked, and those who hired by the week or even the day and lived away from the farm. This division was described as the difference between farm servants, those who 'lived in', and labourers, those who did not. On top of this there was a large group in most counties who held tiny bits of land who were hardly 'farmers' in the normal sense but who worked partly on their own land and partly for others.[42]

Living in farm service was most common in the northern counties of England: Northumberland, Durham, Cumberland, and Westmorland and also in Yorkshire and north Lancashire. In addition farm servants were present in thirteen other English counties.[43] Many historians have argued that 'living-in' farm service was virtually extinct by 1850. As Anne Kussmaul writes, 'service in husbandry did

not evolve into a new form of labour, it collapsed.'[44] However, this is a simplifi-
cation of a complex process. In fact farm service survived until the Second World
War or even later. Indeed in some areas, like the East Riding of Yorkshire and
the northeast Midlands, it even expanded in the nineteenth century.[45] There was
not however only one system of farm service, but three. In Northumberland and
much of the Scottish Border region, whole families hired by the year and lived in
cottages owned by the farmer and near the farmhouse. In the 1880s a government report wrote:[46]

> Each large farm represents a small colony in itself, with accommodation pro-
> vided for labour requirements for all but extraordinary occasions, such as
> hay and corn harvest, when extra labour, chiefly Irish, is employed. This
> concentration of labour is not only economical . . . but the work people are
> more or less under the influence and direct supervision of the employer.

Under this system all family members worked on the farm, indeed it was often a
requirement that wives, sons and daughters worked alongside the 'hind', the
usually male family head.

On most farms, young single men and women also hired by the year. These
single workers lived with other families or sometimes in the house of the
foreman. Bob Hepple's first hiring in 1905 found him living in the house of an
older, unmarried farm worker and eating with the farmer's family.[47] Sometimes
single workers like these were actually hired by a family head who could not
produce enough members of his own family to fulfil the needs of a 'hiring'. This
produced the best-known aspect of family hiring, the notorious (in the nineteenth
century) and over-romanticised (in the twentieth) 'bondager' system. At its most
basic this simply meant that every hired hind had to provide a female worker to
work with him. If she could not be found within the family he hired one. As Mrs
Brown, who was born near Wooler in 1876 said, 'Anybody that hadn't a woman
was hard to get hired . . . and if they had no women workers, well they could
hire one and take her to live with them.'[48] Judy Gielguid has argued convincingly
that bondagers had considerable freedom of hiring and that it enabled single
women to earn good wages on their own terms, something all too rare in the
experience of nineteenth- and twentieth-century rural women.[49]

The second group of farm servants was found in the East Riding of Yorkshire
and parts of the northeast Midlands. As in Northumberland and the Borders, the
remoteness of the farms from village settlements made living in a necessity, while
competition from industry kept wages high. The great difference here however
was that those who hired, although young and single, rarely lived in the farmhouse, but more normally with a foreman or bailiff and occasionally in a separate
building or room over the cart sheds. These young men were hired by the year to
work with horses, the key source of motive power on the great cereal farms of

the region. Two other features need to be stressed. First, living-in in these regions was not an ancient survival but the product of the agricultural revolution – it was a relatively new form. Second, living in was essentially restricted to young men. On marriage they quit the farm, and horse work, to work as labourers, or left agriculture altogether.[50] The young age of the workforce on these farms produced a culture very different from that of the Border regions – it was male and filled with many features of what we would now call a 'youth culture'.[51] At the hiring fairs and in the folk ritual the Plough Play, and occasionally in songs, the young men of these great farms demonstrated and acted out their identity as a group.

A similar system worked in some parts of Wales, and giving rise to similar complaints:[52]

> [the] single men . . . take advantage of their freedom from restraint by spending their evenings until very late elsewhere, or by crowding together into the sleeping rooms of different farms alternately and there spending hours in boisterous talk and revelry.

Also in Wales, especially in the north, married men lived in on some farms.[53]

> One thing, almost peculiar to the district, is that very many married men often work on farms at a distance of from 5 to 15 miles from home, and they only come home occasionally to their families, according to the distance – once a fortnight, or a month, or twice in six months.

The third form of living in farm service was 'classic' farm service, in which one or two sons or daughters of social equals, often other small farmers, lived for a time with a different family and 'learnt a trade'. This was essentially a survival of the early modern notion of the 'servant in husbandry' whose decline is so well addressed by Kussmaul. Nevertheless, it was by no means extinct, especially on the small farms of the upland regions, Wales and the Welsh Borders, parts of Devon and Somerset and even the High Weald of Kent and Sussex as a minority form of hiring. This form was seen by many as a first step on the farming ladder. In Wales, for instance, David Pretty writes 'many' small tenants had 'climbed from the position of agricultural labourer having served their time as servants.'[54]

The system of living in farm service was alive and well in 1914 although it was changing. Hiring Fairs, in particular, were becoming less important as actual points of employment, replaced by written contracts and advertisements in the local press. As early as 1904 it was said that the Alnwick Hirings in Northumberland 'are nearly a dead letter now'. This was mainly 'due to farmers getting their wants supplied by means of advertisements in the newspapers'.[55] Nevertheless, workers and their families continued to attend in large numbers, claiming their

Plate 1 Southern England *c.*1910. English agriculture at its most labour intensive. The numbers employed on the land were to drop throughout the twentieth century but scenes like this remained common until the 1940s. (Reproduced by kind permission of the Rural History Centre, University of Reading.)

'days' of holiday and pleasure. This practice, as is clear from the farm records of the Rutherford family of Dinnington in Northumberland, continued at least until the late 1920s.[56] While the numbers of small farms held up in the upland areas there was always space for hired men and women, and even in 1939 *Farmers Weekly* could complain about the high wages being demanded at the Cumberland Martinmas hirings.[57] Similarly, Stephen Caunce has argued for the continued vitality of living-in in the East Riding well into the inter-war period.[58]

Although living in farm servants were a regionally important group, in most of arable England the land was worked by men and women who hired for much shorter periods, and who lived away from the farm where they worked in villages or small towns. These were the more familiar figures of the 'farm labourer', and they made up about 80 per cent of those who worked the land of England and 40 per cent of those who worked the land of Wales. Again this group was divided regionally, particularly by the kind of farm on which they worked, and by skill. These factors determined wages, conditions, hours and, above all, regularity of work. In general terms those who earned the best money and were most regularly employed were men (and it was usually men) in charge of animals. However, even here regional trends were dominant. Wilson Fox noted that in the largely arable eastern and southern counties weekly hiring was the norm, even where men were in charge of animals, while in the mixed or pastoral western and Midland counties longer hirings were more common. Only the shepherd, an increasingly rare figure outside the far North and Wales, was always hired by the year.[59]

Work with animals also gave better pay and greater status. In arable areas there was a strict hierarchy among those who worked with horses, starting with the senior man (head ploughman or team man) who was the most skilled and usually the oldest, and moving down through second, third and so on to the lowliest of all, 'the boy'. The role of the head team man or head ploughman was ambiguous. He often acted as a foreman, setting the speed of work, arranging who did what jobs and using his skills to cut the first furrows in a field or carry out particularly difficult tasks. On the other hand he often acted as a kind of unofficial spokesman for the rest of the horsemen.[60]

In the mixed and pastoral areas no such obvious figure emerges, although the head dairyman often oversaw a number of workers and could have a similar role to that of the head horseman. In pastoral and arable areas men in charge of animals got extra payments both in money and in kind.[61] These varied enormously from region to region. Horsemen, and those in charge of cattle, often had to look after animals on Sundays and they were paid for that. Men rearing animals, especially prize animals, often got a part of any prize, and extra payments for especially good beasts. Often horsemen and head dairymen got a cheap or free cottage tied to the job and sometimes on or near the farm.

All ranks of the farm labour force were subject to variations in wages by region. In the northern districts, where there was competition from industry for workers, wages were considerably higher than in the south. The exceptions here were the counties immediately around London where, by the mid-1900s, it was becoming very difficult to get men to work on the land. Wages and earnings (wages plus allowances in kind and other payments) are always difficult to assess, but some figures from Wilson Fox's 1905 survey can give an indication of regional differences. In 1905 a horseman in Northumberland could expect to earn about 21s a week, while in Oxfordshire or Dorset the same man would earn only 16s per week, nearly 25 per cent less. The figures are identical for men in charge of cattle. 'Rank' also made a difference. In the case of adult 'ordinary labourers' the average earnings per week in Northumberland were about 20s, while in Oxfordshire the wage was 14s.

Earnings for adult males in the arable counties are clear enough, even if Wilson Fox's figures are a little optimistic, but the question of earnings, conditions and even extent of women's labour, north and south, is a much more complex one. As we have already seen in the Borders regions women were employed as part of the family group, and as bondagers. They were also employed, as they were in the other areas of farm service, as individual workers in the farmhouse and on the farm. This latter distinction, between domestic work on a farm and farm work, is a particularly difficult one to unravel. It is clear, as we shall see below, that even in the 1930s it was difficult to draw a line between domestic and farm work in the case of those employed on the farm. In 1900 it was no easier. In the case of women working on the land the question is no less difficult. It is clear that the number of women employed in agriculture was underestimated by successive censuses. In addition the moral arguments that fieldwork was 'unfit' for women had from the 1870s put pressure on farmers and workers alike to reduce women's field employment. Finally, quite what constitutes full-time work is a problem. Even given all that, there can be little doubt that the number of women employed in agriculture in the 1900s was considerably lower than it had been in 1850, and that probably their numbers had fallen faster than those of men.[62] But to say, as Wilson Fox did, that outside the Borders, 'there are no counties in England where the employment, for wages, of women at ordinary work in the fields is a general custom,' is clearly an exaggeration.[63]

Rural social structure which was, in the 1900s, still dominated in economic and social terms by these three great groups, labourers, farmers and landowners, also showed the Janus face with which we started this chapter. In some ways it was still deeply traditional and local, but in others it was experiencing the beginnings of real transformation brought about by national, and even international changes, well outside its internal control.

Looked at from the point of view of 'continuity' and tradition we can find much, in the social and economic structure of the countryside and the patterns of power and authority in 1900, which would support the popular view that these were the last golden years of the old era. For many country people the world was still a profoundly local place, with fixed social and geographical boundaries and institutions which appeared unchangeable. Despite 50 years of rural immigration to the towns, those who stayed in the country areas lived in what were still small and remarkably self-sufficient worlds. Most villages had a shop and a pub for basic needs. Even in remote upland areas weekly or fortnightly visits by higglers (small traders), tallymen and travelling carts provided a range of goods for sale or barter like the ones described by Mrs Murray from the Kielder area of Northumberland: 'Two carts came up on a certain day and they met them at Kielder Hill Foot, taking the butter and eggs down and coming back with their groceries if they wanted.'[64] Few areas of lowland England and Wales were more than 10 or 12 miles from a town or at least a large village usually connected by weekly carrier's cart. By the 1900s such towns offered a wide range of shops and goods as local directories show. In the late 1890s Hingham, a large village of 1,500 people in Norfolk, boasted tailors, fishmongers, butchers, dress makers, a bank, boot and shoe makers, grocers, a watch and clock maker, corn flour and seed merchants, an ironmonger and photographer, a dozen public houses and two friendly societies.[65] Annually larger towns and even cities offered post-harvest treats. Literally thousands flocked to St Giles Fair in Oxford, Tombland Fair in Norwich, or the great northern hiring fairs every autumn.

These local worlds were reinforced by the apparent permanence of their institutions, especially the Church of England. Yet looking at this very institution the problems of a purely traditional view of rural society begin to appear. Throughout the nineteenth century the Church had been closely identified with the rural elite, but in the 1850s and 1860s a new generation of committed clergy and a revival within the Church had gone some way to at least bringing it in touch with the poor. As E.N. Bennett wrote in 1913:[66]

> The vitalising influence of the Oxford Movement . . . left its mark also on our rural parishes. The improved discipline of the Anglican Church . . . has at least helped to weed out many notorious cases of worthless clergymen . . . while infinitely greater care is exercised in Church patronage than was the case fifty years ago. Services are brighter and more numerous, and the connection between the Church and the social and intellectual life of the parish becomes daily more close.

Yet in terms of numbers, Anglicanism had done little more than hold its ground in the years after the 1870s, and E.N. Bennett estimated that probably only about 30 per cent of the population of rural Oxfordshire attended religious worship on a regular basis, and that most of these were nonconformists.[67] Not that the nonconformists were doing that well. Although there were probably more active nonconformists than Anglicans at the turn of the century, even their numbers were beginning to decline. The old power of the wayside Bethel, for generations of countrymen and women a spiritual home and a political training ground, was beginning to fail.

The reasons for this failure are many, but central was the growing 'respectability' of Chapel. In the 1870s, in much of England and Wales, to be a nonconformist was to take a radical political stand. By the 1900s this was no longer obviously the case. 'Everywhere Methodists grow rich' John Wesley had lamented in the 1780s; by the 1900s that was palpably so in many areas of rural England and Wales. As George Edwards, the agricultural trade unionist, wrote in 1895:[68]

> I will admit at once that nonconformists have not moved along so very fast these few years . . . and that they have far too much ignored the fact that Christ came to redress social wrongs as much as to prepare the way for a higher life.

A movement that had been on the outside of rural life in the nineteenth century had, by the twentieth, become almost a part of the rural establishment. Even if village nonconformity in England and Wales was not rich it had powerful secular interests. Business connections were reinforced by marriage within the chapel to create chapel families and chapel employment networks.

As the twentieth century progressed the chapel moved further and further away from direct involvement in politics and insisted more and more on the spiritual side of religious life. Religious belief became 'increasingly regarded as an individual, even private matter, of no concern to other people'.[69] None of this is to suggest that religion ceased to be an active social force in the rural areas – clearly it did not. Nor is it to suggest that all Anglican clergymen or nonconformist preachers cared little for the rural poor and the social problems of rural areas. Even in the 1950s and 1960s many a rural trades unionist proudly proclaimed his Methodist origins. In the Anglican Church, figures like the remarkable Rev. Conrad Noel of Thaxted in Essex combined the revival of English village life, complete with Morris dancing and folk song, with Marxism and rural trades unionism. And always there were many decent but unsung village priests and ministers who cared for and identified with the poorest of their parishioners and carried on the best traditions of their faith in rural areas. However, they remained an increasingly marginalised minority in most villages.

The declining power of organised religion in the villages and towns of the countryside was in part paralleled by a decline in the power of the aristocracy as a social and cultural force. Declining rent revenues meant that their ability to sustain charitable gifts and a high profile public show were severely challenged, especially among the smaller landowners. By the 1900s many of the larger landowners owned houses in many different counties, in London and on main-land Europe. They moved in an international as well as a national elite. This meant that their fabled and long mythologised special relationship with their estates and with the countryside was stretched almost beyond belief. Despite the frequent, and widely publicised, celebrations of the birth of an heir, the majority of an elder son or the wedding of a family member, sometimes involving the lowliest of estate workers, these were, most often, the mere carnivals of social order. The day-to-day running of these great estates, and many smaller ones, rested formally in the hands of stewards, bailiff and agents.

In addition, their real political power in the countryside had declined. The extension of the franchise to the country worker in 1884 doubled the size of the electorate from just above 3 million men to just under 6 million, while further legislation in 1885 abolished more than 150 small borough seats throughout the British Isles. These measures combined to severely curtail aristocratic power in British national politics. In future in rural England, and especially in Wales, landed magnates had to work much harder than before to maintain their once dominant position.[70] This national dominance was further accentuated by changes at local level. By the end of the century many great territorial magnates held positions in local society which were little more than titular. The office of Lord Lieutenant of the County had lost most of its practical significance after local government reform in 1889. In practice key local government roles, particularly serving on the bench of magistrates and attending quarter sessions, had, even before reform, tended to be performed by the conscientious rather than the simply great. In Cheshire in 1853 there were 556 justices in the commission of the peace but only 176 had taken the oath (which enabled them to act). Strik-ingly, although the number qualified rose by the end of the century, much of the expansion was in the urban areas of the county.[71] In this situation, Lee argues that by the eve of reform 'government by Quarter Sessions . . . was in fact rule by a class of successful business people presided over by the great landowners' retain-ing only 'the appearance of government by the landed gentry'.[72]

It is often argued that the creation of elected county councils had little signifi-cance since those elected were essentially the same as the old non-elected quarter sessions, which made up county government before 1889. However true that was in 1889 it was simply not the case, in some counties at least, by the 1900s. Norfolk County Council, for example, had a dozen 'radical' or Liberal members by 1900; many of them farm workers in origin at least. Even in 1889 six men described as 'workingmen's candidates' had been elected to the Shire Hall.[73] Norfolk cannot 'speak for England' and as a radical county it is in some ways exceptional. Nevertheless, over England as a whole nearly 50 per cent of those elected in 1889 were non-magistrates, that is they were 'new' county politicians. In Wales the results reflected the growing friction between Welsh farmers and labourers and their usually English landlords and, as Cannadine says, 'Almost everywhere, the gentry and the grandees were rebuffed and humiliated. For it was these local elections, that marked the end of patrician ascendancy.'[74]

These changes were even more apparent with the creation of Parish and District Councils in 1894. Although their subsequent history was to show they had little real power these councils were seen at the time as earth shattering. The Liberal/radical paper the *Eastern Weekly Leader* considered theses elections as 'Emancipation Day in Rural England . . . the democratic curfew will ring out the vestiges of feudal power and ring in the new era of self-government.'[75] To an extent the results of the first elections justified this view. As Patricia Hollis writes:[76]

> Across the country as a whole, the *Contemporary Review* calculated in 1895 that between a third and half of the seats were won by farmers, about a quarter by craftsmen, and most of the rest by labourers, with a sprinkling of clergy, gentry, professional men, Nonconformist ministers and women.

The last group, women, also points to another change. Under the 1894 Act, women, where they were ratepayers, could vote, as could married women who owned property distinct from their husband's. Women could stand for election to Parish and District Councils as they already could to school boards. It is possible that as many as 200 women were elected to the new Parish councils in England and Wales in 1894.[77]

This change literally beat on the door of traditional politics and social control, but they were also signs of a broader change. The continuing decline in numbers willing to work the land meant that by 1900, probably for the first time for a hundred years, there were labour shortages even in the arable counties of the south and east. Men and women found their labour at a premium and were less concerned to touch their forelocks than they had been in earlier years. In 1900, the farm labourer used his vote in many rural areas to go against the national trend towards the Conservatives despite the Boer War. In nine out of seventeen rural East Anglian constituencies the Conservatives' share of the poll dropped between 1895 and 1900, and they actually lost South West Norfolk. In the rural seat of the South Midlands their vote dropped in 14 out of 15 seats. In 1906 these minor changes became a rout. In almost every county of England and Wales the Conservatives lost the popular vote to the Liberals. In the rural areas of the South Midlands, only one seat, Mid-Bucks, returned a Conservative and they lost North Bedfordshire, both Berkshire seats, North Buckinghamshire, Gloucestershire East, Huntingdon, North and South Northamptonshire, and all the seats in Oxfordshire. In East Anglia not a single county seat returned a Conservative in 1906. In Wales not a single Conservative was returned for a rural district in 1906.[78]

A less deferential rural working class found other expressions in the first few

Plate 2 The new country worker, station staff, Radstock, Somerset, 1910. Throughout the first fifty years of the twentieth century the railwaymen were modernisers bringing the town to the country, and linking the rural working class to different traditions of organisation and politics as well as respectability. (Reproduced by kind permission of the Rural History Centre, University of Reading.)

years of this century. Rural trades unionism, a powerful and almost millennial movement of the 1870s, had vanished finally and bitterly in the mid-1890s even in its heartland, East Anglia. However, in 1900 there were signs of revival and, in 1906, a 'new' farm workers' trade union was founded at North Walsham in Norfolk. It spread slowly at first, and only in the eastern counties, but by 1913 it had a place in many rural areas. In that year the new union fought its first successful strike in the Ormskirk region of south Lancashire where there were over 2,500 union members, nearly half the Union's total membership. The strike was swift, and won largely because of the support of a new kind of rural worker – the railwaymen. The National Union of Railwaymen supported the strike by refusing to move farm produce out of the strike area. But they played a greater role than that in Lancashire and elsewhere.[79] Unionised, free from the threat of parson and squire, yet often the sons of farm workers, the railwaymen brought the first signs of a new culture into the countryside of England and Wales – a culture that also brought with it the first signs of labourism and socialism. In 1912 the new farm workers' union affiliated to the Trades Union Congress and in 1914 voted to affiliate to the Labour Party.[80]

There were other ways in which the urban world was taking on a greater and greater importance in the countryside in the years immediately before 1914. As rural England, or more accurately agricultural England and Wales, declined in economic and political importance so its representation in various cultural forms became more and more central to the construction of a national identity. It has been widely argued that from the 1880s and 1890s perceptions of a 'crisis' within urban areas led to a fundamental, and critical, reassessment of the process of urbanisation and industrialisation which, contemporaries believed, had been characteristic of the nineteenth century.[81] In this reassessment the urban in particular was found wanting. Urban life, and particularly London life, it was argued, had led to the moral and physical decay of the English race, or rather the poorer part of it – the wealthy and great, it seems, were excluded from such decay. In 1899 Lord Walsingham, a Norfolk landowner, wrote to Henry Rider Haggard:[82]

> I think you will admit that the city breeds one stamp of human beings, and that the country breeds another. They may be a little sharper in the towns, but after all it is not mere sharpness that has made Great Britain what she is, it is the thews and sinews of her sons which are the foundation of everything. . . . Take the people away from their natural breeding and growing grounds, thereby sapping their health and strength in cities such as nature never intended to be the permanent home of men, and the decay of this country only becomes a matter of time.

These ideas were given added impetus by the Boer War, and the revelation that many volunteers were physically unfit for military service. As Kipling wrote in his poem 'The Islanders' of 1902:[83]

> Yet ye were saved by a remnant (and your land's long suffering star)
> When your strong men cheered in their millions while your striplings went
>   to the war.
> Sons of the sheltered city – unmade, unhandled, unmeet –
> Ye pushed them raw to the battle as ye picked them raw from the street.

The solutions proposed to this problem all centred around the 'revaluation' of country life. It was argued that England (and to a lesser extent Britain as a whole) was 'naturally' a rural society and it was necessary for the nation to return to these roots if the decay of national life was to be reversed. This revaluation took many forms, ranging from the rediscovery of British traditional music and folklore to garden cities; from schemes for peasant proprietorship to the invention of a vernacular style in architecture. All were concerned with making the link between national identity and rural Britain.[84] The extent to which this was a uniquely British response is debatable, and does not really concern us here. More important is the extent to which these feelings spread, particularly into the middle and even upper working classes.

In the years before the war these concerns with countryside and national identity had largely rested with the mainly urban elite. Commissioning a 'Tudor-bethan' house by Lutyens, with a garden by Gertrude Jekyll, was well outside the possibilities of all but a tiny minority. Nevertheless these ideas were spreading downwards. The Clarion Movement brought socialism and the open air to the self improving working classes through cycling and rambling, as did the first 'holiday camps' like that set up at Ormsby near Great Yarmouth by Fletcher Dodds in 1906.[85] Similarly, the folk dance and folk song movements, linking the performance of traditional music and dance to national identity, spread their influence – by 1914 Cecil Sharp had persuaded the Board of Education to use folk songs as the basis of teaching music in elementary schools.

This vision though was a particular one. It was not all England which could be seized in this way but only parts. The landscape of Englishness, in stark contrast to the landscape of Romanticism, was a southern landscape – the world of village England. Other parts could be incorporated, the Welsh Borders, for example, with their half timbered houses and Houseman poems. Even parts of the bleak landscapes of East Anglia could find a way in – but the wild, the rugged and the desolate could not. England was a farmed land, a land of churches and greens, of black and white buildings and neat hedgerows. Above all it was a worked and a peopled land – it had to be if the 'race' both had its roots and its rebirth there. But it was also a particular social order – that of the paternalist squire, the ruddy-faced tenant farmer and the loyal worker bound together in a pre-class unity of devotion to the soil. Thus not only were the social Darwinist fears of racial decay confronted but the spectre of class struggle and industrial unrest was banished.

This points to the very unreality of this vision. It was an urban, and before 1914, still a middle-class ideal which had little if anything to do with a country-side which was changing, albeit unevenly. When rural England and Wales went to war in 1914, it still had many traditional social and cultural parts to its character. The old order of landowner, farmer and labourer was shaken in some areas but never broken, except perhaps in Wales. There had been changes in agricultural production, but agriculture's methods were far behind those of the New Worlds of the USA, Canada and Australia which were more and more setting the pace and controlling the market, especially for cereals. Above all the countryside remained firmly regional in its loyalties just as much as its dialects, and this was based on real differences in social and geographical structures. In the national economy agriculture and the countryside still had a place, but it was a place increasingly, and at first unknowingly, circumscribed by the town. In 1914 John Bull was still a farmer – but only just.

2 The Great War and its aftermath, 1914–21

Rural England and Wales confronted two problems on the outbreak of war on 4 August 1914. The first was common to the whole nation – the raising of a volunteer army. The second was peculiar to agriculture – the need to feed the country at war. The relationship between these was to dominate rural life and rural policy until the early 1920s. The relationship was a difficult one because the demands of recruiting could actually work against the needs to increase agricultural output in an industry which was largely unmechanised and thus relied to a great extent on hand labour.

Initially the idea that agricultural output needed to be increased was by no mean universally recognised. Although in 1914 Britain relied on imports for about 80 per cent of its wheat and 40 per cent of its meat it was widely assumed in government and in the industry that war would not disrupt these supplies to any extent. In the immediate pre-war years the possibility of blockade had been discussed, but belief in the invincibility of the Navy led the Committee on Imperial Defence to conclude in February 1914 that 'by maintaining a general control of sea communications this country should in the future as in the past, be able to bear the exhausting consequences of war'.[1] The president of the Board of Agriculture, Lord Lucas, repeated this view on 4 August when he told the House of Lords that there was 'no occasion whatever for public alarm over food supplies.'[2]

To begin with at least, these optimistic forecasts were right. The pre-war switch back to cereals on good lands continued and the yield at harvest 1914 was slightly up.[3] In 1915 the situation was better still. Increased prices, especially for wheat, meant that farmers planted more and the harvest showed an increase of 20 per cent in wheat and 8 per cent in oats. There were problems, however, since little of this was new land and the increase had been met by switching from barley. Worse still, it became clear by 1916 that many farmers had omitted the root break in the traditional rotations, causing a long-term decrease in productivity. Also in 1916, for the first time, overseas supplies began to fail. The harvest of that year was bad all over North America, while the loss of grain imports from the Black Sea areas of Russia, Turkey and Romania, caused by Turkey's alliance with the Central Powers and the closure of the Dardanelles to allied shipping made the situation worse. Finally in the winter of 1916–17 the German U-boat campaign in the North Atlantic began to take a serious toll of shipping. In the autumn and winter of 1916, for the first time, the food supply situation looked serious.

'Business as usual' may have been, as Peter Dewey argues, 'the experience of the farming industry in the first half of the war',[4] and in many ways that was the case throughout the rural community. There was certainly a rush to the colours in rural areas as there was in towns, yet many farm workers found a clash of interest between the needs of harvest or the care of animals and the demands of war. As 'Billa' Dixon from Trunch in Norfolk remembered:[5]

> We were always two or three days nearly longer than anyone else on a big farm . . . we were always three week three days or a month . . . then the war come on just as we started harvest, on the 4th of August, and so I joined up, soon as we finished harvest. They were calling for volunteers, and several of us in the village, I should think about 10 of us, went that morning down to Mundesley and joined up, took the shilling.

Recruitment in rural areas relied heavily, at least in the first months of the war, on appeals to the traditional 'values' of country life and social structure. What Keith Grieves writes of Sussex could easily apply to many counties.[6]

> In August 1914 the landowning social and economic elite of Sussex envisaged a central role in the county's preparations for war . . . predicated on the belief that the paternalistic model of social relations had a relevance beyond the bonding of rural society – involving notions of privilege, duty and responsibility – to the process of transforming Sussex into a county at arms.

The rural elite used both their control of the pre-war Territorial Forces, through their roles as officers and honorary patrons, and their position as landowners, parsons and even farmers to urge men into the ranks.[7]

> Landowners frequently selected likely men from among their servants and farm labourers and transported them to the nearest recruiting office. Lieutenant-Colonel A.C. Borton, who owned an estate at Cheveney in Kent and was a local Justice of the Peace, drove his butler, footman and cowman to Maidstone Barracks to enlist. . . . The Royal Berkshire Regiment included one platoon of butlers and footmen and another composed almost exclusively of gardeners and workers from a peer's estate.

This paternalism, at least at the beginning of the war, worked both ways. In

September 1914 the Norfolk Chamber of Agriculture agreed 'to keep open the places of all those employees who have joined the forces of the King'.[8] In Sussex the Marquess of Abergavenny guaranteed housing 'for the duration' for those who fought, while Lady Margaret Duckworth opened a Post Office Savings Bank account for every man who enlisted.[9] However, such schemes were unusual. As Grieves writes, 'few landowners in Sussex publicly committed themselves to compensating estate workers whose army pay was insufficient to provide an adequate income for their family.'[10] As the war dragged on paternalist pressure to enlist became a source of real grievance and Sasson's bitter lines, 'Squire nagged and bullied till I went to fight/(Under Lord Derby's scheme) I died in Hell — (They called it Passchendaele)'[11] found real echoes time and again in the lives of countrymen and women.

Some went to war for economic reasons. In the rural areas the approach of winter threatened many casual and even some full-time workers with the prospects of unemployment, while in the towns the new Labour Exchanges encouraged the unemployed to enlist.[12] A Private's pay of 6s 8½d a week was less than farm workers earned even in the poorest paid districts, but it was regular, and separation allowances were paid to wives and mothers even if they were slow in coming. However, for most countrymen who joined the New Armies it is clear that a vague patriotism, personal or collective, was the main motive for enlisting. Their feelings were often inarticulate and low key once the shouting died down and, as Peter Simkins points out, their actions were often more considered than the mythology of 1914 suggests. 'Less than one-third of all volunteers were involved in the first rush to the colours in August and September 1914,' which suggests 'a sense of duty and obligation rather than missionary zeal'.[13] George Hewins, who left a life of irregular casual employment in and around Stratford-on-Avon, put it neatly and clearly. 'If you'd asked me why I was going to fight I'd have said, "To save the country". If the Germans won we would be slaves!'[14]

More striking was the fact that the services were now recruiting from all sections of the working class. Before 1914 the army was all too often seen as the last refuge of those in social or moral disgrace. In contrast the New Armies were composed, at least according to contemporaries like V.W. Germains, of 'decent self respecting, industrious working men', while Rudyard Kipling thought the New Armies so superior because the corrupting influence of old soldiers was absent in the new battalions.[15] No such problems confronted the rural elites for whom the Army had always been a respectable career. Officers' Training Corps at public schools and universities provided a military background for most of the rural elite, and even those who missed that found a home within the Territorial Forces. To these young men rural life provided the model for an officer's behaviour. Pre-war officers were, according to Keith Simpson, 'encouraged to follow the pursuits and life style of country gentlemen' and much of that ideal was carried over into the war.[16] To the young officers of the New Armies, especially those from the rural areas, 'my men' or 'my platoon' took on the resonance of 'my village' and 'my workers'. In return their men responded within the same framework of deference and paternalism. It can be no coincidence that two of the most powerful post-war accounts of the war, Siegfried Sassoon's *The Complete Memoirs of George Sherston*, and Edmund Blunden's *Undertones of War*, both function within a rhetoric of the rural.

As the men marched away, rural England slowly adjusted to the business of war. Here 'business as usual' concealed many changes which were at first unclear or even trivial but which were beginning, by 1916, to have real effects on rural society. Although many historians have argued that there was no real labour shortage, at least in the first years of war, this was by no means obvious to contemporaries. As a result employment patterns began to change, especially among women. Before the war the only real employment available to a young woman in the countryside was on the land or in domestic service. The former, as we saw in the last chapter, had been decreasing for decades before 1914 while the latter had been expanding.[17] As men joined up in both rural and urban areas new opportunities opened up for country girls, especially in urban areas and country towns where work had not only been considered 'unsuitable' before the war but also where most trades had been closed to women. In these new areas of employment wages were very good, especially to a countrywoman whose father probably earned about 14s a week in 1914. In Leicester in 1916 a young woman could earn 52s a week plus uniform and a week's paid holiday as a tram conductress, while 'unskilled' work in factories in the same town paid up to 40s a week. Although many of the new jobs were in the great conurbations of the north, many were not. Ransomes of Ipswich was only one of many regional agricultural engineering firms that switched to wartime production. In Warwickshire there were so many munitions factories that 'there was great difficulty in persuading females to take any kind of land work.'[18]

There were also changes for those women who stayed behind in the villages. Two sources of women workers were available. The most obvious were what contemporaries called 'village women'. However, there were a number of factors working against the recruitment of these women. For married women, at least until 1917, allowances to soldiers' wives and families kept up with inflation, and many families were better off than before the war. Additionally, billeting of soldiers provided valuable income in many areas. To single women, as we have already suggested, the urban areas provided higher wages than agriculture. Perhaps most importantly, for 50 years countrywomen had been told by their betters that fieldwork was unwomanly and demeaning, and that could not simply be reversed overnight. Further, in those areas where trade unions had been organised there was widespread opposition to women's work since, it was argued, it lowered men's wages. Even where Union spokesmen appealed for women workers they often got short shrift. When George Edwards, the President of the National Agricultural Labourers Union, spoke at a series of meetings in April 1916 urging women to work on the land, 'A Working Woman' replied in a letter to the press that he had better direct his advice to 'the middle-class and rich men's daughters' as 'some of them have never done a day's useful work in their lives.'[19] However, the government was beginning to act. In 1916 the County War Agricultural Committees were ordered to set up Women's War Agricultural Committees to register countrywomen who were willing to work on the land and put them in contact with farmers who needed labour. By the end of 1916 it was claimed that about 140,000 women were registered nationally. However, the reality was different. Although in theory about 72,000 women had received a certificate saying that they were 'as truly serving (their) country as the man who is fighting in the trenches or on the sea', and about 62,000 had received a 'bottle green armlet marked with a scarlet crown' to show that the wearer had done 30 days' approved service, only 29,000 women were at work under this scheme by harvest 1916.[20]

There was a second area of potential recruits. From at least the 1890s there had been attempts to encourage middle-class women into the 'lighter branches of agriculture', especially horticulture, dairying and poultry keeping.[21] This had been accompanied by the creation of the first women's agricultural college at Swanley in 1880, the creation of the Lady Warwick Hostel, which enabled women to study agriculture at Reading University from 1898, and the founding of Studley College in 1903. All these educational centres were aimed at the middle-class woman with the intention of training her to take a full place in, at least part of, agriculture. Early in the war various groups associated with this movement, most notably the Women's Farm and Garden Union, began both to organise volunteers and to urge on government the necessity of creating an organisation for channelling urban and middle-class women into the war effort on the land and using those women trained before the war to train others.[22] This came into being in 1916 as the Women's National Land Service Corps. By early 1917 the WNLSC had trained about 2,000 women on farms owned or run by sympathisers, at the pre-war women's colleges or at many of the 'county' agricultural colleges set up from the 1890s onwards.[23]

These volunteers, most of whom were middle class and urban, were seen by the WNLSC as having a leadership role. They were trained and skilled and were to train other women, act as forewomen or as recruiters. But in March 1917 a quite different group emerged – the Women's Land Army. This first appeal for recruits was designed to raise 10,000 volunteers; in fact it raised 30,000 and by July 1917 over 2,000 WLA members had been placed on farms. The WLA, as Susan Grayzel has argued, was aimed at 'educated, urban, thus presumably bourgeois women who were then supposed to serve as examples for rural women in local villages'.[24] Nevertheless, the WLA was not simply a showpiece. Its

Plate 3 The changes of war. Members of the Women's Land Army and soldiers in a hay field. Mrs F. Chambers who donated this photo wrote: 'I enclose Photo of some members of the Forage Corps taken with hay-baler during the war. This was taken in Essex in 1917. A friend of mine is on the left and it shows that women did their bit in the Great War as hay-baling was very hard work in those days.' (Reproduced by kind permission of the Rural History Centre, University of Reading.)

volunteers were well trained, had proper uniforms and were paid on a national scale of wages between 18s and 20s a week, not far off the national wage for male farm workers. They were also given extra payments for skills such as tractor driving or ploughing. Additionally, there can be little doubt that they were capable of doing the same work as the increasingly elderly workforce left on many farms.

Initially at least the WLA met with hostility from farmers, farm workers and many village women. Their dress, which included breeches, was a source of horror and much discussion. However, as Grazel writes, 'the "threatening" appearance of these new women on the land, in breeches and puttees, was carefully and deliberately feminised.'[25] More than that, the land girl was appropriated by the on-going debate on rural decline. Here were 'real' examples of what going back to the land could do, urban women 'saved' from the corruption of city life, who in turn 'saved the land and preserved the "Old English Countryside", while the soil of Britain redeemed women, creating a "new" robust yet gentle femininity.'[26]

By the end of the war, with 11,529 women working in a variety of farm jobs, the importance of women volunteers was clear to most in both urban and rural areas. However, perhaps even more important for rural women was another product of the last years of the Great War, the Women's Institute movement. Women's Institutes appeared in 1915 under the aegis of the Agricultural Organisation Society. In September 1917 they were given government support via the Women's branch of the Board of Agriculture and by 1919, when the board handed power over to the WI's National Federation, there were upwards of 1,200 Institutes. Recent scholarship, particularly work by Maggie Andrews, has stressed just how central the WI was to women's experience in the inter-war period by creating 'a women's support network within rural villages' which in turn 'was significant for confidence raising, and helped to challenge dominant perceptions of femininity'.[27] This was clearly recognised by Mont Abbot, a Cotswold shepherd, who, looking back on the war, called the WI 'the biggest revolution of all'.[28]

> Most Institutes in the village before the war had been clubs for working men. Women warnt supposed to club together on purpose. They'd congregate occasionally in the 'Bode of love', the little kitchen at the back of the pub. . . . But coming together on purpose, as a body, and calling themselves 'the WI' – well! . . . They was only doing what we men going to the pub had been doing for years.

Women members of the rural aristocracy and gentry were perhaps less affected by the war, although casualties among the men of the aristocracy were high. Lady Curzon wrote of the period 1914–15, 'there was scarcely one of our friends who did not lose a son, a husband, or a brother.'[29] Many great families, partly in response to these losses, as well as the deeply held patriotism of their class, gave up country and town houses as hospitals or convalescent homes for the wounded, often, like the Duchess of Rutland, taking on the role of 'matron' for themselves. Elsewhere wives and daughters of those who had enlisted ran the estates and farms. The Countess of Airlie wrote in her memoirs, 'my entire horizon was bounded by potatoes. Every vine house was stuffed full of them; even the little hut at the back of the gardens was stacked with potato boxes from the floor to the roof.'[30]

Elsewhere within the elite the concerns were more prosaic and more selfish. Aristocratic and gentry encouragement of servants to enlist, and conscription after 1916, led to a servant shortage. In March 1916 May Harcourt's chauffeur was called up and her butler became ill. 'I have a load of domestic worries but no doubt will weather the storm somehow! It is a gt. bore losing one's Butler, as somehow it is the last male servant one expected to be bereft of.'[31] At Goodwood in Sussex the indoor staff dropped from over twenty in the pre-war years to twelve in 1917, of whom only three were male.

As with the middle and the working class it was the young women of the elite who saw most change during the war. Joan Poynder told Thea Thompson in the

1970s that she had 'a passion for independence . . . and I knew that I wasn't going to get much in the pre-war days except through marriage. . . . But luckily I got it immediately by pretending I was much older and going in for nursing.'[32] Nevertheless London social life continued, indeed took on a more frenetic tone, in some bizarre reworking of 'an anthem for doomed youth'. Both Venetia Stanley, youngest child of Lord Sheffield, and Lady Diana Manners managed to 'come out' in full Debutante style during the war and lead full social lives.

The background against which these changes in women's position were taking place was also undergoing a transformation. Alongside the bad harvests in the British Isles and North America a series of crises in 1916 had led first to a coalition government and then to Lloyd George becoming Premier. 'Business as usual' in agriculture and elsewhere came to an end. In agriculture this was signalled by the arrival of Rowland Prothero, later Lord Ernle, as President of the Board of Agriculture. Prothero was an historian as well as an agriculturalist, who believed that Britain's agriculture needed state support to return it to the position it had been in in the 1870s. His arrival marked the beginning of an organised food production policy – the first in British history.

The first phase of the policy, which ran from January to August 1917, was designed to encourage farmers to plough up grasslands. This was done through increasing the power of the county War Agriculture Executive Committees, giving them power to survey land, urge farmers to sow cereals and bring land up to a higher stage of cultivation. This was to be done by consultation, but ultimately the Committees did have compulsory powers, including the right to remove farmers who persisted in bad practice. In fact these were little used, and by the end of the war only 317 tenancies had been changed.[33] Much more significant was the second phase of the policy enshrined in the Corn Production Act of August 1917.[34]

> Farmers were given guaranteed minimum prices for wheat and oats (up to 1922) . . . barley was omitted out of deference to the temperance movement. . . . During the existence of guaranteed prices there were to be minimum wages for agricultural workers enforced by wages boards. Owners and tenants of agricultural land were to be required to follow cropping directions issued by the agricultural departments, to ensure the use of land in the national interest. There should be no increase in rents as a result of the maintenance of minimum prices.

The success of this food policy has been a matter of debate, but at the most basic level the area under plough in England and Wales increased by about 1.86 million acres in 1918 over 1916. In more direct terms the policy of food control, both rationing and raising the extraction rate of flour from wheat by about 20 per cent were probably more significant.[35] However, the fact that bread remained unrationed throughout the war was widely believed inside and outside government to be a result of the policy, and the farmers were seen as 'Britain's saviours', which was to have many post-war repercussions.

In the short term the most dramatic effect was on the farm worker. Since 1912 the farm workers' unions had been arguing for a minimum wage in agriculture set by Wages Boards. In 1917 this was conceded. County Boards were set up composed of farmers' representatives, farm workers' representatives and 'independent members'. These Boards set a county rate, which was then ratified by the Agricultural Wages Board in London. The first of the County Boards, Norfolk, did not report until May 1918 and in the interim a national minimum wage of 25s was set by London. This wage was a real increase in some areas, for instance in the eastern counties, but in others, especially the north, wages were already well beyond this point.

More importantly the Boards took wage bargaining out of the individual labourer's hands and put it into those of the unions. As Jack Leeder, a Norfolk team man who remembered the Boards coming in said, 'Men were afraid you see. . . . That's understandable. But the union did away with all that sort of thing and that was a good job when they negotiated the harvest wages and your weekly wage.'[36] The Wages Boards marked a transformation in the relationship between master and man — even if it was to be temporary. The farm worker of the first years of the twentieth century developed an increasing sense of his worth and his power. In many areas this found expression in union membership. Between 1917 and 1921 union membership soared. Not since the heady days of Arch's Union in the 1870s had the farm worker had such organised power. In 1914 the National Agricultural Labourers' Union had 350 branches and about 9,000 members, by 1919 it had over 2,300 branches and 170,000 members, while the agricultural section of the Workers' Union had 100,000 members by the same date. Put simply nearly 50 per cent of labourers were union members by the end of the war.

But in some areas it was not simply union membership. There had been strikes throughout the war, which showed the power the union now held in some areas at least. In 1917 Robert Walker, the Secretary of the National Agricultural Labourers' Union, welcomed the Russian Revolution in a series of public meetings throughout the rural areas. Finally in the 1918 election, for the first time, socialist and Labour Party candidates, backed by the unions, appeared in rural areas opposing both Liberals and Conservatives. Their success was limited, but it seemed to many that the mould was broken.[37]

By then, although the war was moving to its conclusion, the near successful German spring offensive of 1918 stretched the resources of the country and the countryside to the limit. The upper age for conscription was raised to 51, and moves were made to reduce the numbers exempt from conscription. In the rural areas the War Agriculture Committees fought back arguing harvest was coming, and that there was already a labour shortage. As a result only about half the men 'demanded' from agriculture had been found when the government dropped its demands in June 1918.

When 'the lights came on' again in 1918 after 4 years of bitter warfare their glow revealed a rural England that was, in many ways, prosperous. All those who had not fought seemed to have done well from the war. This sense of economic success and stability was to last for barely 3 years but was to take on almost the character of a lost golden age in the bitter decades that followed.

However, not all sections of rural society had fared equally well. On the surface at least the landlords had probably done least well. Rents had, by and large, stayed at pre-war levels, and had not risen since 1917;[38] but neither had they been reduced, as they had been in the pre-war period. Further, wartime demand meant that no land needed to be unlet. The end of the war saw this rapidly change. Apparently stable or rising agricultural prices made farm land an even more desirable commodity. However, since suddenly increasing rents might have rendered landlords liable for heavy income tax, the sale of land suddenly seemed an attractive proposition. As a result land sales increased very rapidly. 'The avalanche came with the spring of 1919', writes F.M.L. Thompson and, by 'the end of March about 1,000 square miles or well over half a million acres was on the market.'[39] By December 1922 about a quarter of the land of England had changed hands.[40]

Despite these changes the immediate post-war years did not mark, despite contemporary fears, the end of an old social order; rather it marked, initially at least, a further modification in the spread of landlord capital. While some estates, especially small ones, were sold in entirety, most landlords simply took advantage of the favourable market to transfer parts of their capital into more lucrative stocks and bonds – as their families had often done in the past. For example in 1919 Lord Aylesford sold 2,000 acres of his 17,000 acre estate in Warwickshire; the Earl of Yarborough sold 2,000 acres in Lincolnshire of his 50,000 acres in eastern England; the Marquess of Cholmondleley sold 2,000 acres in Cheshire, about one eighth of his estate, while the fifteenth Earl of Pembroke sold 7,000 acres of his 40,000 acre estate at Wilton.[41]

Yet some small estates did go, and more were to follow in the inter-war period. As in the 1880s and 1890s it was the gentry with no capital but land, and relatively small quantities of that, who suffered most. Those, like the great aristocrats, who held valuable urban property and large portfolios of stocks and bonds, survived even the worst times. Small was also a relative definition. Sir Oswald Mosley's family sold most of the 3,000 acres of their Rolleston estate in Staffordshire in 1919 and the rest followed later, breaking a 300-year relationship with the land and the area.[42]

Moving down the social scale those who had done best were probably the farmers. The end of the Great War saw agriculture in a state of prosperity unparalleled since the mid-1870s. The reduction in imports of wheat, coupled with government guaranteed prices from 1917, had produced a period of stable and high prices for those producing cereals. In other agricultural sectors the story was different. Dairy production, probably the most successful area of farming in the years between 1880 and 1914, suffered badly in wartime although the size of the national herd remained stable.[43] The central problem here was due to decline in output per cow, a direct result of the shortage of imported feed stuffs. A similar problem lay behind the declining livestock output. Again, although the number of animals in the national herd remained stable, their sale weight fell as farmers sold younger beasts because of a shortage of feeds for over-wintering, a practice encouraged by government policy errors.[44]

Thus, agricultural prosperity, although general, benefited some areas more than others. Most obviously those parts of England where cereal production was dominant, notably East Anglia, 'made' most but this concealed the fact that it was often difficult to find extra land to bring into cultivation and so savings and gains were made in other ways.[45] In contrast other areas, some southern counties, Lancashire and the East and West Ridings, for example, found extra land to bring under plough. Here 'both permanent and temporary grass had been ploughed and sown with oats and potatoes, and more wheat planted on the existing arable.' In other areas long established leys were ploughed up, though here, for instance in the north and the southwest, the lack of an arable 'tradition' caused problems because of a lack of plough teams and men or women skilled in handling them – a problem which was to recur in 1940. Also, in Wales, land which had gone out of arable production in the 1880s, was brought back into production especially with oats and potatoes.[46] Given all this few farmers were 'doing badly' at the end of the war except for, perhaps inevitably, the smallest and the most marginal, especially in the upland areas.

Looking at the war period as a whole, Peter Dewy writes, 'farmers were able to raise their share of the income of the industry from about two-fifths before the war to almost two-thirds in 1917–18.'[47] These gains were often reflected in changes in life style. A.G. Street, looking back from the grimmer days of the 1930s, wrote of the years 1918–21:[48]

> I was as bad, or as daft or, possibly more truthfully, as criminally extravagant as any one. I kept two hunters, one for myself and one for my wife; and glorious days we had together with the local pack. . . . We went to tennis parties nearly every fine afternoon in the summer, and, in our turn, entertained up to as many as twenty guests on our own tennis-court, and usually to supper afterwards. . . . In short farmers swanked.

Perhaps, however, the most obvious sign of this new wealth was the rush by tenants to purchase their own farms. In 1909 13 per cent of holdings were owner-occupied, by 1927 the figure was 36.6 per cent. Although as early as 1917 there is evidence of 'an increasing desire (by tenants) to purchase their holdings'[49] the 'main part of the increase in owner-occupation which occurred between 1919 and 1927 occurred in the years 1919–1921.'[50]

The reasons farmers bought land were varied but probably the most important was a general feeling of optimism founded on a perception, among cereal farmers at least, that high prices, supported if need be by price guarantees, as established by the Corn Production Act of 1917, were here to stay. There was good reason for that feeling. Three wartime reports had argued that the future basis of agricultural policy would be government intervention. Most importantly the 'Selbourne Committee', the agricultural policy sub-committee of the Reconstruction Committee, argued that the maintenance of a high level of home-produced wheat was essential in the post-war world.[51] Henry Overman, one of the great Norfolk wheat farmers, summed up the view of many larger tenant farmers to this committee when he said:[52]

> If it was desired to produce more food in this country after the War it was essential that Agriculture should be protected from the criminal neglect of past years. Either a minimum price must be fixed for wheat, or a protective duty imposed on all foreign grain. He favoured the former proposal.

These ideas were picked up by the majority report of the 1919 Royal Commission on Agriculture, which argued for a continuation of minimum prices to be linked, by a new committee of Ministry of Agriculture, to costs of production. The policy of minimum prices, it was argued, should require a period of 4 years' notice before they were terminated, to give farmers the stability they required to plan ahead. In return farmers were to be subjected to 'good husbandry', inspections by County Agricultural Committees, and a minimum wage for farm workers introduced under the 1917 Act would continue.[53] In June 1920 this was given government support in the form of the Agriculture Act.[54]

Even if a section of farming opinion felt the guaranteed wages and conditions given to the farm worker was too high a price to pay for minimum prices, few spoke against a measure which apparently showed that government had the well-being of agriculture at heart. Many, believing this mood and the profits it produced would last, took tentative steps up the farming ladder. Some young men, like Adrian Bell who bought his Suffolk farm, bought their first farms. Others, like Mr Hicks of Trunch in Norfolk, moved up from a 50 acre unit to one of just over 100 acres.[55] Others moved less from choice than from necessity. If a landlord wanted to sell land it was often offered first to sitting tenants. If the tenant refused, another, perhaps less sympathetic, landowner might appear. As Edward Strutt, the Essex landowner and agriculturalist told the 1919 Royal Commission:[56]

> I cannot say they are wise in buying land at the high values of today (but) a great many do not want to lose their farms; they want to stay where they are, and therefore they have to pay the prices in order to secure them.

The purchase of land was not restricted geographically. Sturmey argues that the main determinant of land purchase in the years 1909–27 was availability of land, hence northern counties like the North and East Ridings of Yorkshire, Lancashire and Cheshire all saw rates of purchase above the national average.[57] In Wales the situation was if anything still more striking. Even before the war Welsh tenants had shown a greater wish to buy than their English counterparts, and had had more opportunity since the 'ties' of landownership on the part of a largely English ruling elite do not seem to have been so great as in England. As in England, however, 'after the war the floodgates burst, and in the boom years 1918 to 1922 every major Welsh landowner placed at least part of his estate on the market.'[58] It has been estimated that in those years 26 per cent of Welsh farmland moved into the hands of former tenants.[59]

In England or in Wales, and for whatever reason the purchase was made, nearly all farms were bought on loans and at inflated prices. In Norfolk decent land, which was fetching £17 an acre in 1914, was sold for £28 in 1920, a 60 per cent increase.[60] In Wales, farms that normally went for 20 years' purchase, were selling at 40 years.[61] In A.G. Street's 'novel' *The Gentleman of the Party*, the hero Bob Marsh is forced to buy his farm in 1919 at £25 per acre with an army camp still on the land.[62] It was not so much the price, however, as the necessity to borrow money to buy. In Norfolk, Alec Douet writes, farmers were forced to move outside the normal channels of finance and borrow, often at high rates, from solicitors, auctioneers and even corn merchants.[63] At the other extreme of farming in Wales, as Ashby and Evans noted in 1944, 'many farmers bought their holdings at relatively high prices and with borrowed money.'[64] As Lord Addison, Minister of Agriculture from 1930–1, wrote in 1938:[65]

> All over the country farmers bought their farms because they wanted to retain their home and occupation – but they bought at a high price. They usually had to borrow two-thirds of the purchase price on mortgage and, for the rest, often put in all the money they had. Not infrequently some of the balance came from bank overdrafts on the security of their stock or general credit. The rate of interest payable on these mortgages was usually 5 or $5\frac{1}{2}$ per cent.

However in 1919, or even 1921, that did not seem much of a problem. Prices were high, profits had been good during the war and farmers lived better than they had since the 1870s. As R.R. Enfield wrote of the farmer in 1924, '[he was] doing very well out of the general buoyancy of prices and the relatively low cost of production, and for one brief space he found himself, perhaps to his surprise, with very little to complain about.'[66] Even in Wales, although profits were not those of the great grain growing areas, there was prosperity, and even a sense of political triumph. As Kenneth Morgan puts it, 'the gentry subsided as if they had never been.'[67]

The growth in owner-occupation marked a speeding up in the transfer of power from one class to another. In the early 1920s the farmer who was also the owner-occupier of his, or occasionally her, land begins to emerge as a separate and distinct political and social force. This is clearly indicated by the growth of the National Farmers' Union, an organisation which excluded landlords from its membership. Emerging from the tenant right and anti-trade union movements of the 1880s and 1890s, it had 80,000 members and 58 county branches by 1918 forcing the *Estates Gazette*, the voice of the County Landowners' Association, to admit, 'it is clear that the landed interest is now not even strong enough or real enough to make itself felt and respected.'[68]

For the mass of the working population in agriculture, the farm workers, the story was a mixed one. Nationally money wages had increased through the war. In early 1918 it was stated by the Agricultural Wages Board that wages had increased by between 56–61 per cent. However, given wartime inflation, and the fact that with little overtime pay farm workers wage rates were close to earnings, Dewey concludes that taking the war period as a whole there was a decline in real wages.[69] In the immediate aftermath of the war this changed slightly. Rationing and prices controls had slowed the course of inflation by the summer of 1918, and the national minimum wage introduced between May and October that year narrowed the gap further. In March 1919 the weekly half-holiday introduced the possibility of overtime on Saturdays. As with minimum cereal prices, nationally fixed wages were continued by the Agriculture Act of 1920. To an extent these changes helped the worker. Minimally they began to even out the long-term differences between the 'high-wage' counties of the north and the low-wage ones of the south, a division that had dominated during the nineteenth century. For example, by 1920–1 Suffolk and Norfolk had county minimum wages fixed at 46s per week, only 3s less than northern counties like Northumberland and Lancashire. However, many regional differences persisted until the Second World War and may even have been reasserted in the inter-war years.

A final area where the war hastened change was in the area of ideology. We saw in Chapter 1 how, in the years immediately before the Great War, sections of the artistic and intellectual elite had turned to the countryside, and to things rural, as the basis of a new England. The war seems to have speeded this process up. Paul Fussell has argued eloquently for the importance of the 'pastoral' form not only in the writing about the war but in shaping the sensibilities of those who fought.[70] The most eloquent testimony comes, of course, from the elite in the writing of Brooke, Sassoon and Blunden most obviously. In Blunden's *Undertones of War* particularly, the horror and waste of the Flanders landscape is constantly set against a soothing and restoring land of England, and in the 'simple' life of the East Anglian family of his first wife.[71] Sassoon pictured the ultimate escape for his men in a pastoral (or perhaps picture postcard) reworking of his Kent childhood. 'I wish,' he wrote in 1917, 'I could write a book of Consolations for Homesick Soldiers in the field.' Not surprisingly his landscape is a stereotype of the 'South Country' with grey church, village green and ultimately the 'rose grown porch of some discreet little house', with 'a girl in a print dress . . . waiting, waiting for the returning footsteps along the twilight lane, while the last blackbird warbles from the may tree.'[72]

However, although the evidence is hard to find, there is no reason to think these feelings were restricted only to the elite. The antithesis of battlefield and home were just as great for many 'ordinary' soldiers as for their officers. Post-cards from the front as often show soldiers dreaming of a 'rural' home as they show patriotic motifs. Further, as George L. Mosse has argued, the rural was a necessary part of the immediate post-war world. For many who had fought on all sides nature 'healed' the dead land by restoring it, in the same way as the ex-soldier protagonists of J.L. Carr's powerful novel *A Month in the Country* search for healing in rural England.[73] However, it was to be in the inter-war era that the 'long, long trail' found its resting place in a rural Britain. As Hardy and Ward write in the study of the plotland settlements of the immediate post-war period:[74]

> After the First World War, many a survivor suffering from the effects of gas was urged to get out of London, while there were others, terribly disfigured, who wanted to avoid the daily encounters of city living. And there were yet more who, counting themselves fortunate to have survived, resolved not to go back to the life of the urban toiler, but to invest the gratuity paid to demobilized soldiers in a new life in the country. . . . Dreams of chicken farming or market gardening may have been easily shattered, but the patch of land and the owner built house on it remained.

More still turned to the countryside as a site of recreation and escape. The empty Downlands of the South Country that had attracted pre-war artistic ramblers like Edward Thomas soon echoed to thousands of south London ramblers and cyclists. Most of all the towns themselves came to the countryside. As the 1921 Census noted, rural population appeared to have fallen since 1911 but in fact it had grown because of 'the gradual extension of the urban at the expense of the rural districts'.[75] The suburb was coming of age; 'gradually', writes Peter Mandler, 'the cities flowed out into the country'[76] and the 'countryside' was under siege in a way it had never been even at the height of industrial and urban expansion in the middle years of the nineteenth century.

In the spring of 1921 much of this was still to come. However, to those who looked outside the prosperity of their farms and their villages there were ominous signs of change. Internationally cereal production picked up, and imports of cereals started to seriously affect British prices. On the Wages Boards the farmers' representatives started to talk about reductions in wages. In Norfolk, the county where wheat prices mattered more than anywhere else, a series of meetings in February 1921 called for a 'general reduction' in wages, while nationally Mr George Mutimer, a Norfolk representative at the NFU said 'farmers in his county were at their beam ends owing to the slump in corn prices.'[77] In the country districts, as elsewhere, unemployment was increasing rapidly, and in the same week 1,800 men and women demonstrated outside Norwich Workhouse. Many of those present were 'wearing service badges'.[78]

Most in the rural districts, however, probably believed it was a temporary hiccup – after all there had been many before, and the Government had offered price guarantees. But it was not to be. For most of the next 20 years British farming was to go though a profound depression, which affected all those who lived in the rural areas, and many who did not. It is to those years that the next four chapters of this book are addressed.

Part II

The 'locust years', 1921–39

3 The misfortunes of agriculture, 1921–37

In 1931 Adrian Bell, the Suffolk farmer and author, wrote of the autumn of 1921:[1]

> Trade had been adverse since I started farming, but in those precipitous times probably less so than many other kinds of trade. Farmers pulled long faces, but they had not yet realized that their wartime pat on the back nationally was but a panic impulse; the Corn Production Act's immediate repeal gave them a taste of political wriggling, but still they thought it was but a momentary sinking of the prosperous breeze. I, too, hoped.

His hopes like those of many engaged in agriculture were short-lived. The repeal of the Agriculture Act in the summer of 1921 marked symbolically at least the end of agriculture's 'special' wartime treatment. Internationally, cereal prices had been falling since the winter of 1920 and the Government faced the possibility of having to pay some £20 million in subsidy to agriculture, a 'minor' industry, while refusing to help other sectors of the economy. On 7 June 1921 Sir Arthur Griffith-Boscawen announced the Repeal of the Agriculture Act with effect from the following August ending all price guarantees, although making short-term compensation payments, and abolishing the Wages Board and hence the national minimum wage.[2]

Repeal was met with a mixed response, initially at least. The farm workers' union was violently opposed to repeal and George Edwards, the union's founder and Labour MP for South Norfolk gave a phrase to farming history when he said that repeal had been 'the greatest betrayal of the agriculture industry that any government has ever been guilty of'.[3] Farming opinion though was largely in favour of repeal. The main reason for this was that the removal of the Wages Board meant that wages could be cut, thus reducing the cost of a major input which had, it was argued, been biting into farming profitability. As the *Mark Lane Express*, the main national farming paper put it in July 1921 during the debate over the Bill, 'the absolute right of two free-born Englishmen to make a business contract with each other must be affirmed.'[4] Further, the short-term subsidies offered as a sweetener effectively continued to protect cereal, and especially wheat prices, for 18 months. Not for the first (or the last) time did it seem the Government protected the farmer at the expense of the worker.

As a result of repeal wages fell by about 40 per cent between the autumn of 1921 and the spring of 1923. However, so did cereal prices and farming opinion began to change. Many farmers, as we have already seen, had bought their farms in the immediate post-war period, often at high prices and on mortgage. As the prices of imported cereals continued to fall these men began to feel the pinch. However this experience was a regional one. In East Anglia, where owner-occupation had increased from about 11 per cent to about 37 per cent by 1922 and large arable farms with high labour costs found themselves in direct competition with imported cereals, the situation was probably worst. But other areas, which had relied on wheat, suffered badly, especially Oxfordshire and the chalky downlands of Hampshire.[5] It was in these areas, and in Norfolk in particular, that farmers were beginning, by 1923, to talk about a 'great betrayal'.

Prices of cereals stabilised in 1924–5 giving rise to some optimism on the part of cereal farmers, especially in the eastern counties of England. Here, an additional ray of hope was provided by government subsidies for sugar beet production in 1924. As Douet writes, 'in the uncertain conditions of 1924, such a guarantee was manna, and the announcement was made in time for growers to sow 7,000 acres.'[6] Norfolk and north Suffolk benefited first from this subsidy, but by the early 1930s factories processing beet were to be found in most eastern counties, the West Midlands, Yorkshire and Cupar in Fife.[7] This stability was short-lived; by 1926 prices began to fall again. By 1927 when S.L. Bensusan toured England in the footsteps of Sir Henry Rider Haggard's 1902 agricultural tour, he found parts of Norfolk virtually waste.[8]

> The area of desolation, that embraces Methwold and passes eastwards to Watton and descends by Tottington, Wretham and Croxton in the direction of Thetford, did not seem to belong rightly to England; it recalled to me in part the backlands of Ontario and the bare plains of Manitoba before the settlers came. . . . The only crop to be seen was weeds, and a multitude of these were seeding generously; houses there were none for miles . . . nor was there any traffic.

Cereal prices continued to slide throughout the rest of the decade inducing what Jonathan Brown has called a 'peasant like' response – 'keeping to more or less established routines and avoiding the spending of any money'.[9]

However, as we saw in Chapter 1, English and Welsh farming remained firmly regional and in the non-arable areas the story was very different. Cheap grain prices meant a reduction in feed costs for cattle thus increasing the profitability of both meat and dairy production. Alongside this there was an increasing awareness of the nutritional value of dairy products growing out of wartime dietary surveys. As a result a growth in urban demand for milk led to a considerable expansion in dairy production in the immediate post-war period, especially near large towns. In the established dairy counties, however, growth was considerable and often successful. Gloucester saw an increase of 40 per cent in dairy production over pre-war level by 1930, while other traditional dairy counties increased by 20 to 30 per cent. There were also increases in production in less firmly dairying areas, like parts of the South Midlands, stimulated by urban growth. Conversely, as Taylor says, 'reflecting the industrial depression afflicting much of the north, dairy herds grew by a mere 5 per cent in Derbyshire and the West Riding of Yorkshire while in Lancashire the increase was less then 1 per cent.'[10] Alongside this growth in production came increasing specialisation in dairying and the careful and selective breeding of herds. The most important element here was probably the spread of the Friesian strain, produced solely for milk production, and the growth of a number of pedigree herds. By 1930 one of the most famous of these, that of E.G. Barton at Soundby in Yorkshire was producing as much milk from 14 Friesians as from 24 ordinary dairy cows.[11] In general, in the 1920s, dairying did well as Messer wrote on the agricultural depression of 1931,[12]

> two features [are] most consistently mentioned in the present circumstances of agriculture . . . the stability of dairy farming generally and the extension of this type of farming where ever it is possible.

Fatstock farming in the 1920s suffered from mixed fortunes. The declining costs of feedstuffs in the early 1920s benefited the meat producer but increased imports, especially of frozen meats, undercut the selling prices often between the purchase of the animal for fattening and its eventual sale. Alec Douet gives a Norfolk example: 'Nine beasts bought by a farmer in October 1920 at over £40 a head were sold in Norwich market a year later for £35.4s each.'[13] The loss after feeding animals for a year was clearly crippling. In Cheshire and elsewhere outbreaks of foot-and-mouth disease in the early 1920s were 'a great blow to the county's pastoral farming', with over 1,300 outbreaks in the years 1923–4 alone.[14] Although these outbreaks clearly affected dairy and well as fatstock animals, fatstock producers found them especially hard in the face of increasing imports.

This problem was heightened in a dramatic way by the Canadian cattle crisis of 1922 – what one historian has called 'the real great betrayal'.[15] To protect the British herd from disease the import of live cattle had been prohibited since the 1890s. This had had the effect of banning Canadian imports. During the war the Government had assured the Canadians that once peace came the now 'clean' Canadian herd would be free of these restrictions. There were also strong urban interests in Britain who argued that by preventing the import of Canadian cattle, and keeping cheaper 'Empire' meat from British workers' tables, the Government was increasing the price of meat and subsidising British fatstock producers. After a bitter campaign which involved the first agricultural appearance of Lord Beaverbrook as champion of the Canadian producers, Empire and the workingman, the embargo on Canadian imports was lifted in December 1922. Although the lifting of the embargo made little difference to imports its political significance was great, especially following the repeal of the Agriculture Act. Perhaps even more decisively than in 1921 the structural weakness of the agricultural lobby had been exposed. Worse still it showed that farming opinion could be divided, since the large farmers of the eastern and some northern counties were in favour of imports as a source of cheap winter store cattle. Possibly for the first but certainly not for the last time divisions between the 'wheatocracy' and the smaller pastoral farmer showed the hollowness of an 'agricultural interest'.

In the 1920s other areas, what we have already called 'alternative husbandry', began to have a significant impact on English and Welsh agriculture. Changes of this kind had a long history, and some aspects of this were discussed in Chapter 1; however, in the inter-war years these husbandries took on a new importance for a whole range of farmers. A good example of this is egg production. Traditionally egg production, because of the difficulties of transport and storage, had been small-scale and usually the area of the farmer's wife. In Devon in the early years of the century eggs and butter were sold at the farm gate, to a higgler or at market. This money 'was used to keep house. As a source of income for housekeeping, this money was important to farmers' or small holders' wives alike.'[16] A similar situation was found in West Wales and Northumberland. Good prices during the war were maintained throughout the 1920s and 1930s encouraging growth in flock sizes, since hens brought in a decent profit with the use of family labour. By the 1930s many mixed family farms had flocks of 400 birds providing valuable additional income. On top of this, as with other branches of agriculture, some regions began to specialise. Lancashire in particular became the home of British egg production. By 1931 the President of the Preston Farmers' Co-operative could claim that the Preston area produced one-third of all the eggs in England.[17] These were produced on small often specialist farms, buying feed co-operatively and marketing in the same way. By 1924 the volume of egg production had increased by a third over post-war figures.

Other crops had similar histories in the inter-war period. Fruit and vegetable production had also increased rapidly in the post-war years, especially vegetable production; this took advantage of new canning methods, which capitalised on changes in working-class diet. Again there were areas of regional specialisation. Lancashire had a long history of vegetable growing and especially potato production, which in cash terms at least dominated the farming of much of Lancashire and Cheshire. In East Anglia pea and bean production were well established in Essex, Suffolk and Norfolk before the Great War, but it was in the production of cabbages and sprouts for human, rather than animal consumption, that real changes came. Indeed, looking at the situation nationally in 1937 W.F. Darke argued that this was 'one of the chief changes in the structure of English agriculture'.[18]

There were more problems with fruit production. Reliable and disease resistant strains were still in their infancy and soil type was crucial. Thus in the fens of East Anglia and Cambridgeshire soft fruit production was well established before the war and this provided a good base of inter-war expansion especially into strawberries, while Chivers at Histon near Cambridge continued their semi-industrial fruit growing and jam production. In the Vale of Evesham and much of Kent plum and apple production increased in the 1920s although the level of profitability of many small holdings remained questionable. Despite this Bensusan found a very successful fruit farm of 130 acres near Tewkesbury in 1927. This produced high-quality pears, apples and plums and a smaller quantity of strawberries for the 'most profitable markets', including 'some of London's leading hotels'.[19]

The picture for alternative husbandry was not all rosy. Cheese production suffered throughout the 1920s from both foreign competition and an inability to market English produce. The Preston area of Lancashire, as we have already noted, was enormously successful in egg production, but the other interest of the Preston Farmers' Co-operative, indeed the one for which it was in part founded, cheese production, was little short of disastrous. The Co-op saw as one of its aims the buying and selling on of Lancashire cheese and in 1916 they reported with some satisfaction that they had launched into the 'business of cheese factors ... [and] have been the means of introducing Lancashire Cheese into districts where previously it was unknown.'[20] However with the end of the war and the growth of imports the 'cheese side' started to do badly. By 1924 the AGM was told 'the loss in the Cheese Department has been occasioned by the fact that there have been large importations of Kraft Canadian Cheese at such low price as to make it impossible to sell Lancashire Cheese in any quantity and at a profit.'[21] Nevertheless they continued to act as cheese factors through the 1920s to a decreasing number of members, and at a loss. Elsewhere, although small amounts of traditional cheeses continued in production, more and more farmers switched entirely to the more profitable and ever growing trade in liquid milk. For example, in Wensleydale the opening of a railway branch line encouraged liquid milk production and led to the creation of a producers co-op which seems to have quickly reduced cheese production, although cheese was still farm-produced in the dale until 1956.[22] There were some successes though. In Wiltshire the creation of factory cheese production in the 1890s ensured that county's cheese production continued although, ironically, it was cheese of the Cheddar type that was produced – not Wiltshire cheese. Similarly factory production of Stilton ensured its survival and continued success through the inter-war period.

Plate 4 Dairying, even on a small scale, was one of the few areas of real success in the inter-war years. A woman worker on a small farm in Wensleydale, Yorkshire in 1934. (Reproduced by kind permission of the Rural History Centre, University of Reading.)

Through these difficult years government played little part. The attitude of all governments in the 1920s is well summed up by the Conservative Prime Minister, Bonar Law's replies to a joint farm workers' and farmers' deputation in March 1923 asking for support for agriculture. He said:[23]

> I do not see what can be done, or what you could expect the government to do. You come to me and say the position is very bad, and you ask the government to put it right. We should only be too glad to if we were able ... but I cannot see any practical scheme by which that can be done. ... I think that the agricultural industry is in a worse position than almost any other industry, but they have all suffered; but the question is, is agriculture to be self supporting, or to be supported by the State? I think the latter is impossible. If there were any way we would like to help you, but it seems to me that agriculture must lie on an economic basis.

Coming in the wake of the repeal of the Agriculture Act and the lifting of the embargo on Canadian store cattle such statements were a slap across the face for the once great 'agricultural interest'. Britain, even its traditionalists now recognised, was an urban society. For all the inter-war maundering and sentimentalising of Stanley Baldwin, amongst others in the Conservative Party, agriculture was, if necessary, to be sacrificed in the interests of cheap food.

By the late 1920s government faced 'more serious' problems with growing urban depression. Compared with them agriculture's difficulties were seen as naught. In addition the Labour Party, the 'new' opposition, had, as Clare Griffiths has shown, little sympathy or understanding of the rural areas in the early 1920s at least. At best Labour saw the countryside as a 'sleeping nation', which needed to be awakened by socialism. In this view 'the rural constituencies were the "backward areas". . . . The epithet reflected the low levels of organisation in rural areas, but it also implied that the political culture of the countryside itself was underdeveloped.'[24] At worst the countryside was seen as hopelessly reactionary while agriculture was, as Phillip Snowden said, 'the pampered darling of the Conservatives' and 'a parasite upon the general industry of the country today'.[25]

A little was done. The Sugar Beet Subsidy had a fundamental effect on farming in the eastern counties as we have seen, and the reintroduction of the Wages Boards by the 1924 Labour government did help the worker a little. Beyond that there was virtually nothing. A grant of £1 million over 5 years was given to improve drainage; the Agricultural Credits Act of 1923 gave very limited aid; and grants to rural councils for road building and cottage building were measures to help the unemployed. Right at the end of the decade the promotion of grading and marking to distinguish British products and guarantee their quality was begun, although it was not really effective until the early 1930s and in some sections of agriculture and horticulture much later.

More striking in its effect on the countryside if not on agriculture was the creation in 1919 of The Forestry Commission. By 1929 it owned 104,100 acres in England and Wales and managed a further 120,000 acres of Crown lands. Its policy of planting quick growing conifers, rather than native deciduous trees attracted criticism, especially in the Brecklands of Norfolk and Suffolk, the North Yorkshire Moors and at Kielder in Northumberland. As early as 1927 Besusan commented:[26]

I recalled Julius Cæsar's description of these islands – 'one horrible wood'. Now after 2,000 years in the course of which the English land has been brought under cultivation so successfully that for centuries it supplied the needs of the entire population, we are permitting a vast acreage, that could produce food at need to revert to the condition old Julius Cæsar found it.

The bare outline of agricultural change in the 1920s given in the last few pages suggests a mixed picture. For all the improvements in many areas cereals still dominated the agriculture of Britain emotionally and politically, if not in terms of acreage, and cereals suffered. Against this contemporaries saw the relative success of dairying and small-scale alternative husbandry as insignificant even if historians stress these gains. However, by the end of the decade what Richard

Perren has called a 'precarious balance' had been achieved, and many in the country areas felt a slight confidence that maybe things were going to get better.

They were to be bitterly disappointed. As in the depression of the last years of the nineteenth century, what to some seemed an end to the bad time proved simply a temporary respite. The Wall Street Crash of 1929, coupled with increased world production, particularly of cereals, led to a collapse of farm prices. This was made worse for England and Wales by export bounties paid to many overseas producers which led to low-price dumping by a whole range of agricultural producers but especially cereal producers. Even the dairy producers did not escape this time. Since the early 1920s large national dairy companies like United Dairies had bought from farmers at guaranteed prices. Although this tended towards monopoly the farmers had benefited from the regular and pre-dictable payments. By 1930 dumping of cheap milk had led to the complete, if temporary, collapse of the guaranteed price system.[27] In addition, as in the 1880s, a run of bad weather, including one of the mildest and wettest winters on record in 1931, made conditions even worse.

Those who had weathered the first storm faced the second ill prepared for its blasts. As in the 1920s those who suffered worst were the cereal farmers of the eastern counties. These men and women, 'whose capital and credit had already been eroded by the falling trend in grain prices during the previous decade,' now faced disaster.[28] These conditions were repeated throughout the cereal growing areas, but the situation in livestock areas was little better. Initially cheap feed had helped the livestock producer, having the net effect of transferring income from the arable east to the pastoral west; however, in the winter of 1931–2 livestock prices fell again.

In this rapidly worsening situation government was forced to act, although initially slowly. In November 1931 tariffs were imposed on soft fruit and potatoes, and this was extended in January 1932 to other agricultural products, although the staples remained unprotected; no government, even in what was now regarded as an agricultural crisis, was prepared to 'tax the people's food'. This was rectified indirectly by the Wheat Act introduced early in 1932. This essentially returned to the old principles of the Corn Production Act with deficiency payments to guarantee a minimum price. However, unlike the old Agriculture Act, the money was raised by a tax on milled flour, both home-produced and imported, and it was in fact, as Brown says 'a disguised tariff'.[29] The effects were remarkably swift. In 1933 and 1934 there was a large increase in the area sown to wheat. In 1934 the subsidy to sugar beet was renewed thus removing another fear of the arable farmer.

More important in the longer term was the creation of Marketing Boards, in 1932 and 1933, especially that for milk. The principle grew out of the 'National Mark' Act of 1928 but took it much further. The principle was simple. A vote was taken on demand of all registered producers in a particular branch of agriculture. If two-thirds voted to establish a scheme it went ahead. The main point of the scheme initially was to restrict imports of commodities covered by the Boards but moved, by the mid-1930s, to have substantial inputs, and even control, in areas of production, pricing and marketing.

These changes were not simply short-term reactions to crisis, or to the growing farmers' protests in the winter of 1931–3, but did represent, to some extent, a change of heart. As K.A.H. Murray wrote:[30]

> The motives were many; one was to give agriculture some assistance equivalent to the protection afforded to other industries in 1932; another was to meet the increasing interest in nutritional problems which developed during the decade; a third was a traditional dislike of the decline in the rural population and of agricultural land going to 'waste'. There was also present in some people's minds the needs of national defence.

At the heart of these changes lay a contradiction. On the one hand agriculture needed to be protected if it was to survive, on the other there could be no 'taxes on the people's bread' which would cause unacceptable price rises for the huge urban majority of the population. This was clear in what Cooper sees as new Conservative policy after 1929 as a result of Neville Chamberlain's report on agriculture for the Conservative Research Department. His conclusions were that some form of state involvement was inevitable to stop agriculture 'going under', but that such intervention must be directed at the restructuring of agriculture to make it more efficient as a producer of food by a 'reduction in the number of marginal and inefficient producers'.[31] The notion here of large-scale and efficient farms working broadly within state plans, if necessary aided by subsidies on a carrot-and-stick basis, was to form the foundation stone of agricultural policy for the rest of the century – although few can have seen it at the time. This streamlining would, it was believed, increase productivity and efficiency, thus avoiding price rises. However, in reality, as Venn pointed out in 1933, this change represented a transfer from the pockets of the non-agricultural consumer to the farmer. Assuming, as was the case, that the cost of the quota of 2s 9d charged upon every sack of flour was passed onto the consumer of bread, this added up, on the basis of a farthing a loaf, to a charge of 10s a year on every family in the country.[32] The charge was minute but like the principle involved it was the beginning of a policy which no subsequent government was to alter or even seriously challenge.

The passing of the Wheat Act, the renewal of the Sugar Beet subsidy and the enormous success of the Marketing Boards, especially the Milk Market Board, turned agriculture round. As Newby writes these measures together were 'largely successful in raising farm incomes'.[33] This was clear even in the worst affected areas, the cereal producing counties, and by 1935 the acreage under wheat was back to the level of 1923. However, much of this increased acreage was the result of replacing other crops, rather then bringing in new land, and most of the increase was in East Anglia. Elsewhere the acreage under wheat continued to fall. It was replaced largely by a continuing switch to dairy farming, supported by the efforts of the Milk Marketing Board and urban demand for liquid milk which was largely impervious to overseas competition. As a result the balance of agricultural production finally, and decisively, shifted. By 1939 milk and milk products represented 31 per cent of the value of the gross output of agricultural holding in England and Wales as against 4.5 per cent coming from all grain crops.[34] As Jonathan Brown writes, 'it might still lack the glamour, but after nearly seventy years expansion dairying was coming to occupy the eminent place in agriculture held before the Great Depression [of the 1880s and 1890s] by cereal farming.'[35]

Nor was it only dairying, although other sectors lacked the high public profile provided by the Milk Marketing Board. Poultry and egg production accounted for twice as much of gross output as grains by 1938–9, although when the wheat subsidy was added they were about the same. In 1935 a subsidy was given to fat cattle, which increased production in that sector, and although the Pig and Bacon Marketing Board was a failure owing largely to the inability of the Board to control production, that sector also expanded. In 1937 farming was given a further boost by a new Agriculture Act which was, according to W.S. Morrison the Minister of Agriculture, to 'increase the productivity of our own soil, with a view to ensuring increased food production in time of war'.[36] This Act covered grants to increase the productivity of land but also increased the acreage under wheat on which subsidies would be paid, and extended subsidies to barley and oats.

The fortunes of agriculture in the 1920s and early 1930s had a profound effect on those who lived and worked in the rural areas. They also served as the backdrop to new versions of rural England and Wales in which agriculture was coming to have a less central part. The experiences of those who lived through the 'locust years' are the flesh on the bones of the often grim accounts of economic change. It is to these people that we shall now turn, starting at the 'top' with the wealthy and great, the landlords and then moving to the farmers. We will then look at the rural working class and the 'new' countrymen and women.

4   Landowners and farmers

In the spring and summer of 1921 in many rural areas they were still finishing the memorials to the Glorious Dead. Most of them carried the names of the local squire or squire's son. More of these found their names on private memorials. In Chester Cathedral there is a monument to thirteen members of the Grey-Egerton family of Oulton Park who fell on active service. Although this scale of family tragedy was rare the rural elite suffered terrible casualties. As David Cannadine writes:[1]

> The British aristocracy was irrevocably weakened by the impact of the First World War. Not since the Wars of the Roses had so many patricians died so suddenly and so violently. And their losses were, proportionately, far greater than those of any other social group. . . . Of the British and Irish peers and their sons who served during the war one in five was killed. But the comparable figure for all members of the fighting services was one in eight.

This carnage contributed to the changes in land ownership in England and Wales in the first two or three years of peace. Yet there were many other reasons for sale, most, as we have already said, economic and carefully considered, a fact lost on many contemporaries as well as subsequent histories. Further, we need to be cautious about the extent of this supposed cataclysm. Put simply, if a quarter of the land of England and Wales changed hands, mainly away from the aristocracy and gentry, three-quarters of it remained in their control. In that sense, if no other, 1918–21 did not mark the end of the landed estate, at least on a national scale. Further, although precise figures do not exist, land sales nationally decreased rapidly as agriculture entered the period of crisis in 1922–3 and farmers in particular were unwilling to buy land in a less certain market situation.[2] Moreover, although land sales rose again in 1924–5 when agriculture revived the period of relative stability, these were on a small scale and, after 1925, land sales practically ceased.

None of this is to deny that in some localities there were real changes. In Nottinghamshire and Derbyshire sizeable areas were sold off – up to a third of

Derbyshire's great estates were sold off by 1930, and by 1939 all the major landowners of Nottinghamshire had left their estates.[3] In the absence of real national figures it is difficult to know how these figures compare with other areas, but recent regional histories give the impression that many left the north, and even the Midlands, in part at least because of the 'problems' of industrial areas, what John Walton has called 'the drift to fairer climes' away from Lancashire.[4] Elite members described Nottinghamshire as 'uninhabitable' by the 1930s, while Phillips and Smith in their history of Lancashire and Cheshire write that 'industrial pollution threatened old family homes (for example, Norton Priory and Madbury Hall in Cheshire were reportedly pulled down because of it).'[5] In Staffordshire the Duke of Sutherland had sold Trentham before the war as it was too urbanised and in 1917 sold his other Midlands house, Lilleshall, and moved to Surrey, 'where I could enjoy the beauty and peace of the countryside'.[6] This is supported, to an extent, by Heather Clemenson's figures for country house demolition since 1880 which shows a slightly higher rate of country house demolition and non-replacement in the northern counties in the period 1880–1980.[7]

This is not to suggest the sale of estates, whole or in part, was an exclusively northern or Midland phenomena – clearly it was not – but the general sense, drawing on the examples in recent studies, suggests that very few whole or even large estates were sold in the southeast in the immediate post-war period, while many seem to have been sold in the north and Midlands. Sales in the southeast tended to be on a smaller scale and for specific purposes, usually housing. For example, part of the Lovelace estates at Leatherhead had been sold just after the war to 'Tommy' Sopwith, the aircraft manufacturer, but in 1925 the farms were being advertised as 'excellent sites for the erection of first-class houses'.[8] Similarly in the area around Shere, the Bray family had been selling and letting land for villas since the 1880s, including the arts and crafts paradise of Holmbury Saint Mary. By 1922, realising that land for large-scale housing was used up, they turned their attention to more modest developments on the outskirts of Holmbury. There were even worse fates. In 1923 a small estate and pheasant shoot of 300 acres, known as Selsdon vale, was bought by the Surrey Garden Village Trust – it produced a plotland settlement.[9]

In Wales the effect of landed sales and aristocratic flight seem to have been more obvious than even in the north of England. Although not one of the estates in Wales of over 20,000 acres in 1883 had ceased to exist by 1922, many were seriously depleted and some middle-sized and gentry estates did vanish completely. The process in Wales though had been a longer one, and the social structure of rural society very different. As John Davies writes:[10]

In rural Wales, the non-economic perquisites of landownership had been more severely and suddenly undermined by democracy than had been the case in rural England. After 1868, and particularly from the 1880s onwards, there can be little doubt that those who had both English and Welsh estates found it more rewarding, in terms of local prestige and influence to concentrate upon their lands in England.

It was also, in the long term, to go much further. In 1887 Wales had a structure of land ownership similar to that of the north of England, but by 1970 owner-occupiers in Wales had reached 61.7 per cent while in the north of England they had not reached 50 per cent.

What these regional difference show, even in the case of Wales, is that nowhere to any extent was aristocratic and gentry landholding abolished. This suggests that in economic terms at least, there were many more continuities with pre-war First World War Britain than is often suggested by concentrating on the apparently huge figures of 'change'. This is further emphasised by Heather Clemenson's careful work on a sample of 500 great estates from 1880–1980, really the only source we have for long-term change. She emphasises the extent to which 'decline' is dependent, as we have already suggested, on which section of the landed elite is being discussed. Her work suggests that:[11]

> the extent of decline has been greater for estates of private landowners in the 3,000–10,000-acre size range, that is the greater gentry. On the other hand, the break up of estate property appears to have been less severe for the great landowners, especially the long-established landed aristocracy.

Further, the great territorial magnates tended, as is well documented, to sell off sections of their estates, often the outlying parts, rather than break up the estate as a whole.

These regional and other changes open up questions of social, economic and political power which are difficult to resolve. Estate sales had very different social effects in different areas. The Victorian notion that a great house was the centre of a whole socio-economic and cultural community clearly was true in some places but not in others. For example, while many areas of Surrey remained rural in 1921 they were already within the orbit of a newer suburban world where the traditional 'norms' of agricultural society were considered unimportant in reality, even if the incomers saw themselves as living in a rural idyll of parson and squire. In areas like this sales could have relatively little impact. This was also true of parts of Essex where the agricultural depression of the 1870s–1890s had already led to the break up of some estates. On the other hand in more purely agricultural districts, for instance rural Oxfordshire, it is clear from some accounts that an active elite presence, often seen as a nineteenth-century phenomenon, continued important throughout the inter-war period. At Waterstock in the 1920s 'most . . . villagers worked for Squire Ashurst, lived in his cottages and were ruled by him.'[12] At Goring 'on the last day at school the local gentry came round and offered jobs.'[13] In Worcestershire Fred Archer, the son of a small farmer, wrote of his village in the 1920s, 'at the top of the tree in power and respect was Mr John Baldwyn, the last of a family of squires who had been looked up to for 600 years. . . . Apparently he was quite an accessible gentleman, but to me he was just a little lower than the King.'[14] Nor was an active gentry or squirearchy a purely southern phenomenon. When Bill Denby moved to a farm at Heslington near York in 1930 he found:[15]

> you had to behave yourself – it was a known thing. You were supposed to go to church on Sunday, and you hadn't to cut ivy off your house, because his Lordship liked to see it. . . . Then you hadn't to chop branches off trees, and you'd to leave a good big wide hedge bottom for game purposes.

On many great estates the public rituals of deference continued unchanged. At Arundel in Sussex, in June 1929, the coming of age of the sixteenth Duke of Norfolk was marked by several days of celebration throughout the estate, including the traditional meals in the Castle grounds for the tenants and their families, treats for the children, bonfires and fireworks. As late as 1933 in Yorkshire 'thousands' of tenants from Earl Fitzwilliam's estate were transported to Dublin for his son's lavish marriage in Saint Patrick's Cathedral.[16]

Against this there were clearly important cultural shifts, which are difficult to document. At the simplest level the aristocracy in particular appear to have withdrawn from an active cultural role in many country districts. The reasons for this change are numerous and the costs of estate ownership was certainly one of them. Yet one has a sense of deeper changes. When Henry Evans Lombe, 'the descendant of an ancient and well endowed gentry family, sold Bylaugh in Norfolk he gave his reasons as not only the death of his son in the Great War but also, to spread the money over a wider range of investments.'[17] Of the situation in Wales, John Davies writes, 'the majority of landowners who sold in both the pre-war and post-war booms were doing so, not because of severe financial difficulties, but rather in order to diversify their investments.'[18] The wisdom of such a move was not to be doubted, especially in the 1930s, but it does demonstrate a shift away from the imperatives of duty as inscribed in Victorian ideals of the gentleman. It was not simply investment. Country life became 'boring' and 'old fashioned', particularly among those who had gone through the war. As Madeline Beard writes:[19]

> While hunt balls, comings of age, and Christmas gatherings continued in style after the war, there was also a reaction by landed society against the old pre-war world. Many expressed boredom with the life accepted for so long. London society and county society merged with great frequency.

Plate 5 Continuity. The aristocracy and the gentry follow the old pursuits here at the Golden Retriever Club Sanction Show near Pangbourne in Berkshire 1934. (Reproduced by kind permission of the Rural History Centre, University of Reading.)

Nor was it only London society. The aristocracy was becoming 'internationalised'. Although travel and even periods of residence abroad had long been common, the 1920s brought into being an international smart set:[20]

> . . . for many . . . patricians, travel and recreation had ceased to be an interlude from or a preparation for the more serious business of estate management, local leadership, and national politics. Instead they had become an escape, an alternative, and even a substitute, as social life abroad was inflated to a full-time activity, an end in itself, which left little time for the performance of traditional functions at home.

Where, and for whatever reason, an active paternalist presence ceased there certainly were changes. The departure of a well established gentry family from a Lincolnshire village ended Christmas treats for children, dinners for tenants and local charity. As one of their tenants remembered, 'we thought a lot of Sir John and Lady Fox, and they did of us; we were *their* [sic] people. We didn't need no sick club to look after us, not with having Sir John.'[21] In the end though it is difficult to assess in any quantifiable way the 'decline' of the aristocracy and gentry as a social and cultural force in the countryside of the 1920s. There were certainly changes in landholding but even at the outbreak of the Second World War the majority of rural England was still in the ownership of gentry or aristocratic landlords. In many places they continued the rituals of the Victorian period and practised the codes of paternalism and the Lady Bountiful. The group that suffered most were those who relied mainly on agriculture for their income with estates of between 3,000 and 10,000 acres – what Clemenson calls 'the great gentry'. These were precisely those who kept up the traditions of paternalism, as they were reliant on agriculture and were thus more likely to be resident in the countryside. The perception of 'decline' was then in fact the decline not of all the aristocracy but of a vulnerable and traditionalist section of it. There remained, throughout the whole of the twentieth century, an enormously wealthy and powerful landed aristocracy. What Roy Perrot wrote of the aristocracy in 1968 was even truer of the 1920s:[22]

> While there may be a very gradual annual decline in acreages, I think most estates are well placed enough to last a long way into the foreseeable future. There will certainly be enough to give the aristocracy a strong enough semblance of the old, landed character, for a good many generations yet; which is one good reason for thinking that the reports of the disappearance of this elite have been premature.

However, the ways in which the elite sought to use this wealth and power were changing. Parallel with the withdrawal of sections of the aristocracy from local social and cultural life was a more striking withdrawal from local politics. Although there were, as it has often been argued, real continuities between the old county government and the new county councils, there were many real breaks even in purely agricultural areas where non-landowners were elected in increasing numbers. This process continued in the inter-war period in response to both to increasing bureaucratisation and the withdrawal of aristocratic interest in local government. As Cannadine writes:[23]

> By the 1930s, the county councils were no longer the old rural oligarchy under a new name, but a professional hierarchy and structured bureaucracy which might – or might not – be sheltering behind a façade of patrician authority . . . [T]he aristocracy's part in the government of the countryside was increasingly moving towards that non-contentious and essentially ornamental role that during the same period, they were perfecting and practising in the towns and the empire.

The collapse of farm prices in 1929–32 and the Wall Street Crash of 1929 were further blows to the landlords. For those who lived in the rural areas, and especially those who lived on rents or farmed themselves, the collapse in prices could be disastrous. Although, as we saw above, rents rose at the end of the war they began to fall again in the 1920s. By 1933 they were back to pre-war levels and in 1936 reached their lowest point since 1870. Since 1921 they had fallen by 25 per cent. Although costs had fallen they had not fallen so far or so fast and Thompson estimates the estate expenditure was about 70 per cent lower than it had been before 1914, and 'that the residual income of landowners was about half its pre-1914 amount.'[24] This had knock on effects. Falling rent rolls meant less estate expenditure, while the effects of the price collapse on farmers meant they were unable to buy land. In that sense many landlords were caught in a vicious circle.

In this situation the already declining role of the aristocracy and especially the gentry took a further plunge. Even the very wealthy cut back as the continued demolition of country houses showed. Equally symbolically, the death and funeral of Viscount Cowdray, with the body on a horse-drawn cart followed by the estate workers and tenants six abreast, was not only probably the last funeral of its kind in Sussex, but seems to mark the end of a certain kind of paternalism. In this situation some probably simply withdrew further, gradually 'settling down to a circumscribed style of living, which had previously been typical only of the impoverished arable land-owners.'[25] Some, only a few, turned in anger to defend the system which they had lost, and we shall come across them again. Viscount Lymington, later the Earl of Portsmouth, espoused the revival of a paternalist order based around an 'English' fascism and organic agriculture and found a hero and friend in another disillusioned landowner, Sir Oswald Mosley. These were exceptions. In general one is left with a sense that the collapse of 1929–32 simply continued, or perhaps speeded up a process of aristocratic and gentry withdrawal from the society they had once dominated.

Nevertheless, 'county society' continued to function. Indeed, 'country house life' in the inter-war period has taken on in many memoirs the quality that an earlier generation ascribed to the years before 1914. We have already noted that many of the public shows of deference continued in some areas, but more centrally the private lives of the aristocracy and gentry continued to have many aspects of the pre-war era. Hunting, the London Season, and country house weekends all retained much of their exclusivity even if the really grand 'do's' were the exception. Few new country houses were built in the 1920s and early 1930s and many were demolished or sold for non-residential use, yet through all the wailings and gnashing of aristocratic teeth, again, a powerful sense of wealth and privilege remain, even in the ranks of the gentry.

The fact that much of this was 'new' money made little difference given the long-term ability of the aristocracy and gentry to absorb the right kind of incomer – commercial occupations and the professions had long been acceptable sources of wealth and new blood. They were also, provided they remained 'gentlemanly', acceptable in social circles. A good example of this can be seen at Anglesey Abbey near Cambridge. Here between the late 1920s and the 1950s, Lord Fairhaven, benefiting from the money made by his father in America, recreated on a modest scale a garden and house of near eighteenth-century splendour. As Sir Arthur Bryant wrote:[26]

> Our age is not without rich men ... yet Huttestion Fairhaven must be almost unique in having created in the middle of the twentieth century a garden which can compare with the great masterpieces of the Georgian era. With patience, single-minded devotion and flawless taste, in an age of war and revolution he has endowed the England of tomorrow with a landscape garden worthy of her past.

Ironically the garden was furnished with mostly eighteenth-century statuary from a number of houses all over England. Some of it came from Stowe, the great Grenville house, whose sale to a school in 1922, was seen by many contemporaries as the end of the old order – *plus ça change*. ... More publicly the society created at Polesden Lacey in Surrey by Mrs Greville in the 1900s, and financed by her millionaire brewer father, continued into the inter-war period with lavish house parties, even if some thought these 'old fashioned'.[27] What is significant about Polesden Lacey, as was the case with many Edwardian and inter-war country houses and their occupants, was that there was little economic relationship with agriculture. There are a number of reasons for this. F.M.L. Thompson pointed out some years ago that the costs of acquiring a large- or medium-sized agricultural estate from scratch, even at the depressed prices of the immediate post-war years, was well beyond the wealth of all but a tiny minority of 'new comers', but more importantly few wanted one. What those from industry, the professions or the 'purple of commerce' wanted was country life not agriculture. Farming or renting farm land was increasingly less economically viable in the inter-war period, indeed, as we have seen, by 1930 had became suicidal, but the charms of country sports, relaxation and an essentially idyllic view of country life still held many attractions, especially in the southeast of England. Here in a 'modest' house the banker, lawyer or company director could entertain in style with the additional advantages of the air of the squirarchy. Lesley Lewis's account of growing up in the 1920s in Essex presents an idyllic and charming view of the life of such a family.[28] Her father was a successful lawyer from a long-established family firm in the Inns of Court who bought, in 1912, Pilgrims Hall near Ongar, with a home farm of about 100 acres, which was then suitably modernised by a pupil of Lutyens. Here Lesley Lewis was privately educated and sent to Paris at seventeen to complete her education. On her return, 'I did what my neighbours and contemporaries did ... hunted when there was a horse to be had, played tennis and stayed in houses which for the most part were run like ours. I did my stint in local good works such as the Red Cross. . .'[29] In 1927 she was presented at Court and went through a London season. By employing indoor and outdoor servants, and as cottage owners, her family played a minor local gentry role, a position reinforced by her father's position as Chair of the Parish Council. To cement this, small-scale rituals of deference were also carried through. At Christmas those who worked for them were given presents, 'joints of pork or beef to married men, probably money to single ones, and the maids usually had dress lengths to make up themselves.'[30]

Some withdrew, some failed, but some remained, and to an extent, at least in the inter-war period, some came in their place. Thompson's view of some years ago that 'on the whole the social balance of the countryside was not greatly disturbed between 1921 and 1939,'[31] has much merit in the face of recent accounts of aristocrat and landlord decline, but it goes too far. There were ways in which that balance was disturbed, some of which we have already looked at, and others will form part of the accounts that follow. In particular the growing power and influence of the farmers, although still in its infancy in the 1920s and early 1930s, was in the longer term to provide a real disturbance in the countryside. It is to them that we now turn.

In 1927 there were 401,734 farm holdings in England and Wales of which 146,887 were owner-occupied.[32] The rest were held from usually larger landowners. The first point to make is that there was clearly a difference between the experience of those who owned their own land, although often via a mortgage, and those who were tenants. This is an important difference between the depression of the last years of the nineteenth century and that of the inter-war years. In the 1880s and 1890s the vast majority of farmers were tenants. This meant that the costs of the depression were often borne by the landlord in the form of rent reduction. This was still true of the inter-war period for something like 63 per cent of holdings. In Norfolk, for example, rent abatements begin to appear as early as 1923–4. By 1929, on three estates examined by Douet, rent abatements of between 2 per cent and 16 per cent had been granted to tenants, while there were also rent arrears of a similar order.[33] For those who had purchased their farms the situation was very different. There were something like 90,000 ex-tenant farmers confronting the problems of the 1920s plus some 55,000 established owner-occupiers. For these farmers falling prices and profits had to be met from within the resources of the farm and the family, even where they were supported by sympathetic creditors. This group dominates narratives of the depression both by contemporaries and historians but, as with other cultural factors, this cannot deny the reality of the hardship of those who bought their farms often at inflated prices between 1918 and 1922.

There can be little doubt that those who suffered worst in the 1920s and again in the early 1930s were those in the cereal growing areas, and within those areas probably those who had bought farms in the immediate post-war years and were

thus saddled with debt. For all the first reaction was to let land go out of cultivation and this was widely done. Between 1921 and 1929 in the mainly arable areas
of the northern and eastern counties over half a million acres went out of arable
cultivation, much of it, as in the 1880s and 1890s, going to permanent grass.
While to some extent this figure reflects a shift to pastoral farming – the classic
'down corn, up horn' solution, which is reflected in[34] increased numbers of cattle
– it also showed some land effectively going out of cultivation altogether. This
was particularly so in the light lands. Mr G.M.T. Pretteyman, farming near
Orwell in Suffolk, abandoned to rough grazing nearly a 1,000 acres of heathland
that had been under wheat during the war. Eventually some of this land ended up
in the hands of the Forestry Commission, as did much of the Brecklands on the
Norfolk/Suffolk border. Further north in the East Riding of Yorkshire, the
Wolds, formerly good cereal land, suffered from the falling demand for barley,
which left the chalky uplands with few real alternative crops, since the land was
unsuitable for non-cereal production and a long way from markets. In addition
this land had been heavily farmed during the war, which further weakened it. In
1936 it was suggested that this area suffered from 'a more marked and more baf-
fling state of depression . . . than elsewhere in farming'. In contrast in the Glendale area of Northumberland, the most northerly area of English cereal
production conditions were much better, which prompted a University of Newcastle survey of 1936 to describe it as 'a small district of really high class
farming'.[35] In the far north the land which had gone out of cultivation was 'intermediate land between the low land and open hills', for example in the area east
of Wooler where, as a result of the decline of arable production, 'some of the
enclosed land bordering on the moors is practically derelict, even on the lighter
soils of a useful, workable type. Much of this land is becoming bracken
infested.'[36]

   Letting land go out of cultivation or into semi-dereliction was one cost cutting
exercise, reducing the size of the workforce was another. Even with wage reductions in the early 1920s, wages formed a very large part of farming costs throughout the inter-war period. Jonathan Brown and others have argued that the
inability to control labour costs was a significant contributory factor to the inter-
war depression.[37] In 1931 a survey on arable farms in eastern England showed
that labour was the single largest item of outgoings at 37.7 per cent. The obvious
response here was to shed workers and replace them with either family labour,
machinery or cheaper casual labour. Again the figures speak volumes. Between
1921 and 1931 about 60,000 workers left agriculture and between 1931 and
1939 a further 100,000.[38] To the farmer this was reducing costs; to those who
worked the land it was the loss of livelihood and often a way of life.

   The final short-term solution was simply going into debt. Farming debt is very
difficult to get at. We have figures for bankruptcies which show them increasing
through the inter-war period. In 1914–20 farming bankruptcies averaged 82 per

annum; in 1921 they rose to 285 and to 401 in 1922. They reached a high point in 1932 at 560 but by 1934–9 they dropped back to 240 per annum.[39] Tragic as each of these cases were, in total they are insignificant seen in a national context. There were 343,000 farmers in 1921 and, although the figures had fallen to about 300,000 by 1931, a total of about 7,500 bankruptcies in 10 years represents about 2.5 per cent of the farming population. As J.A. Venn noted as early as 1933, the notion of 'widespread bankruptcies' across the whole farming community was clearly a wild exaggeration.[40]

For those who did not go bankrupt, but who were suffering from economic problems, going into debt with the landlord (if a tenant) or with the bank or mortgage company (if an owner-occupier), and with tradesmen (for all) was another alternative. While material of this kind is difficult to go by it is clear debt was widespread. In Norfolk, as we have already seen, the Holkham Estate and the Blickling Estate had 8.5 per cent and 29 per cent of tenants in arrears of rent in 1932, and even in 1939 both still had significant numbers of tenants behind with payment.[41] The banks fared little better. It was reported in December 1932 that £3.5 million was owed by farmers to Barclays Bank in Norwich.[42]

If rent reductions, debt, laying down to grass or sacking men were immediate solutions there were longer-term ones for the farmers of the arable areas in the 1920s and 1930s. These were most obviously the use of machinery, to cut labour costs and increase output, and diversification into crops where there was a market with high, or at least stable, prices. Both of these were tried with varying degrees of success. Mechanisation was surprisingly little used. In the 1920s tractors tended to be heavy and unreliable. Even following the introduction of light American machines in the early 1930s initial capital costs prevented many farmers from buying machinery. Further, it was very difficult to convert horse 'gear' to tractor use giving additional costs that the small- or medium-sized farmer could ill-afford. Nor were tractors necessarily more efficient on many holdings and, where they appeared, with some notable exceptions, they appeared in small numbers and alongside horsepower, with tractors being used for ploughing and horses for carting. In the North Norfolk village of Trunch Mr May, who farmed just over 100 acres, was the first man to have a tractor at the end of the 1920s. 'Mr May had one tractor, you see, which did the hard ploughing, and then he had horses as well.'[43] As a result of all this there were only about 40,000 tractors in England by 1938, and those mostly on holdings of over 300 acres. As Charles Rawding had written about the Lincolnshire parish of Binbrook:[44]

On the Wolds, tractors first appeared in significant numbers in the early 1930s, principally on the larger farms, although some contractors had tractors, which were taken around the smaller farms to work the land where the farmers themselves were still using horses only. Smaller farms generally had to wait until the Second World War.

Gains in labour replacement or output were also uncertain. In 1939 an East Anglian survey found that tractors did not lower costs per acre but did increase output, increasing profits by lowering costs per unit of output.[45]

The most significant change from the pre-war era was probably the widespread use of the reaper binder. Although used before the war, older forms of taking the harvest, most obviously the mechanical reaper still dominated in most of England. In 1919 Harold Hicks remembered that 'there were one or two big farmers' who did not have self binders in the area north of North Walsham in Norfolk where his father farmed, and 'in very laid conditions, where the corn was flat on the ground', even big farms still resorted to the scythe.[46] Reaper binders represented a real gain over mechanical reapers by reducing the workforce required at harvest and by the 1930s they were general for cereal harvest. In contrast the combine harvester made very little progress. It was a very expensive machine and could return its costs only on very large farms. Even in Norfolk where in many ways conditions were ideal, there were only about 30 combines working in 1939, which probably accounts for a large percentage of those available and in general use.

There were of course exceptions to the rule that mechanisation was seldom 'total'. The most famous of these was the Alley brothers' Bluestone Farm near Fakenham in Norfolk. By 1935 it was worked entirely by machine, including caterpillar tractors, combines and grain dryers. The farm created huge interest, appeared on cinema news and farming documentaries, and was frequently written up in the farming press. The Alleys also produced their own wheat flakes sold under the name 'Farmer's Glory' and sold direct to Woolworths – in every way a very 1930s set-up. There were other less spectacular experiments. William Parker at Babingley Hall near Kings Lynn was using a wide range of machinery including a grain dryer in 1934,[47] but this level of mechanisation remained unusual.

If wholesale mechanisation was little tried, changes in cropping, even in the most arable of the eastern and northern cereal growing areas, were widely practised. The simplest course was to modify the arable system in some way, and this was done widely, especially in East Anglia, by the introduction of sugar beet. With a government subsidy, and guaranteed purchase by the factories, sugar beet had become central to the survival of much eastern counties farming by the mid-1920s. Nor was it only East Anglia. The factory at Cupar in Fife enabled the arable areas of the northeast to go into sugar beet; even A.G. Street in Wiltshire tried the crop in the early 1920s, but as transport costs involved in sending the crop to Norfolk for processing and unsuitable soils cut down the profits, he stopped after 2 years. He did however return to limited beet cultivation in the 1930s.[48]

If sugar beet had a regional impact moving into fruit and vegetable production was wider spread. At one extreme there were semi-industrial enterprises like Chivers at Histon near Cambridge, which had impressed Henry Rider Haggard even before the war. In 1935 the Chivers factory covered 14 acres and during the busy season it employed over 3,000 workers making jam, bottling and canning. Although Chivers owned about half of the land which grew this crop, about 2,500 acres came from other producers.[49] In the Lea Valley there were, according to *Farmers Weekly*, 'thousands' of glasshouses in 1935, and the industry had 'grown considerably in the last few years'. Rochford's at Broxbourne had 30 acres of glass and employed 250 people, including forty single men who lived in a hostel with its own clubroom and bar.[50] These however were extremes, and more usually it was a case of changing within the arable system by substituting a vegetable crop. Here soil type was of central importance. The fenlands of Norfolk, Lincolnshire and especially Cambridgeshire had a well-established vegetable growing industry before the war and expansion continued into the inter-war period. Elsewhere Brussels sprouts and cabbage, which had often been grown in the past for animal feed, were added to the rotation and sold for human consumption.

Fruit was more difficult, since the change involved was more comprehensive, although there were notable successes in the cereal areas. In the Fens strawberries were grown on a large scale and a 1,000 tons a day were going to the Midlands and north from the area in the mid-1930s. Further east around the Wroxham area of Norfolk blackcurrants were grown on a large scale. In 1927 Bensusan visited one of these farms, a unit of 150 acres formerly down to wheat. As well as growing blackcurrants the owner raised bushes as stock for nurserymen and in 1927 had sold 100,000 of them. He was also growing daffodils.[51]

The most obvious change for those with problems in the cereal growing areas was a switch to dairying, usually as part of a mixed farm rather than going solely into milk production. This course was widely followed even in the heartland of arable England, Norfolk. The Norfolk dairy herd almost doubled between the wars, often using the by-products of arable cultivation including sugar beet. As a Norfolk farmer told A.G. Street in 1934, 'You can't farm wi'out muck, and you can't get much wi'out cattle, and in these days you can't get any money to buy cattle unless you grow sugar beet.'[52] The Milk Marketing Board was vital, not only in providing a market and the regular milk cheque, but in improving standards, especially in relation to the tubercular testing and pasteurisation of milk and a general cleaning up of milk production methods. By the end of the 1930s the kind of dairy conditions described by Arthur Amis in the 1920s were becoming a rarity. 'Milk then was not produced too cleanly. Round your knees an old sack apron was considered good enough, and only discarded for a clean one when it could stand on its own.'[53]

The switch to dairying, though, was not always welcomed. There was a continuing belief that dairying, or for that matter growing vegetables, was not real farming. Even Street, a firm advocate of the change to dairying wrote, 'this grass farming was an uninteresting business as compared to the older ploughland system. The romance of farming was gone.'[54] But it was not only romance. Dairying was traditionally women's work and of much lower status than cereal growing at least. As E. Lorraine Smith wrote in 1932, 'it was a common opinion among farmers that corn farming is a more interesting and less arduous occupation than dairy farming, and that it had superior social standing.'[55]

Size of holding was a key determinant of many of these changes, and crucially how these changes were experienced. For many large farmers in the eastern and northern corn growing areas the impression frequently comes through that things were not as bad as they were painted. Like the largest landowners they were able to cut down at the edges while keeping the 'centre' whole. They also had capital available to make cropping changes more easily than their smaller neighbours. When this was combined, as it was in many cereal counties with rent reductions for tenants, the worst of the depression could be weathered. A minor indicator of this can be seen in the fact that the number of domestic servants in rural areas actually increased in the years of the depression. While many of these were certainly employed by incomers and by the rural bourgeoisie many must have continued the traditional route into 'farmhouse service'.

As one moves down the social scale the experiences were different. Although the small or medium farmer could adapt by use of family labour, as well as by modification of cropping, changes in life style were more obvious. The experiences of Harold Hicks and his father were similar to many in this group.[56] His father had had 75 acres of land as a tenant of the Jex Blake family at Swanton Abbot in Norfolk during the war, but in 1919 he bought Brick Kiln Farm in Trunch, a farm of 96 acres also in Norfolk from the Buxton family.

> At that time they were selling up the estate and the farmers who where in occupation had the opportunity to buy the farms you see. Well the old gentlemen who lived here didn't wish to buy, and so it came on the market at public auction, and my father bought it. . . . (My) father paid £30 an acre, about the top price for good land in Norfolk at that time.

However, as for many the optimism which had led to the purchase soon evaporated. 'After the first war everything seemed to break down, farmers' guarantees by the Government were slashed, and so that when harvest came round they didn't get only half what they was supposed to get.' In this situation Mr Hicks began to adapt. Two of his brothers returned from Canada and replaced hired workers. When Harold left school he replaced another full-time worker and eventually his younger brother joined him. By the mid-1920s the farm that had had three hired men had none and was worked entirely with family labour.

However, for the Hicks family, even that was not enough in the really bad years of 1930–2 and further changes had to be made. First, since they lived near the coast his mother took in visitors – a common resort of farmers' wives well outside the cereal growing areas. Second, his father took the road also followed by many and moved towards alternatives to cereal, which had dominated his farming until then. 'Father built some greenhouses and sold tomatoes and cucumbers.' They also grew blackcurrants. Thus, with family labour and some diversification, the Hicks family survived as farmers but, as Harold Hicks said, 'there were times when he wondered what to do next.'

At the lowest level the tiny farmers – those barely above small holders – adapted the long tried strategies of survival. The Jones family from Alpington, west of Norwich, farmed about 50 acres on a near-peasant system mixing fruit, cereals, dairy cattle, chickens and ducks. A core workforce of Mr Jones and his wife plus his son and his wife worked the farm. They occasionally employed two men but relied on the irregular work of Mr Jones' two sisters and one of their husbands. They sold milk in the village, butter and cream to stallholders on Norwich market, and general produce at auction. This was combined with dealing which involved 'a run into Norwich City on Fridays . . . and he would take produce in when people in the village, knowing he went in would come and say "I've got too many carrots, or I've got this fruit. . ." and he would take it in and charge a percentage.' Finally they bartered with other small farmers exchanging eggs, vegetables, butter and fruit for hay or straw.[57]

In marked contrast to the experiences of the east and northeastern cereal growing areas the western and even some Midland counties did reasonably well in the inter-war period even if few, especially small farmers, remained untouched by the chill wind of depression. Nationally, as we have seen, in terms of output at least, England and Wales became pastoral economies in the inter-war years. In 1938–9 milk and its products accounted for £64.6 million of gross national output, and livestock and wool £68.8 million. Against this grain crops, potatoes and sugar beet added up to £25.8 million. Within these general figures, as in the depression of the 1880s and 1890s, those areas which were able to move into dairying, and especially liquid milk production, did best. If we wanted an 'ideal type' of successful farmer in the western areas, he would be farming about 250 acres of good grass, near a town, or at least a good rail link, with a pedigree, perhaps Friesian, herd. By the late 1930s such a man could be producing pasteurised milk with the aid of machinery, have a 'milk contract', guaranteeing income and his own milk delivery business. This is of course an ideal type as with our earlier 'worst case' eastern counties farmer and few fitted the stereotype absolutely. As in the cereal areas, region and size of holding made a huge difference to how the inter-war years were experienced.

Probably the smallest farmers were to be found in the upland areas of western and northern England and above all in Wales. Here the precise nature of the land was of crucial importance. In the upland areas the inter-war period saw a growth in the number of sheep, although on the lower slopes and valley bottoms cattle, either as 'stores' or dairy cattle, were also kept. There were also changes in type of sheep, away from the traditional 2–3-year-old wether sheep to the leaner and younger lamb, in response to changing consumer demand which gave 'leg of lamb' a place on the Sunday dinner table. In these areas the small family farm dominated. In Wales over 60 per cent of those engaged in agriculture were farmers and their relatives;[58] in England and Wales as a whole the figure was 35.4 per cent. These were also by and large small farms, although in Wales, and in parts of northern and western England, the availability of moorland grazing causes confusion as to actual acreage.

The inter-war history of these upland farms was mixed. Sheep prices rose, and the national flock increased despite imports of frozen meat especially from New Zealand, yet the living was always a struggle. What Richard Moore Colyer writes of Wales could well apply to many upland areas.[59]

> For the hill farmer, the inter-war decades represented a period of largely unrelieved physical and financial struggle. The rigid structure of the hill system, limited to outputs of wool and store stock by the combined rigours of altitude, elements and soils . . . meant that farming at any level was a constant and unremitting challenge.

It was men and women like this who Bensusan met in the North Riding of Yorkshire in 1927.[60]

> In the first place he is a tremendous worker. His wife and his children, if they are the right age, help him; he has, in his devotion to the land, something that makes him akin to the French, Belgian and German small farmer; he shows a fine contempt for hours and is rich in the assistance he receives from his family towards the efforts he makes in every direction to wrest a living from a small and reluctant acreage.

Many hill farmers continued to follow other occupations where they could. Some still travelled to industrial areas in search of work as they had done in the nineteenth century. However, the industrial depression closed down the lead mines at Allenheads, which had helped support Allendale's farming community, and put the pits of South Wales on short time, which had contributed to the farming economy of West Wales. In this situation those near enough to large farms found day work as labourers at hay, corn harvest or potato harvest. In Wales a survey of Carmarthenshire in 1923 suggested that of just over 4,000 farms of less than 50 acres 45.9 per cent were held by people with other occupations, the largest number being coalminers. Ashby and Evans write:[61]

> The coal miner occupying a small family holding was fairly common in some parts of Carmarthenshire, as was the slate quarryman with similar attach-

ments in parts of Caernarvonshire and Merioneth. This system, which was also found in Cardiganshire and Glamorgan and in small areas of other counties, tended to swell the proportion of auxiliary holdings in the county.

Nor was it only Wales. Growing up near Evesham, on the borders of the highland and lowland farming regions, Fred Archer recalled Hugh Clements, baker, publican and small farmer. 'It used to be said that Hugh Clements was involved in every trade except that of coal merchant.'[62]

Hill farms and higher land could be improved, where it was possible because of the nearness of towns or railheads and decent or moderately good land, to switch to a larger number of dairy animals. This route was followed widely throughout the 'upland' areas of England and Wales and, more especially in the Midlands and southwest. In many areas this was a change of scale rather than an entirely new operation. Nor was it open to all. A small farmer, especially one who had bought a farm immediately after the war, would have found it difficult to raise the capital to invest in major changes, especially in view of the increased standards of hygiene demanded by the Milk Marketing Board (MMB) after the mid-1930s. Nevertheless, even in remote districts, a guaranteed price and a guaranteed demand encouraged many to make the change.

The effects, particularly in 'traditional' communities in Wales and the west of England were profound and went far beyond the simply economic. Both David Jenkins's study of Cardiganshire and Mary Bouquet's of north Devon point to the displacement of women by men as dairying ceased to be the perk of the farmer's wife and became the mainstay of farm incomes. In Devon:[63]

> before 1933 the Torridge Vale Creamery collected only cream and butter, which were traditionally made in the farmhouse dairy by the farmer's wife. After 1933, it was the policy of the MMB to collect milk and manufacture dairy products industrially, and eventually farmhouse dairy production by farmers' wives was phased out.

Jenkins links these changes to other technological transformations:[64]

> On farms the change-over to bulk milk sales and the introduction of the tractor eroded the connection between women and the milk cattle, and the men and the horses, which had been one of farm work's most prominent customary features.

Milk produced in the southwest and Wales went mainly to local creameries, but nearer to centres of population many farmers combined MMB sales with local dealing. Tony Harman was typical of these. He began farming in 1931 in Buckinghamshire and in 1932, as a result of the refusal of a local dairy in Hemel

Hempstead to take his milk, he began his own retail business. Although he started in a small way, by carefully buying the goodwill of other small roundsmen and farmers he built up a considerable business by the mid-1930s. Building on this by 1936, he added vegetable production to his crops and then went to owning his own greengrocers.[65] Nor was it only in the south of England that units like Harman's prospered. In 1935 *Farmers Weekly* wrote of the large numbers of small mixed farms and dairy producers on the 'bad land' around the industrial centres of Lancashire and the West Riding, quoting farms of 100 acres keeping 90 cows, 200 head of poultry and fattening 200 pigs per annum with much of the produce going direct to the consumer.[66]

Dairying and other livestock production looked much better in the inter-war years than other sections of farming. Moreover, as we have suggested, they were becoming progressively more and more important. By 1939 poultry production had moved from being the 'pin money' resort of generations of farmers' wives and daughters to accounting for over £21 million per annum, greater than the non-subsidised values of all grain crops. In some areas of Britain, as we have already suggested, poultry and eggs accounted for a large part of all farming profits. In Lancashire the area around Preston supported a huge and well-organised poultry industry, as well as one of the most successful of all farmers' co-operatives – the Preston and District Farmers' Trading Society – now Amalgamated Farmers. Founded in 1911 to buy poultry feed collectively for small and medium producers, it had an annual turnover of over £1 million by 1937 on the basis of Lancashire poultry.[67] Even in 1930, one of the worst inter-war years, the President of the society said: 'Notwithstanding the depression in most of our important industries . . . I have to report a year of steady progress.'[68] Nevertheless even in this successful district there were problems, especially for small producers who concentrated solely on eggs. In 1935 the annual report commented:[69]

> It is very difficult to obtain anything beyond a bare livelihood no matter how hard they work. There are a favoured few who have mixed farms, or who can obtain a fair output of hatching eggs and chicks, who no doubt do alright, but we are satisfied it is extremely difficult for small Poultry Farmers to obtain an adequate return for their labours.

Lancashire also suffered from competition, partly from overseas but partly also from the growing part of the national flock elsewhere. Poultry farming was a favoured resort of the 'new' small holders created by government legislation after the Great War. Poultry farming appealed to many on the edges of the great cities as needing relatively small amounts of capital, and producing apparently high returns. These small producers, scratching a living from farm gate sales, were perhaps typical in terms of numbers of poultry farmers, but before war broke out the first intensive rearing units were beginning to appear, pointing to a new and very different future for poultry.

Equally fundamental to the fortunes of agriculture in the inter-war period was the changing nature of the farmers' self-consciousness of themselves as a group with political and economic clout separate from that of the landowners. As landowner power declined, albeit unevenly, so the power of the farmers grew. The most obvious aspect of this, which we have already briefly mentioned, was the growing power of the National Farmers' Union. Founded in 1908, its membership grew from 10,000 in 1910 to 60,000 by 1918, reaching more than 100,000 by the end of the 1920s.[70] Formally, the NFU took no part in politics despite various attempts in the 1920s and 1930s by sections of the movement to create an 'agricultural party', especially in East Anglia. Its power lay much more as a pressure group working locally, and especially nationally, to influence agricultural policy. Like the farm workers' unions the NFU gained considerable power and prestige under the control of agriculture instituted by the Corn Production Act of 1917 and the Agriculture Act of 1920, experiences which gave them formal and informal ways into government policy. Although this power declined in the 1920s with the end of government intervention, the NFU had learned valuable lessons which were to reap their rewards in the growing self confidence which marked campaigns after 1930–1 to 'do something' about the state of agriculture. These changes in attitude to farming, already noted, had a good deal to do with the NFU. Street's view in 1931 put this clearly when he wrote that 'the National Farmers' Union is a responsible body with which any Government can discuss agricultural problems . . . To present a united front to any Government on a national question is . . . a difficult job, which the Council of the Union accomplish far better than is usually supposed.'[71]

At local level the NFU, or rather farmers, gradually came, in the inter-war period, to replace the gentry and aristocracy as local elected representatives. Lee's study of Cheshire shows the local NFU emerging as an 'independent party' on the County Council in the 1920s, a pattern which seems to have been repeated elsewhere. The changes were not always easy. In the areas of small farms, and especially in Wales, an anti-establishment attitude was more common among farmers than in the areas of large farms where they tended to follow gentry traditions of a conservative paternalism. Indeed in Wales the small farmers' vote, both in local and national politics, tended to encourage regional nationalism.[72] More spectacular, if less long lasting, were the brief forays into active politics, which marked various farmers' movements in the late 1920s and 1930s. The brief flirtation of Lords Rothermere and Beaverbrook with agricultural protection in the early 1930s produced in 1931 the Norfolk Farmers' Party, later the Agricultural Party, which was supported by the Norfolk county NFU and, notably, by its energetic secretary J.F. Wright. It attracted some support and by 1932 had 113 branches in East Anglia. However, it was unable to draw

Plate 6 Continuity. The spectacle of the Hunt, here at Dunster in Somerset in 1922, could still apparently unite county society and find many followers even in the darkest years. (Reproduced by kind permission of the Rural History Centre, University of Reading.)

widespread support away from the established political parties and, with the gradual onset of protectionist policies after 1932–3, lost its raison d'être and vanished.[73]

Longer lasting was the Tithe Campaign. Despite the 'abolition' of the Tithe (payments to the established Church to support the church and vicar) in 1836 many farms were still liable for Tithe payments. In the early 1930s this became a live issue as profits fell and many new owner-occupiers found themselves liable for payments often carried in the past by landowners. The usual form of resistance was a refusal to pay the Tithe followed by seizure of goods. The campaign was national but focused especially on the eastern and southern counties where local associations and later the National Tithe Payers Association organised often spectacular demonstrations at Tithe Sales. These ranged from other farmers buying seized stock and returning it to its owners, to the kidnapping of auctioneers and eventually to heavy police presence at farm seizures.[74] The campaign bore fruit. With sympathetic support from the farming press a Royal Commission met in 1935 and in 1936 produced a Tithe Bill, which resulted in the Government buying the Tithe and passing on the costs via long-term taxation to those farms which had previously paid tithe.

The Tithe War also brought the farmers unlikely allies in the shape of the British Union of Fascists. Figures like the novelist Henry Williamson, who farmed in Norfolk in the late 1930s, and the Dorset landowner Rolf Gardiner, saw in the farmers, and in the tithe campaign, the basis of a rural, and peculiarly British *fascisti*. Blackshirts were especially active in Suffolk where they organised to prevent tithe seizures but, although they were welcomed, and in some places are still remembered with affection, their impact was slight. A more likely leader was a Kent small landowner and Methodist Minister, the Rev. R.N. Kedward, whose hostility to the tithe was based on his religious conviction as well as a concern for agriculture and his own deeply held Liberal politics. At the great anti-tithe demonstration in June 1936 Kedward shared the platform with Stafford Cripps rather than Oswald Mosley.[75] Although the Tithe Bill was opposed by the National Tithepayers' Association and seizures continued through the Second World War and into the late 1940s, the cause was dead. The NFU grumbled but accepted the Act as the best that could be got at the time, and the majority of farmers, now beginning to feel the benefits of protection, voted with their feet by marching away from the campaign.[76]

Perhaps symbolic of the new confidence of many farmers was the appearance in 1934 of *Farmers Weekly*. In stark contrast to older farmers' papers, *Farmers Weekly* presented a confident and public image aimed first at working farmers and their families but also at the countryside as a whole. It covered a whole range of country life issues and presented an increasingly unified voice on agricultural politics, becoming by 1939 an able advocate for the farmers' 'cause'. While it remained studiously 'non-political' it more often than not represented the views of the NFU and, even before the war, a particular section of the Union: the larger tenant farmers. It had little time, for instance, for small holding schemes and land settlement, preferring instead to follow the view that large means good. It did however provide a site for popularising experiments with its 'successful farm' series, while its non-farming coverage opened up a wider worldview to farming families. It also, from the start, encouraged a nostalgic ruralism alongside its practical hints, carrying pictures and articles which stressed the continuities of (usually) English rural life. This mixture was to continue throughout the war, and only began to vanish in the 1940s.

Looking back at the inter-war period, and at the fortunes of agriculture as a whole, the picture is a mixed one, with a great deal more success than many accounts allow. Why then do contemporaries accounts, and indeed memoirs, suggest a picture of unrelieved gloom? The most important element here was the presentation of the 'depression in agriculture' as a cultural phenomenon through a whole range of books and articles. This is especially the case in relation to accounts of the 'collapse' of cereal farming. Although cereal production represented only a small and diminishing sector the influence that East Anglian farming in particular had on the cultural presentation of farming as a whole was absolutely fundamental. Books like Adrian Bell's farming trilogy published in the 1920s and 1930s, and appearing as a single volume in 1936, presented a picture of a decent way of life blighted by government inactivity and urban neglect. Even

A.G. Street's *Farmers' Glory*, which is very critical of wheat farming, supported this view. Although more 'academic' studies like Bensusan's *Latter Day Rural England* did present a more mixed picture, the dominant image of chapters with titles like 'Derelict Acres' went a long way to supporting the pessimistic view. Politically from both right and left this grim view was given support in the 1930s by Lord Addison's *A Policy for British Agriculture* of 1938, published by the Left Book Club, and Viscount Lymington's *Famine in England* of the same year, published by the Right Book Club. Few writers, like J.A. Venn in his 1933 edition of *The Foundations of Agricultural Economics*, challenged this view, pointing to the relative success of some areas of production and warning of the consequences of fetishising cereal production.

Yet this writing fell on deaf ears. By the mid-1930s the farming press had constructed a recent history, which came to dominate public thinking and many historical accounts. In August 1934 *Farmers Weekly* looked back to 1914 and the years that followed under the headline 'Does Britain So Easily Forget?' Beginning from the sacrifices of 1914–18 (with little mention of profits) it took the reader through the 'Great Betrayal' to the derelict acres and to the prospect 'that only a European war can remind our people how great is the service that the farming industry, given fair treatment, can render.'[77] The message was clear. Britain's staple food was bread; bread could and should be produced from British wheat, and in the event of war would have to be. Emotionally and politically cereal production was linked to national need, almost to national being. Rolling acres of corn had always been more attractive than pens of chickens or fields of beet, and rolling acres were East Anglia. Not for the first, or the last time, the fortunes of a section of British agriculture had come to stand for it all, and the success, or in this case the failure of that sector, had been made to speak for the whole of agriculture.

5 The traditionalists

Farm workers and domestic servants

At the Census of 1921, the largest number of 'workers' in the rural areas were those employed in agriculture, although as a group their primacy was already being threatened by other workers. It is with those who worked the land, usually held by or owned by others, that we shall begin. In 1921 there were 572,000[1] men and women in England and Wales described as agricultural labourers or farm servants. They were already a declining group and had been since the 1850s, when agricultural employment was at its height. The inter-war years were to see the numbers decline still further.

By using the statistics provided by the annual agricultural returns, although they produce higher numbers employed throughout the inter-war period than the census does, we can get a clear sense of relative decline over the 20-year period. Between 1921 and 1930, that is up to the onset of the 'worst' years, the number of male and female farm workers declined by about 10 per cent. Between 1930 and 1939 numbers fell by a further 18 per cent. Looking more closely still we see that numbers employed dropped rapidly from 1919–23, when they picked up, remaining fairly constant until 1932 when they fell again, and continued to drop very rapidly until 1939. This fits crudely with part of the chronology of agriculture discussed in the last chapter, but also suggests modifications of it. Crucially these modifications relate to the regional nature and experience of farm work and farming systems, and how they adapted to the processes of change.

A key determinant in how the inter-war period was experienced by farm labourers continued to be the nature of their hiring – how and when they were employed and under what conditions. In this the broad regional trends, which were discussed in Chapter 1, remained fundamental throughout the 1920s and 1930s and had a persistent effect during the Second World War. Perhaps surprisingly for historians who believed that living-in farm service vanished with the eighteenth century, in many northern counties as well as Wales, the system whereby 'servants' were hired by the year and lived on or near the farm continued dominant. This was true of the counties of Cumberland, Westmorland, north Lancashire, Northumberland, Durham and Yorkshire. Living-in service was also present, in some form, in many other areas.

Again, as in the pre-Great War period, 'living in' was not a homogenous system; rather the term covered three main varieties of hiring. First, the classic system of the sons, and sometimes the daughters, of social equals living in the farmhouse as part of the life cycle, and learning a trade. As we saw this was certainly in decline by the late nineteenth century, was increasingly rare in the inter-war period and was probably restricted to areas of small farms where work group co-operation was high. This was true, for example, in parts of west and mid-Wales. Here, as with other areas of very small family farms, if a son could not or did not want to work on his parents' holding, he moved away to a nearby farm to earn money hoping to set up on his own account, or at least bring savings back when he took the family farm. This tended, in theory at least, to blur the distinction between farmer and worker, especially where a unit employed only one or two men. As Ashby and Evans wrote in 1944, 'it is still very common for labourers to live in the farmhouse and receive board as well as lodging from their employers. Sleeping accommodation is not always of the best, but meals are usually shared with the family.'[2] Similar conditions were found in Westmorland as *Farmers Weekly* wrote in 1935:[3]

> The farms are chiefly from fifty to sixty acres in extent. . . . Labour is usually hired at half yearly hiring fairs, and as a rule men live in the farmhouse, taking their meals with the family. In some cases the men draw a small weekly allowance and the balance at the end of the period, but more generally they draw the whole of their wages in one lump sum at the end of six months. The majority are young single men, and when they marry they either take a small farm of their own or they work in town.

Winifred Foley worked on a mid-Wales farm in 1930. The farm was run by the farmer, his wife and a nephew as well as Foley. Her food was 'dry bread and cheese or dry bread and broth' for supper with occasional cider and potatoes or swedes with bacon for dinners, 'day in day out weekdays and Sundays, it was always the same'. All the food was produced on the farm but 'nothing that could be taken to the market on Tuesday was ever used at home'.[4] Foley's account is a salutary reminder also of the continuing 'hidden' nature of women's farm work. Although employed as a domestic servant to work in the house and look after a baby, she worked in the dairy everyday and helped in the hay harvest.

Moving away from 'classic farm service' was the practice of hiring young, single men by the year that lived in the farmhouse, or more usually the house of a foreman. This was the system in the East Riding of Yorkshire, although it was also present in Lincolnshire and parts of the East Midlands. In Lincolnshire in the 1920s Mr Cottingham remembered the foreman 'usually had single men lodging in his house. They were looked after by the foreman's wife, sometimes with the aid of a young girl who had just left school.'[5] Unlike most other cereal growing areas of England and Wales on these farms young men looked after the horses beginning as young as 13, with their first hirings as a 'boy' and reaching the height of their trade in their early 20s. As they grew, and changed farms at the hirings, they increased in seniority, with each lad being given a fixed place in a rigid hierarchy. Living in meant long hours.[6]

> We started work at six o'clock each morning and worked until six o'clock at night with one hour's break from twelve noon till one o'clock. We fed our horses before breakfast and again at night, then groomed them.

At harvest the hours could be longer still.[7]

> In clover or hay time we got our horses groomed and harnessed up, ready for going out cutting with the reaper at 3 a.m. and worked until 1 p.m. Then we changed with the second lad who went from one o'clock until dusk.

At marriage they often left the farm or worked as labourers, living off the farm and working on shorter contracts. Occasionally the lucky ones would get to be a foreman:[8]

> . . . I had been courting the parlour maid who lived in and worked for the boss's wife, for three or four years. The boss he was moving the foreman I lived with to another farm. So he would like me to take his place and be foreman at the farm I worked on. So after a long talk I said I would, if my young lady agreed to get married. She did and I came to live in the cottage where I had lived with the other foreman.

The third form of farm service was family hiring. This was most common on the Border regions of England and Scotland, particularly in Northumberland where it was a highly formalised system, but it was also present in Kent and Dorset, although it was of little significance in the latter county even in the 1900s. In the cereal areas of Northumberland the system involved the family head – usually a male 'hind' – being hired for the whole year to live on the farm in a tied house. The family group then provided both regular and casual workers. In 1921 the farm workforce on Castle Heaton Farm in the Glendale area of Northumberland was based around six family groups who lived on the farm and were employed regularly throughout the year. The households were all headed by men who were paid a weekly wage, and in most of the families there was also at least one regular female worker.[9] This was a direct survival of the 'bondage' system in which a hired man had to bring with him 'a good and sufficient' woman worker.[10]

In family hiring payments to the family members were recorded separately but seem to have been paid, on occasion at least, to the family head. As well as a rent-free house, the family members also received payment in kind. In 1921 such payments at Castle Heaton included oats, land to keep a cow, coal, seven pigs and two lots of mutton. In addition the farm employed a number of casuals from within the families already hired and outside, including migrant Irish workers.

If we move away from the north, the west and Wales the dominant form of hiring was by the week, or even by the day, although there was often a longer-term contract implied in these hirings. East Anglia, most of the Midlands and the southeast were dominated by this system. Unlike the areas of farm service in these counties men lived away from the farm on which they worked and, although the number of tied houses was growing in the inter-war period, they usually had no formal living arrangement through their employers. Again in contrast to areas of the north and west, and especially Wales (though not with Yorkshire or Lincolnshire), there was a wide separation between master and man. The farms were large, and so were the workforces. William Womack Ringer, admittedly an extreme example, farmed some 7,000 acres in northwest Norfolk in the 1920s with a workforce of over 200. The farm workers of these great eastern farms had little or no chance of ever becoming farmers themselves and had, on the surface at least, little reason to identify with their employers.

However the farm workforce, whether on the huge cereal farms of the eastern and northeastern counties or on the dairy farms of the Midlands, was not an undifferentiated mass. Hierarchies of skill, and sometimes of age, marked men off, one from another. Again, in the inter-war period as in the 1900s, regional experience was vital here. On the cereal farms the horseman was still king. His skill, especially with the plough, was still sought after and rewarded both by better wages and real status among his peers. Nor was his position substantially challenged before the war outside of some of the larger East Anglian farms. Stephen Caunce notes that the decline in the number of horses in the East Riding for most of the inter-war period was related not to their replacement by tractors, and hence a decline in the role and status of the horseman *per se*, but rather to a decline in acreage under crops.[11] In Sussex, Harold Canning started on the farm in 1917 working with horses, and it was not until 1935 that the first tractor appeared. However, even then it was not used in winter. 'At the end of summer, about October time, the tractor was put to bed for the winter. This was the practice on most farms, as you didn't want them on the ground when it was wet. I carried on through the winter with horses.'[12] This is borne out by George Ewart Evans' classic studies of the East Anglian horseman whose decline he dates to the post-Second World War period.[13]

In the dairying areas the position was more ambiguous. Dairying had been 'women's work', and in much the same way as many farmers thought that dairy farming was 'not real farming', so many farm workers seem to have objected to 'retraining' for dairy work. When Mr H. Green who farmed at Walsgrave-on-Sowe near Coventry switched to dairy after 1921 he 'discharged all his men with the exception of one young man' and replaced them with boys direct from school. 'It was not so much because their wages were lower, but because they were keen and willing to adopt new methods.'[14] However, skilled dairymen soon came to demand as good wages and nearly as much prestige as good horsemen. Particularly as the demands of government for more and more hygienically produced milk became insistent, indeed central to profitability, after the early 1930s the name 'dairyman' replaced 'cow keeper' even on the most arable of farms in Norfolk, marking a grudging acceptance of the new status of milk and milk production.[15]

More traditionally shepherding remained little changed except in terms of numbers. In the Border regions shepherds seem to have continued to have been paid almost entirely in kind, with a share of the flock, a house, coals and oats provided, until well into the 1930s. In southern England in contrast the shepherd was a hired worker paid a weekly wage but supplemented with various payments for the number of lambs. He also earned extra, well into the inter-war period, by sheep shearing, done by the piece by organised shearing gangs. These, headed by a man called the Captain, with a good reputation as a shearer, and the trust of both the rest of his gang and those farmers who employed them, moved from farm to farm sleeping rough in barns. The hours were long, from dawn until late at night, when they sheared by candlelight, but the money was good. At the end of shearing they met in a pub and the Captain paid them what was due.[16] However, these men were at the end of an era. The fall in wool prices in the 1920s hit the Downlands badly and by the 1920s the number of sheep in the Rottingdean area of Sussex, for example, had dropped to a third of their pre-war level. In the same village the last great Downland sheep farm was sold and broken up in 1928. The Downs were no longer grazed, and in many places reverted to scrub, while the ever-powerful march of house building spread from Brighton and Peacehaven.[17]

The position of women in the farm workforce also varied regionally. In percentage terms the largest number of women were employed in Northumberland. In 1921 the number of women farm labourers was 36.6 per cent of that of men as against a national figure of just under 6 per cent.[18] This figure reflects, as we have already said, the continuance of family hiring in this area, as it does in Durham where the same figure was 33 per cent. What we have in these areas is a continuation of 'traditional' women's employment patterns dating back to at least the beginning of the nineteenth century, and although they were to continue through to the 1930s, they were entering their last phase. However, even in the first years of war *Farmers Weekly* continued to report on women at northern hirings.[19] In terms of numbers a different kind of women's employment was beginning to dominate, especially in the eastern counties. The highest numbers of women employed were in the Isle of Ely with the Holland area of Lincolnshire coming next. Here women were widely employed in the relatively 'new' areas of fruit and vegetable production. Similarly in the counties around London, and especially Middlesex and Kent, market gardening and fruit production provided work for many women.

Although much of this work was 'casual', accounts from within these areas show that if all periods of casual work are added together many of these women were working something like a full-time job. As Mrs Ruth Brockwell, who grew up on a Kent farm in the 1930s wrote:[20]

> We used to have two women who came in nearly all the time, unless the weather was very bad, to help with the work on the fruit trees – pruning and that sort of thing. We had a group of women from Tenterden who used to come in all through the summer for fruit picking and packing and they used to come in year after year. It was always the same women.

These women also weeded the strawberry plants in early spring and then put straw down on them, while in the winter months they pulled docks and thistles.[21]

If these women were effectively working full time there was another group for whom work, although central to the income of labouring families, was more obviously casual. Few operations of the agricultural cycle functioned without the work of women, and for that matter children, at any time during the inter-war years. An old Essex man sketched out the year round in an interview in the 1990s:[22]

> See in them days boy, see in this village alone women used to go out and start sugar beeting in May, thinning the sugar beet out . . . then they used to go on the pea-picking. They reckon they used to start pea-picking 1st of June. When they finished pea picking, they used to go on the sticks, and after they finished the bean picking they'd probably go on the potato picking, see? So they were going from May, well, as long as the weather kept open, say to the end of October.

Work like this remained hidden from the census taker, and indeed from officials in general since much of it was low paid, and paid in cash. This was also true of children's work. Throughout England and Wales until at least the 1950s school holidays varied with region to accommodate the different harvests. In the north and parts of the east it was potatoes, for much of East Anglia it was cereals, for the London region and for Kent and Sussex it was hopping. Together the earnings of children, and especially women, were a vital part of the social economy of the rural poor. An account from the daughter of a jobbing gardener, farm worker and (very) small holder who grew up in Ditchling in Sussex in the 1920s shows just how vital the combined income of the whole family was.[23]

With the money that he earned and the garden produce from our own plot of land, we were much better off than before. To supplement father's income mother made jellies, jams, pickles and wines. They were much in demand. . . . The sugar was brought by the cwt. sack. . . . We children had the task of picking the wild fruits in season. . . . We also had to take our turn stirring the great pans. The jars had to be washed. . . . Rex wrote the labels (and) we made the covers. . . . Some of the ladies in the village would buy a jar but most of it was packed into wooden crates and these would be collected by Carter Paterson the carrier and taken to the various universities that were attended by the young gentlemen of the village.

Strangely enough, perhaps the most traditional women's work of all, work in the dairy, was, as we have said, passing out of women's hands in the inter-war period. Again this was a long process beginning in the nineteenth century, and one which was associated with the commercialisation of dairy production. The 1921 Census shows how far this change had gone; while just over 10,000 women were described as 'in charge of cattle', 57,000 men followed the same occupation.[24] However, women's dairy work did not vanish. Mrs Emily Owen grew up on a Cheshire farm with a herd of 90 cows, which were hand milked in the early 1920s. 'Most women in the village turned out as a matter of course,' she wrote, 'partly to earn extra money but also it was expected of them as the wives of farm labourers.'[25] With the gradual spread of mechanisation women were further pushed out of the workforce in the dairy sector, ultimately leaving the control of the milking machine in the hands of a male, full-time worker.

Wages and conditions, for men and women, varied with regions and with hiring. From 1917 to 1939, with the brief exception of the years from 1921–4, wages, conditions and hours were set by the Wages Boards. However, this did not mean that wages were uniform nationally, even where the minimum was actually paid. The north of England had, in the nineteenth century, been a high-wage area. This was due largely to competition from industry, but also simply to the sparsity of population and hence available workers, and this continued to be the case in the immediate post-Great War period. However, after the re-establishment of the Wages Boards in 1924 these regional disparities tended to disappear. Nationally, wages had risen in the last years of the Great War, peaking at between 45s and 50s per week in 1920, with regulated hours including a Saturday half-day.

Wages dropped dramatically in the aftermath of the repeal of the Agriculture Act and the end of the first Wages Boards in the summer of 1921. This was met by spasmodic strike action, even in high-wage areas of the north, as in the East Riding in 1920 and 1922.[26] In Norfolk wages fell from 45s per week in that year to 30s by the winter of 1922. This led, in March 1923, to a bitter strike in the county when a further reduction to 24s 9d was proposed. The strike had some of the character of a set piece battle between the best-organised farmers and the best organised workers in the county. At the height of the strike, which lasted a month, some 7,000 men were out, mainly in the north of the county.[27] The strikers used 'cycle pickets' to move around the county going onto farms where men were working, but where the pickets were not known, to prevent strike breaking. Six hundred extra police were brought into the county but were, by their own admission, unable to protect those working on distant farms. The strike also showed, as had the unemployed demonstrations of the previous winters, that attitudes of a section of the farm workers had changed from those of their supposedly deferential fathers and grandfathers. At Rougham, for example, a farmer's son, Eric Hockley, who was a 'farm pupil', was working with a team of horses with a farmer, Mr E.H. Ringer, when a group of strikers arrived. Hockley later told the magistrates:[28]

> They swore at me and called us blacklegs, telling us we were taking bread out of their mouths. I undid the horses, and as I was bending down to do this, one of them hit me with a stick across my back; another struck me a blow with his fist in my ear.

Ringer continued the story:

> One of them asked Hockley, 'Where were you in 1914?' He replied 'I am not 18 now'. One of the strikers then said, 'We have been through five years of war. You made your pile in the war and we are going to have it now.'

At the end of the strike some 2,000 workers were still out, blacklisted for their solidarity. It was to be the last major strike of farm workers in the twentieth century. In 1924 the Wages Board was restored and with it a national wage. For this reason the strike was seen as a victory by many who took part. As 'Billa' Dixon, a Norfolk worker, said:[29]

> That was the turn of the tide, after we went back, and we asked for, the farmers had had enough, they got chopped over the strike, we asked for another 5s, and we got it and went on. . . . Then more went into the union, and it got hold then, up to where we are today. They were the start them days, getting the wages, and we had to do it on nothing.

However, the farm workers' leadership saw it differently. In the aftermath of the strike it quickly became the accepted wisdom that the farm worker could not go it alone. Rather, it was argued, that those who worked in agriculture needed to stand alongside the farmers and fight for the 'interests of agriculture'. Particularly important here was Edwin Gooch who virtually rebuilt the policy of the Union after 1928 when he became President. As Howard Newby writes:[30]

during the 1930s (Gooch) convinced his Executive that the farm workers' interests were not necessarily identical with those of the industrial workers. He was also brave enough to lead his union into the political wilderness which the break with the Labour policy implied. Thereafter Gooch sought common cause with the NFU on agricultural policy matters.

Not that this implied an easy course for the 'rank-and-file'. Although the 1923 strike and the return of the Wages Board saw a halt in wage reductions in the short term, the price collapse of 1930–2 saw wage reductions across the United Kingdom, bringing wages in some counties down to those of 1923. In addition unemployment rose dramatically. Figures are difficult to come by since farm workers remained excluded from the provisions of the National Insurance scheme until 1936, but there are some regional indicators. In Wales, Ashby and Evans calculated that unemployment was about 10 per cent of the workforce in 1931.[31] In Norfolk, Douet writes, 'the county workforce fell by about 3,000 between 1929 and 1931, almost exactly the number on outdoor relief in 1931, nearly all of whom were agricultural workers.'[32]

With no unemployment pay the farm workers turned, as their parents and grandparents had, to the hated Poor Law. An unemployed Norfolk man wrote in *The Land Worker*:[33]

> I have worked on this farm fourteen years . . . we were discharged a fortnight before Christmas. All Christmas with no pay. Only remedy to go to the relieving Officer which was three miles off. . . . He gave me a card and I had to go round to six farmers and get it signed . . . (then) back to the Relieving Officer and hand in our cards. . . . After another week had passed we were told to report to the roadman and started work.

In the 1970s a Norfolk farmer remembered the same period. 'The unemployed were required to work four days a week in the local gravel pit where, with pick and shovel, they raised hoggin for the local road making and received the sum of 3s per day.'[34]

For many, though, leaving the land forever was preferable to digging stones. This was especially true for the young. In the East Riding of Yorkshire there was a 41 per cent reduction in the number of under 21-year-olds at work on the county's farms between 1921 and 1938.[35] This figure was repeated nationally with a drop of 39 per cent in the same period, while those over 21 declined by only 18 per cent. In Wales the figures were slightly different. Here, the decline among older workers was slightly higher, but the decline had set in earlier. Most striking in Wales was the decline in the number of women workers, whose numbers fell by over 50 per cent between 1929 and 1939 alone. As Ashby and Evans wrote, 'movements of this magnitude can only be described as a veritable flight of hired labour from the land.'[36]

Plate 7 Farm labour. Even in the late 1930s the horse and machinery designed in the nine-
teenth century dominated most of English agriculture. Cutting oats near Ipsden in
Oxfordshire in 1938. (Reproduced by kind permission of the Rural History Centre,
University of Reading.)

    As the fortunes of farming began to pick up after 1935 so did wages; however,
conditions in the rural areas still remained worse than the towns in many
respects. In 1937 Rowntree's survey of working-class family budgets, based on
minimum standards of nutrition laid down by the British Medical Association,
calculated that a wage of 41s per week was needed to support a family with three
children in rural areas. In that year average weekly earnings set by the Wages
Board were 35s 3d for ordinary workers, 40s 10d for stockmen and 38s 4d for
horsemen.[37] The problems of rural living standards were also shown John Boyd
Orr's classic study of the national diet *Food, Health and Income* of 1936.[38] While
the most spectacular results of Boyd Orr's work on children's diet were from
urban areas, they also demonstrated widespread rural nutritional deficiency
resulting from low wages.

    Certainly in some areas there were 'perks'. In Sussex Harold Canning got 36s
a week, a cottage and a hundred faggots a year in 1928.[39] In the north and Wales
a portion of wages was paid in board and lodging, but money wages in these areas
had fallen to less than £1 a week by the mid-1920s for living-in workers. Much is,
and was, made of 'free' cottages, but the number available was actually always

small, and most tied housing was not rent-free. Even where housing was free or cheap, conditions were bad. In 1928, Harold Canning's cottage, by no means the worst around, had no gas, electricity or mains water. A woman writing of Kennington in Oxfordshire in 1925 remembered:[40]

'Cottages' conjures up a very rural 'roses round the door' picture, but they were nothing like that. . . . There was one large room downstairs, with a piece partitioned off for what we used to call a scullery, which was the kitchen really. Upstairs there were two bedrooms, one of which you had to go through to get to the other one. . . . The bedrooms were very cold – very cold. . . . It wasn't idyllic really, like they think.

To an extent the inter-war period saw some slight improvements in working-class housing as a result of government grants to local authorities, however this was limited. The Parish Council minutes of Heathfield in Sussex tell an all too familiar story. In September 1918 Hailsham Rural District Council, their controlling authority, wrote, under the terms of the Housing of the Working Classes Act, asking what the housing requirements of the parish were. The Parish Council responded that the 'the nominal requirements of the parish was (sic) met at present but the opinion was expressed that it was desirable to consider what could be done with certain cottages which were not considered fit for human habitation.'[41] In 1919 two pairs of houses were built, and soon after another four pairs. However, Heathfield now considered this inadequate and a scheme was put forward, and accepted by Hailsham RDC to build twenty-two houses. The scheme was short lived; as a minute laconically puts it, 'this scheme was dropped in 1923 owing to the action of the Ministry of Health.'[42] Heathfield, like thousands of rural and urban parishes, had fallen victim to 'Geddes Axe', the sweeping cuts in public expenditure which ended so much of the dream of a 'land fit for heroes' and marked, in housing, the switch from government support to 'private enterprise'. Nevertheless, in 1927, using the 'Wheatley Act' brought in by the Labour Government of 1924, some houses were built in Heathfield, though not the twenty-two asked for, and within a year there were six families on the parish 'waiting list'.[43]

Another problem was caused by the deterioration of existing housing stock, especially in areas where landlords and farmers were unwilling, or unable, to repair or improve housing as a result of the agricultural problems. The 1926 Rural Workers Housing Act and especially the 1933 Housing (Financial Provisions) Act and the 1935 Housing Act could help in these cases. These enabled County Councils to give grants for improvement of existing properties as well as to purchase, compulsorily if necessary, houses or buildings to convert and rent to 'rural workers'. How far they were used nationally is difficult to know. Cambridgeshire Labour Party complained in 1929 'in 1927 only TWO [sic] houses in the whole county were reconditioned, under the Tory Rural Workers Housing Act, and very Few Since [sic].'[44] In Sussex the 1930 Acts, though limited by restricted funds, seem usually to have been used well, especially to improve existing dwellings. Grants were used to add staircases, windows, access and re-dig wells. Standards were usually high, and enforced, as in July 1931 when a landlord was refused a grant for a cottage improvement unless the changes included an extra bedroom and a new well.[45] Some Sussex landlords seem to have made extensive use of these Acts to improve at least some dwellings. Lord Gage at Firle received £139 in 1939 to convert the old workhouse into flats, and Harold Macmilliam got a grant in the same year to convert a 'cottage for a farm worker'.[46] However, even with the grants some estates would not comply with Council standards, as, again in 1939, when the Sheffield Park Estate applied for £494 to renovate twelve cottages but were only given grants for two since they were unwilling to enlarge the cottages, by joining two into one and thus reducing their number.[47]

To some farm workers 'the land fit for heroes' appeared to promise just that. Going back to the years immediately before the Great War the issue of the land had loomed large in British politics. A particular aspect which had attracted wide-spread discussion was the question of 'the land for the people' — some version of redistribution of the land via small holdings. There had been limited pre-war leg-islation of a permissive kind, but during the war demand grew for government action as part of reconstruction, which would enable ex-soldiers to become small holders and eventually farmers. In 1918 the 'Selbourne Committee' had made recommendations that alongside a minimum wage and a minimum price for cereals the Government should promote colonies of small holders, many recruited from ex-soldiers. At the end of December 1919 County and Borough Councils received a circular from the Board of Agriculture instructing them to 'proceed at once to consider what land can be acquired in your county for the settlement of ex-servicemen'.[48] Land could be purchased and, subject to Board approval, central Government would cover losses between income and expendi-ture up to 1925. After that date 'the position will be re-considered as regards any subsequent schemes.'[49]

The response was mixed. Nationally about 250,000 acres were bought and nearly 17,000 tenants eventually settled on holdings of various sizes, many of which contained no buildings at all. Locally some councils were better than others, and while no study of the scheme as a whole exists, provision of holdings seems to relate more to the willingness of the council to act than to real demand for farms. The contrasting experiences of Sussex and Cambridgeshire highlight the successes and failures of the scheme. Both counties had numbers of council-owned small holdings before the war, although Cambridgeshire, with a strong, if relatively new, tradition of market gardening and fruit and vegetable growing had more. Cambridgeshire also reacted quickly to a perceived post-war demand for land and in May 1918 put in motion plans for acquiring land for ex-servicemen.[50] In December 1918, however, the problems which were to bedevil a scheme which relied largely on the votes of farmers and landowners on the County Council for money, were already clear. While admitting the demand for land and the justice of the cause the War Agriculture Executive Committee resolved 'to order the County Council to take steps to acquire any land required for the Settlement Schemes at a change of tenancy rather than by exercise of compulsory purchase in order not to disturb the normal security of tenure.'[51]

Despite this, Cambridgeshire CC went ahead acquiring land for holdings and also a farm, Shelford Bottom Farm, to train disabled ex-servicemen in agriculture, which was bought by compulsory purchase from Caius College, Cambridge.[52] By June 1919 Cambridgeshire CC had requests for some 15,300 acres from 952 applicants, just over half of them ex-servicemen.[53] A year later despite extensive purchases they still had demands for over 4,000 acres from 374 approved ex-service applicants.[54] Sussex followed a similar path but with both less enthusiasm and, initially at least, many less applicants. In February 1919 there were 144 applicants, the vast majority ex-servicemen, for 840 acres of land.[55]

If the largest group of workers in rural areas in the inter-war years were those employed in agriculture, the second largest was another 'traditional' group, domestic servants. In 1921 there were 427,798 men and women employed in 'personal and domestic service' in England and Wales. The vast majority of these were women (369,407) and indoor domestic servants (16,663 men and 309,337 women).[56] As with most occupations there were profound regional differences in distribution. In the rural areas nationally 11.9 per cent of employed women were in personal service making it by far the most important inter-war occupation for women in these areas. The highest concentration of women in personal service was in the southeast, and within that area in the counties of East and West Sussex (20 per cent and 18.6 per cent respectively). The reasons for this are fairly clear. Even in the inter-war period there were a very high number of elderly and retired people in these counties, which created a demand for servants. They were also holiday areas, which at least produced seasonal demands for hotel workers. In addition these counties, along with many others in the southeast, contained a high proportion of traditional gentry and aristocratic households, which also created a demand for servants. Furthermore, here, as elsewhere, the spread of the suburban population into the countryside with the continuing growth of commuting provided 'places' for many young women. This is clear in the high percentage of domestic servants in Surrey (16.8), Buckinghamshire (16) and Hertfordshire (13.2).

At the other end of the scale the largely industrial counties show a low proportion of domestic servants. Only about 7 per cent of occupied women in the West Riding of Yorkshire were domestic servants, as was the case in Lancashire and Nottinghamshire, while the lowest level of employment was in Leicester-shire. There are other counties though where the figures reveal a continuing contradiction in the description of women's work. Most Welsh counties show a very high level of women employed in domestic service as do some northern counties, for example Northumberland and Westmorland. Given the social structure of these areas it seems likely that many women described as 'domestic servant' were, in fact, either part- or full-time *farm* servants. This was certainly the case in the Devon parish of Hartland where, according to Mary Bouquet, young women going into service in the 1920s carried out both domestic duties including cleaning and cooking as well as milking, butter making, bringing in the cows from the fields and cleaning the dairy.[57]

It is near impossible to generalise about the conditions under which these women worked, since so much depended on the precise nature of their 'places'. Traditionally there was a fairly clear career path. Country girls began on leaving school with service in a local farmhouse or in a nearby town. In theory they 'learned their trade' in places like this and moved upwards to larger and better places. At the same time they might move up through the complex hierarchies of the household with a few, unmarried, ending up as housekeeper to a great house. In practice, of course, few followed this route. Most, like Winifred Foley, moved through a series of jobs among largely middle-class households where only 'one servant was kept', her only real gains being those in wages, and these usually based on age. Such employment was hard and seldom rewarding. Winifred Foley writes of a house in Cheltenham where she went into service in the late 1920s.[58]

> They were in need of a strong young fool – one who could be housemaid from six till one for cleaning the house, then parlourmaid for waiting at table, then nanny for the children's afternoon outings, the washerwoman in the evening. They needed a creature that would run on very little fuel and would not question her lot. Instead they had me; but at any rate I *was* a fool.

It is difficult to know if this kind of experience became more common in the inter-war years as the number of servants kept in the 'great' houses probably declined while the number working in one or two servant households, especially in the new suburbs, probably increased. Certainly the studies done by Jean Beauchamp for *Women Who Work* in 1931 suggest conditions in a single servant household could be terrible.[59]

> D. does all the work of a small house, including the washing and ironing. She works from 6.30 a.m. till after 9 p.m. with one half day off a week and alternative [sic] Sunday afternoons. She sleeps in a tiny bedroom which is very hot in summer and bitterly cold in winter. Her wages are 14s a week, and her food is weighed out for her in niggardly portions by her employer.

Given these conditions Beddoe suggests, as does Roberts, that resistance to going into service was growing in the inter-war period, especially among women from the industrial areas and from other urban centres.[60] If this is so the fact that the number of women in personal and domestic service actually increased between 1921 and 1931 means that country women must have made up the gap, although there is some evidence of older urban women entering service, especially as non-residential workers.[61] The reasons for this are not far to seek. For most working-class girls leaving school in the country areas there was little opportunity to do anything else. As a woman from Oxfordshire wrote, 'on the last day at Goring school the local gentry came round and offered jobs. My first job was as a between maid.'[62] Another woman from the same county says 'domestic service was the job open to most country girls 60 years ago, (1930s) who went to the nearest town or city and lived in with a family. I went into such a job in a residential suburb of Oxford.'[63]

By the mid-1930s there is a sense that even this had begun to change. We have already noted that as the economy improved the number of women employed on Welsh farms fell dramatically, and many of these would probably have been 'domestics' as well as farm workers. Also in the 1930s the 'servant problem' began to take on a new dimension of horror for the middle classes suggesting a subtle change. E.M. Delafield's fictional 'provincial lady', whose diary first appeared in 1929, was in constant fear of losing her servants and, as Alison Light comments, 'a note of muffled outrage starts to creep into many of the writings of well-to-do women, confronted by such "desertion".'[64] Nor were these feelings without reason. Even if Winifred Foley went into service, it was because there was little else, and she did not relish it. Further, as a 'good' domestic she was constantly approached by many a current employer's 'friends' to leave and come and work for them, suggesting that notions of servant shortage were not all in the minds of the idle or wealthy.[65]

Despite these conditions, domestic service, like farm work, retained a traditional deferential, and even idyllic, character. At the most brutal end of this both groups were reliant on their employers to an extent few other groups in society were – this reliance stretching at its most extreme to the very roofs over their heads and the food in their bellies. Both groups were also 'outside' the welfare system until the late 1930s in that they were excluded from the National Insurance scheme, which left them unprotected in times of unemployment. In this situation workers were forced to rely on the paternalistic side of employer/employee relations. Where this functioned, as it frequently did, it was represented in idyllic tones. The memories of a 'good' master among farm workers or a gentle and caring mistress among servants are not simply to be taken as golden age inventions – they frequently represented a very real part of lived experience.

That experience was lived out within social milieu, which still retained many traditional elements. The most obvious of these was the village, yet, as we have already seen, the village was by no means the only or even dominant rural settlement pattern in England in the past, or for much of the twentieth century. In the north and west of England and throughout most of Wales men and women lived, and continue to live, in scattered farmsteads or hamlets, while it is only in the south and east that the 'classic' village dominates.[66] Yet for many, especially in the areas away from the Home Counties, farm, hamlet or village remained occupational communities throughout the inter-war period. What change there was was often subtle and hidden. For example, the growing political and local power of the farmers, and conversely the relative decline in that of the aristocracy, was often difficult to see as anything other than immediate personal experience. The great house might close; in extreme cases it might be pulled down; there were more farmers than gentlemen on County Councils; but seen through the narrow prism of one community these changes were difficult to quantify.

Intangible changes, some of which are touched on in the next chapter, perhaps broadened the worldview, especially of younger villagers. The radio reached out into country districts and even with the relative poverty of the farm worker few were untouched by it. The cinema was different. For most villagers 'going to the flics' meant a journey by bus or even in a carrier's cart to the nearest town. The dreams of the silver screen touched few, outside the young, in the rural areas of England and Wales. Holidays were even rarer. The Saturday half day was by no means universal in rural England and Bank Holidays in the summer were always ignored because of the necessity of farm work at busy seasons. Few of the modernising influences of the 1930s touched the rural working class.

In the market town there were more changes. At the end of the nineteenth century there seems to have been a decline in village-based trades supplying goods and services to the community – for example boot and shoe makers, tailors, even some kinds of food shops. In their place the relative power of the market town grew in influence over its surrounding *pays*. This was also true of the social and cultural institutions of late Victorian England where religious, political and leisure organisations increasingly saw the country town as a centre. The country towns also bred their own 'working class' and their own elites of shopkeepers and tradesmen.[67]

In the inter-war period some of this began to change as smaller country towns began to lose out to larger or even to 'the' county town. Although they remained few until the 1930s the growth of rural bus services here was a key. People whose parents had perhaps gone only once a year from rural north Oxfordshire to Oxford City for St Giles' Fair, or to Tombland Fair in Norwich, now went four or five times a year 'to shop'. They were attracted, especially in the 1930s, by the products of what was the beginning of a retail revolution. As Aldcroft writes:

Plate 8 The country goes to the town and the town to the country. A 'charabanc' outing preparing to leave Reading in the 1920s. (Reproduced by kind permission of the Rural History Centre, University of Reading.)

Estimated retail sales in real terms rose by nearly 38 between 1920 and 1938, and much of this increase in business went to larger retailers. The growth of large scale retailing was primarily a twentieth-century phenomenon.

Before the Great War the vast majority of shops were locally owned and run, with large multi-outlet chains accounting for less than 20 per cent of retail sales. By 1939 this had risen to nearer 35 per cent, while in some areas such as footwear, women's clothing, groceries and provisions, dairy produce and chemists' goods, they accounted for more than 40 per cent of the market.[68] It was in the 1930s in particular that chain stores spread out from the cities and suburbs to the county towns. Even before the Great War Sainsbury's had shops in large county towns like Norwich, Ipswich, Oxford, Eastbourne and Folkestone. In the inter-war period, although Sainsbury's remained essentially a southern and eastern phenomenon, shops had appeared in much smaller towns like Colchester, Cambridge and Chelmsford. Importantly, these were large shops by the standards of the day and sold branded and standardised merchandise under Sainsbury's 'own label'. By 1938 'almost all the groceries sold in Sainsbury's were own brands.'[69]

Not all welcomed the changes in country and market towns. In 1929, Dr H.A. Mess, Director of the Tyneside Council of Social Service wrote:[70]

> The country towns dream no more. The rattle of the motor has roused them. The char-a-banc are parked in their market places. The multiple shops have invaded them. . . . The roads between the towns are thick with traffic; the entrance to the towns is through a barrage of unsightly advertisements and the sides of the roads are fringed with villas and bungalows.

Yet like the case of the village, such change was uneven and regional. Sainsbury's seldom moved far outside the south and east before the Second World War, although there were of course other regional chains. Even when they appeared, especially in the smaller towns, the chain stores stood alongside older and family established business for many years. In Bicester in Oxfordshire the 'International Stores' stood alongside a whole range of locally owned shops in the main street, including at least two 'grocery' shops.[71] Yet these changes in market towns, however slight, marked the beginning of a new countryside and the arrival of new countrymen and women.

6   New countrymen and women

Workers and trippers

It is now a well worn cliché of historical writing that for some – perhaps even a majority of the working class – the inter-war period, and especially the 1930s, was a period not of depression and despair but of growing prosperity.[1] This was clearly not true for those who worked the land, and whose average weekly earnings were half those of skilled urban workers in 1937, and 30 per cent lower than even urban labourers. However, there were new groups of workers in the rural areas and especially in the southeast, who were benefiting from some of this improvement. Adding to this group were others who sought out a country life or at least a country holiday and who brought to the countryside a part of the financial improvement of the late 1930s. In this respect the inter-war period marks the slow beginnings of the change, which was to come to fruition in the last decades of the century when the majority of country dwellers ceased to have any contact with the land, at least as workers.

The most obvious example of this is 'sub-urbanisation' – the tendency for cities to grow on their outer edges, not only as a result of growing population and the demand for inner-city land for commercial purposes, but also as a result of changing desires. Suburban growth was of course not new in the 1920s and 1930s. The gradual spread of railways, trams and, in London, the underground had been opening up the countryside to the commuter since at least the 1880s and the outer areas of London grew at a rate of more than 50 per cent per decade from 1881–1901. In 1905 Henrietta Barnett wrote, 'every year London grows, stretching out into the country long and generally unlovely arms.'[2] Nor was it only London. As Peter Hall has shown, Merseyside, Bristol, the West Midlands, Greater Manchester and the West Riding all showed signs of suburban expansion in this period.[3] Indeed there are few cities, or even large towns, which would be exempt from such a list.

However, it was London and the southeast which dominated inter-war thinking about suburbanisation. The reasons for this are clear. At the most basic level the gradual movement from an economy based on heavy industry and manufacturing, to one based on light industry and commerce led to population

Plate 9 The 'octopus' which conservationists and others feared was strangling rural England. New bungalows at Boreham Wood 'Garden Village' *c.*1930. To those who lived in them, they were the taste of a rural idyll; to their usually wealthy critics they were the end of the Garden of Eden. (Reproduced by kind permission of the Rural History Centre, University of Reading.)

movements away from the areas of the industrial revolution. As property prices in inner London grew (outside the slum areas at least) both businesses and their workers moved out. In 1921 the Census had noted that 'increases above the average are recorded for all the Home Counties with an exception in the case of Kent.'[4] By 1940 the Barlow Report saw this trend as a major change.[5]

> The continued drift of the industrial population to London and the Home Counties constitutes a social, economic, and strategical problem, which demands immediate attention.

Those who moved out came in search of rural or at least semi-rural England. As Thomas Sharp wrote in 1932:[6]

> People have lived too long in dreary streets. They had seen too few trees and too little grass in their sordid towns. They were tired of the squalid paved back yards. They wanted gardens of their own, back and front, with a space between their house and the next.

They also, however, as Best and Rogers argue, wanted modern houses near to shops, schools and transport; hence it was the hamlet, the small town and the village which were the epitome of rural life.[7]

Where they came they built in country style. As Barret and Phillips write in *Suburban Style*:

> It was this rejection (in the inter-war period) of the uncompromising images of the neo-Georgian and the Modernist style favoured by the architectural establishment that provoked the most acute criticism. . . . The haphazard combination of architectural details – mock beams, lattice windows, weather-boarding, pebble dash and fancy brickwork – created, in Osbert Lancaster's words an 'infernal amalgam' of the 'least attractive materials and building devices known in the past', a view shared by the architectural profession and social commentators alike.

'By-pass variegated' was a middle-class invention, or rather reinvention of the rural. 'Moderne' houses, like those built by Laings between the wars, were far out-numbered by 'traditional' or 'cottage' styles. The visual evidence of this remains with us today in every city, town and even many villages, in the form of the 'mock-Tudor' house.

In culture in general, though, it is often argued that the inter-war period saw a complete defeat for ruralism and Englishness. The modern movement in art, letters and music had little place for the 'traditional'. Yet such an easy judgement misses huge areas. The inter-war period saw, especially in the south and east, the regionalisation of the country life ideal through magazines like *The Sussex Magazine* founded in 1923. Although 'rural' in its content it was edited from Eastbourne by a solicitor and firmly aimed at an urban or at least suburban audience. It carried articles on folklore, country crafts, country houses and short stories with a 'rural' setting. Most counties had identical magazines.

In literature pre-war writers or writers in the pre-war style like Sheila Kaye-Smith and Mary Webb continued to be enormously popular, indeed much more popular than most modernist writers, whose readership remained firmly upper class, bohemian and metropolitan. Nor was there much sign in their writing of the modern movement conservatism that Alison Light detects in the writing of Compton Burnett, Christie or Jan Struther. Others, like Francis Brett-Young continued to create and recreate the 'imagined' world of a recent lost past as a comment on the current collapse of England. And to top it all, A.E. Housman sold more copies of *A Shropshire Lad* in the 1930s than Auden or Eliot sold of all their poetry.

It seems the inter-war manifestations of ruralism and identification of that with some essentialist notion of Englishness are a continuation, indeed a building on, the pre-First World War movements which were touched on earlier. What is striking, though, is the extent to which these manifestations are less to do with the avant-garde of high culture than in the pre-war period, and more to do with 'mass' middle-class and even working-class culture. What we see here is what

Alison Light calls 'the representations of Englishness traded in familiar tropes' but 'displayed across new forms and modern reproductions'.[8] But that does not change the fact that they represent a kind of Englishness.

Behind these cultural ideas of an essentially 'English' countryside was a new economic reality. The economic growth of the 1920s but especially the 1930s was, as we have already indicated, a regional and occupational one in which the 'traditional' skilled manual and male industries of the nineteenth century declined while the new, and especially the commercial and largely southeastern, prospered. The impact of this was swift. Even in 1921, white-collar workers were the third largest occupational group in country districts after those working in agriculture and domestic servants. If we take together commercial, public and professional occupations in that year we find these groups employed 483,656 men and women in the rural areas.[9] These figures are even more striking when we return to the Home Counties. In 1921, the largest number of white-collar workers lived in Surrey with about 21.5 per cent of the population in these occupations. Middlesex follows this with 21 per cent and Essex with 16 per cent. This meant that there were more white-collar workers in Surrey and Middlesex than in London. Nor was regional spread solely a southern phenomenon. Cheshire, perhaps Manchester's equivalent of Surrey, had 13.2 per cent of its population in white-collar occupations, although no other area in the north comes anywhere near this figure. The other point that needs to be made about this figure is the large number of women involved; women made up 172,721 or 36 per cent of the white-collar workforce even in country districts.

Quite how startling this change was, even at the beginning of the inter-war period, can be shown by a simple comparison. For much of the nineteenth century the third largest group of workers in the rural areas (after agricultural workers and domestic servants) was coal miners, 297,968 of them in 1921 (all the figures are for men and women workers). In fact there were over half as many coal miners living in rural areas as there were farm workers. If we add other quarrying employment there were 336,485 employed in these trades – a group over a third of the size of those in agriculture. The next largest group, and one which was also growing in importance, were transport and communication workers (177,521). Already by 1921 the majority of these were working in road transport, although railway workers constituted an important, and homogeneous, group. Close behind transport workers came metal workers (168,798). This presents an interesting group with both 'traditional' and modernising elements. For instance, there were 28,860 smiths and skilled forge workers – a firmly traditional group. However, they had already been overtaken in the fast lane by the future with 59,637 men and women who worked in branches of the motor trade and mechanical engineering. The only other group employing more than 100,000 people in rural districts was the building trades (135,218).

In the southern areas of England many of these new 'rural' workers were commuters, travelling daily from the rural areas to London by railway. The Southern Railways assiduously promoted Kent, Sussex and above all Surrey with posters illustrating slogans like 'Live in Surrey Free From Worry' and 'Live in Kent and Be Content'. In the early 1930s it published a guide, *Country Homes at London's Door*, arguing that as a result of electrification there were great areas in easy reach of London which were 'actually in and surrounded by the real and beautiful country', where 'London's daily workers can spend their leisure, and sleep, in pure air and in a beautiful country which before was more or less inaccessible'. The guide gave details of housing, lighting, soils and schools and even gave advice on how to borrow money to buy or build a house.[10] The growth of the railways was followed by, and sometimes went hand in hand with, suburban development. The population of Epsom and Ewell increased from 22,953 in 1921 to 35,228 in 1931 and 62,960 in mid-1939; Leatherhead expanded from 11,233 in 1921 to 21,170 in mid-1938, and Caterham and Warlingham from 17,108 to 27,100 in the same period.[11] At Stoneleigh, also in Surrey, the development was even more remarkable. It barely existed in 1930 when two farms were sold to developers, who contributed half the cost of a new station, which was opened in July 1932. By 1935 313,647 people were travelling from Stoneleigh each year – the vast majority to London.[12]

Not all these new countrymen and women were the same. At one extreme there were the hated noveaux riches of John Betjeman's poem 'Slough'.[13]

It's not their fault they do not know
The birdsong from the radio,
It's not their fault they often go
    To Maidenhead

And talk of sports and makes of cars
In various bogus Tudor bars
And daren't look up and see the stars
    But belch instead.

These were perhaps the typical inhabitants of Stoneleigh with its typically unpretentious 'semi's', its grand new roadhouse/pub by the station and, by 1938, the 1,462 seat Rembrandt Cinema, or perhaps Oxted which expanded vigorously in the 1920s and 1930s. Here 'Tudorbethan shopping parades' sprang up in station approach along with another cinema, the 'new Kinema', also in Tudorbethan style.[14]

Elsewhere in suburban England, and even in Surrey's crowded land, lived wealthier and, one assumes from other of Betjeman's suburban poems, more acceptable commuters. St George's Hill near Weybridge, the site of the Diggers' doomed and heroic experiment of common ownership of 1649, became from the late 1920s one of Surrey's most exclusive estates. Here in contrast to the humble 'semi' of the clerk, grand houses built by the developer Walter G. Tarrant stood in grounds of never less than an acre and enjoyed two eighteen hole golf courses and private tennis and croquet clubs.[15] Grander still were the houses making up what Jackson calls 'high quality residential scatter'.[16] In the area around Leith Hill in Surrey, F.E. Green wrote in 1914, 'I can point out to you the residences of people who have amassed wealth out of ships, law, tea, pottery, ink, banking and "contracting".'[17]

Nor was this solely a southern phenomenon, although it was at its most obvious in the south and east of England. In the English Midlands the demand for cars, bicycles, household and electrical goods saw all these sectors increase in size. As in the south and east this led to a largely middle-class move out of the cities of the industrial revolution to the countryside around. Around Birmingham and Wolverhampton suburban development of a kind familiar in the south and east spread into the rural districts. By the mid-1930s the decline of the rural population in both rural Staffordshire and rural Warwickshire had been reversed while, for example, the population of Stoke-on-Trent declined as the areas around 'began to attract young couples who worked in Stafford or the Black Country and travelled daily to work by bus, train or car.'[18] In the former industrial village of Neston in the Wirral the 1930s were remembered as a time of similar change, with 'the building trade . . . one of the few steady occupations'.[19]

> The whole area in the 1930s was slowly but surely changing, if not already changed, into the irreversible dormitory town for the city gent . . . while the rank and file of the populace had to follow suit. The city was where the new work was, and new staff were needed, from manager to office boy, from manageress to typist. . . . To town they went on trains and crowded buses everyday.

Even in the northeast, one of the areas worst hit by the depression, the Council for the Preservation of Rural England could still bemoan the development of the Jesmond area of Newcastle. 'There is a pathos in the rush to build dwellings in green surroundings, which, through lack of early planning, blots out those green surroundings.'[20]

What these new countrymen and women had in common was that they were in the country but not, at least in the traditional sense, of the country. The men of these families, and a substantial part of the unmarried women, travelled daily to an urban place of work, returning for evenings and weekends. The women and children of the new suburbs and suburbanised villages and towns stayed at home. This has led many historians to see these places, particularly for women, as 'a cultural desert', providing a 'life of extreme monotony':[21]

These estates embodied a way of life which was atomised and individualised, that lacked social cohesion except of a passive, flock-of-sheep, variety, and which generated no networks of associations or communities to stand between individuals, or families, and the state.

Yet this seems more to do with what Andy Medhurst has called 'the sheer vitriol which cultural practitioners and commentators have felt compelled to pour over the suburbs' than with historical reality.[22] What few memoirs there seem to be of suburbia talk about endless clubs and societies, from the ubiquitous amateur opera society through to rambling and cycling clubs – indeed as Medhurst writes, 'clubs and societies' were in some ways the defining feature of suburbia.[23] It was not only the elite of St George's Hill that had tennis, golf and even croquet clubs. No new suburb was complete without a 'Tudor Bar' or two, and even the Left Book Club, as George Orwell reminds us, found a cosy niche in the world of 'Dunroamin'.[24] Nor were the women and children quite so trapped at home as is often suggested. Between 1927 and 1935 the number of ordinary tickets sold at Epsom Downs increased from 329,778 to 859,794 as the suburb grew, and the wives and children of the largely male commuters went 'up to town' for the day.[25]

The new white-collar countrymen and women were not the only modernisers in inter-war England and Wales. In many ways, especially in the remoter districts, the transport workers were the most obvious modernisers, bringing in to the rural areas new skills, different traditions and expectations, and even ways of life. Of these 'new workers' the oldest established were railway workers. Their role in rural communities was a complex one embracing, especially before the Great War, aspects of both modernisation and traditionalism. Frank McKenna in his work on the Victorian railway men emphasises the deferential, paternalistic and quasi-military aspects of railway employment.[26]

> From the earliest days, the railway companies sought a new type of loyalist, nothing less than a prototype, an 'organisation' man. They achieved an outstanding success, and for more than a century the workers demonstrated a loyalty to newly founded traditions and working methods unique in British industrial history.

Yet, as we saw briefly in Chapter 1, this was only one side of their being. From at least the 1900s the railway men had been unionised and in the forefront of union militancy. Although they were often the sons of rural workers, they were also mobile workers going where the company sent them, which brought urban workers and the sons of urban workers into the country areas. With them they brought different ideas and different traditions.

Raymond Williams grew up in Pandy in the Welsh Borders, the son of a railway signalman, who was himself the son of a farm labourer who had been sacked and evicted from his cottage. Williams' father started life as a farm worker and then moved on to the railways, working first in the South Wales valleys and then returning to the area of his birth in the early 1920s. Williams had an acute sense of the unusual place of the railway men:[27]

> I grew up in a very peculiar situation – a distinctly rural pattern of small farms, interlocked with another kind of social structure to which the railway workers belonged. They were unionized wage workers, with a perception of a much wider social system beyond the village to which they were linked. Yet at the same time they were tied to the immediate locality, with its particular family farms.

In this situation the railway men ceased to be the deferential workers of McKenna's account and became real forces for change, especially political change.[28]

> The interesting thing is that the political leaders of the village were the railway men. Of the three signalmen in my father's box, one became clerk of the parish council, one the district councillor, while my father was on the parish council. They were much more active than anyone else in the village. All the railway men voted Labour. Most of the farmers, by contrast, voted Liberal. Within the village, there would be local divisions of interest between the two – typically over expenditure. The railway men were a modernizing element who, for example, wanted to introduce piped water and other amenities.

This experience was repeated over much of rural England and Wales as Clare Griffiths has shown in her work on the Labour Party in the countryside.[29]

> The general assumption (in the Labour Party) was that a railway man would be the first choice to organise a rural party, like the signalman Harry Allen, who was the founder and first honorary secretary of the Norfolk Divisional Labour Party. George Ridley, M.P. for Clay Cross, suggested that half the rural parties in the 1930s could not exist but for the substantial contribution made by the N.U.R.

Other apparent representatives of a newer, 'modern' world 'grew' out of the existing communities and their pre-existing economic structures. For example, during the inter-war period the carrier with his horse-drawn wagon, carrying goods and passengers from village to market town and back, was almost universally replaced by the motor bus. In Binbrook in Lincolnshire there were seven carriers in 1900 all using horse-drawn vehicles. By 1937 there were three, all using motor buses or lorries. In Binbrook, as elsewhere, these were often ex-army lorries bought in 1919–20 and 'converted' by adding seats. However, striking continuities are concealed by this bald statement of change. All three families running buses in 1937 had been carriers in 1900 and all retained small-scale farming interests. One family, the Starks, continued dealing – buying and selling on a small scale – characteristic of nineteenth-century carriers and far from a world of modernised motor coaches and arterial roads.[30]

> Robert Stark was also a general dealer, particularly in commodities such as eggs and butter, which were bought at Market Rasen market on a Tuesday and sold at Grimsby on a Friday. He was a horse dealer and breaker. . . . In addition the family bought the water mill and land surrounding it in 1926 which they grazed and farmed. . . . At the same time, Robert's wife Rose, ran a shop selling crockery and some food including monkey nuts and bananas.

This kind of account could be reproduced time and again in the 1920s and 1930s throughout rural England and Wales. Yet against the continuities of family and social situation there were real changes. Stark's bus service, which returned from Louth to Binbrook at 10 o'clock on a Saturday night, enabled those young men who 'lived in' on Binbrook's wold farms to escape at least one night a week from their work place.

The appearance of the private motor car made little direct difference, before the war at least, to those who worked the land. However, its indirect effects were enormous. Many, if not most garages in rural areas started off in black-smith's shops – the village smith being the only person in most villages with any real experience of machinery.

More spectacular, although less obviously rural, was the growth of the motor industry itself. This was overwhelmingly situated in the south and Midlands, often in new suburban areas or even, as at Luton or Oxford, in towns which had at least in part a rural character and hinterland. What R.C. Whiting writes of Morris Motors Cowley is emblematic of these moves. Before 1914, he argues, the rural population had little do with Oxford. However,[31]

> [a]fter 1920 the interpenetration of rural and urban was far more marked. . . . There were certain ways in which Oxford as a town within a largely rural area was bound to have some attraction as a centre for social activities once rural transport improved. In this way there were general changes, which brought the rural, and urban worlds closer together; the impact of the Cowley works, located within what was still an outlying village, was more specifically economic.

The primary economic effect of the Morris works and its associated supply companies was to increase opportunities for employment. Arthur Exell, who worked at Osberton Radiators, one of Morris's suppliers, remembered the workforce in the late 1920s.[32]

> They were mostly locals at Radiators, though there were a few Cockneys. We had ever such a lot who had been farm labourers, and some had worked in the [Oxford] colleges. They were thankful for the work because it paid better wages.

Increased employment opportunities were reflected in the decline in the number of farm workers in Oxfordshire. Between 1921 and 1931 the number of farm workers, male and female, in England and Wales fell by about 10 per cent. In Oxfordshire the number fell by 32 per cent. By 1936 Whiting estimates that about 3,000 ex-farm workers were working at Cowley, out of a total workforce of about 5,000.[33]

Much more striking were the indirect effects of the car. In 1922 there were just over 300,000 private cars in the United Kingdom; by the outbreak of the Second World War there were nearly 2 million. Much of this growth took place in the late 1920s and early 1930s when a 50 per cent decrease in real prices encouraged Morris, Austin and Ford to produce small cheap cars for the middle class. In 1930 you could buy a new 10–15 horsepower car for about £100. With the aid of hire purchase this put a new car within the reach of those, especially white-collar workers, who were benefiting from the relative prosperity of the commercial sector, particularly in the southeast of England. Buying a car meant buying into a new world. As John Lowerson has written, 'ownership and pride in a marque identity was provided by "own brand" magazines which turned increasingly to the leisure use of cars.'[34] Once a month throughout the late 1920s and 1930s *The Morris Owner* informed the proud owner of a new Morris Minor not only how to fix his carburettor on a lonely road but how to find that lonely road in the first place. As the *Morris Owners Road Book* of 1926 put it, buying a car was buying a 'modern magic carpet'. Using it took the motorist to 'the pretty villages, the old farmsteads, besides numberless quaint features to be found in our old towns (which) all reach out from those bygone centuries and captivate us with their reminiscences of ancient peace'.[35]

However it was not only, or mainly, the car owner who came to the countryside but also those who came by train, bus and bike. They came in search of the same, often idealised rural Britain that drew the owner of the Morris, Austin or Ford car. In 1920 the *Cyclists' Touring Club Gazette* wrote of the Ashdown Forest area of Sussex:[36]

> You will see a dozen different types of scenery every day; woodland scenes ... great landscapes of hill and valley clothed in fine trees ... quaint old

village-cities . . . tiny hamlets suffocated by their own flowers. . . . It holds one of the richest stores of wild life in the country. . . . You can get right away from people and cars.

The Ramblers' Association founded in 1935, and its predecessors, organised country rambles, campaigned for cheap railway fares for walkers, especially on Sundays, and laid on special excursion trains. By the late 1930s many local Ramblers' Association federations had negotiated special point-to-point 'Walking Tour Tickets' which enabled the walker to get off at one station and return from another. In August 1938, for example, a group from south London took a day ticket from Waterloo to Farnham and returned from Haslemere. They carried a picnic lunch and bought tea in Hindhead walking 12 miles for a cost of 5s 6d. On

Plate 10 The new countrywoman or a dreaded urban invader? My mother Lillian Howkins (nee Lowe) in the Cotswolds *c.*1935. Like many urban working-class young people my parents spent most weekends and all of their holidays in the 1930s on a tandem looking for a bit of rural England (author's photograph).

a larger scale in April 1938 two special trains brought walkers to Hartfield in Sussex to walk in the Sussex Weald.[37]

This influx, especially of the urban working class, brought with it inevitable conflict, which, as with the case of housing and suburbanisation, prefigures many of the battles of the post-Second World War era. C.E.M. Joad, philosopher and urban-born back-to-the-lander, despite his reputation as a radical, precisely echoes Betjeman's petulance and snobbery:[38]

> There are the hordes of hikers cackling insanely in the woods, or singing raucous songs as they walk arm in arm at midnight down the quiet village street. . . . There are tents in meadows and girls in pyjamas dancing beside them to strains of the gramophone. . . . There are fat girls in shorts, youths in gaudy ties and plus-fours, and a roadhouse round every corner and a café on top of every hill for their accommodation.

In many areas of southern England, Joad's view of the 'uneducated' townsman and woman found echoes in organisations like the Surrey Anti-Litter League which reported those who dropped litter to the police and on occasions instituted private prosecutions, as well as campaigning (successfully) to get Surrey County Council to revise its bye-laws on litter. They also campaigned against unsightly advertising. In 1933 the League's annual report said proudly that there were similar societies in seven other counties.[39]

Conflict could and did become more serious. Parish and District Council Minutes from many country areas are full of minor disputes, especially over rights of way and access throughout the inter-war period. For example, about 50 per cent of the business conducted by Heathfield Parish Council in Sussex in those years concerned questions of footpath closures, rights of way and responsibility for maintenance of footpaths and tracks.[40] On the Sussex/Kent border at Withyham in 1938–9 a year-long battle was fought to persuade the Parish Council to take action to re-open an illegally closed footpath which involved a very large part of the village.[41]

Most of these disputes involved locals in local battles, although most had leisure rather than traditional economic or work origins. In other cases national organisations were involved and the issues transcended the merely local and centred much more on the recreational. The Council for the Preservation of Rural England, founded in 1926, brought together various learned societies and voluntary bodies around the question of how best to 'preserve' rural England. It initially saw itself, according to David Matless, as a kind of advisory body of the elite who were constituted as a body of specialists whose 'insights might be pooled' rather than a pressure group.[42] However, once the organisation allowed individual members, primarily to provide financial support, it seems its role began to change, especially at local level, into a much more interventionist body.

John Sheail points out that by 1929 the Thames Valley branch had produced a detailed report on the Thames Valley from Cricklade to Staines which included suggestions for preservation of the 'more attractive parts of the area' as well as attacks on ribbon development and plot land settlements at Bablock Hythe.[43] From the late 1930s the Isle of Wight Branch campaigned vigorously against holiday camps on the island as, although the branch was in 'general sympathy' with camping, they 'do not consider that permanent holiday camps should be placed in or near a good class residential area, or in an area of outstanding natural beauty.'[44] Nor was it only a southern phenomenon; as we saw above the Northumberland and Newcastle areas were opposed to ribbon development and the 'destruction' of market towns and villages.[45] There were other organisations whose 'defence' of a particular view of the countryside caused problems in the inter-war period. Throughout the 1920s the Commons, Open Spaces and Footpaths Preservation Society fought battles to prevent the sale of common land and parkland and took on local authorities and the War Office as well a speculative builders. The Ramblers' Association kept a watching brief on closed or ploughed up footpaths and pressured local councils to create 'rights of way' maps for their areas.[46]

Most spectacular of all the battles, by far the best known, and the one which opened up the whole issue of rural/urban relationships, were the 'mass trespasses' in the Pennines in the early 1930s. Here organised and urban working-class rambling associations, including the Communist Party, led by the British Workers' Sports Federation, asserted the right to roam on open moorland which was private and mainly used for grouse shooting. On 24 April 1932 a group of several hundred ramblers, led by a BWSF activist Benny Rothman, walked onto Kinder Scout from the village of Hayfield. At the top of Kinder they were met by a group of keepers and temporary wardens. 'The pushing and shoving that followed saw only a few open fights; and then they left.'[47] On their return to Hayfield five 'ringleaders' were arrested and were subsequently imprisoned for between 2 and 6 months. The campaign continued however, with demonstrations and attempts at trespass elsewhere in the Peaks.

To the rural working class and even to many farmers these 'trippers' were at worst a source of mild irritation or envy, at best a chance to make an honest shilling. Cafés and tea rooms sprung up wherever there was a demand. In September 1930 the CPRE wrote to the Design and Industry Association that:[48]

> We feel that the number of these [tea] shops is increasing rapidly and their untidiness almost rivals that of the average garage, and is often worse. The owners are small men and anxious to attract attention, and have neither means or education to build anything very decent.

'Men', was frequently a misnomer. Many cyclists of the 1930s in the Pennines and Dales remember hill farms where a good 'scoff' could be had from farm ingredients prepared by the farmer's wife or daughter. If the customer could not afford that, a dry place to sit and hot water for a 'brew up' from tea brought in a screw of newspaper could be had for pence. A café or tea room, which cost relatively little to set up, was a lifeline for many farming families in the hard years of the late 1920s. This was also the case, in some areas at least, with the growth of 'bed and breakfast'. Particularly in Wales, the southwest and southeast of England, the uplands of the north and all coastal areas the provision of cheap accommodation for the urban working and middle class became widespread in the inter-war years. In many places, as with 'farmhouse teas', bed and breakfast became an essential, if hidden, part of the income of farming and labouring families.[49]

As we have already suggested, suburbanisation and the slow but certain movement of 'incomers' to the country districts put pressure on farm land. In many areas before the Second World War this appeared to matter little, at least in agricultural terms, since the pressure was regionally uneven, concentrating mainly in the southeast. However, in these areas especially there was increasing pressure for building on what had previously been agricultural land. At one level this did not matter. Agriculture was in decline and many a rural landlord was happy to sell land for development even in places a fair distance from the capital. In 1923 the Master of Waveney sold land near Haselmere to be developed into 720 building plots designed by a local architect Harold Falkner. George Sturt, despite a long friendship with Falkner, was outraged, calling him 'the evil genius of the countryside'.[50]

> The road yesterday, lonely to be sure, gave glimpses of the old delicious path-way he had helped to shut us out from and spoil. Half the villas were of his designing, and at the end of the garden full of his buildings and flower-beds is his tasteless replacement of what was once the beautiful acclivity – tree rimmed, gorse-covered – atop of Vicarage Hill.

By the late 1920s many other voices were added to those of Sturt, and appeared to have increasing support from a largely urban 'conservation' lobby arguing that unchecked and uncontrolled urban development was destroying the essentially rural nature of much of Britain, but especially southern England. Some of these have already been discussed, for example the CPRE, but they were given a new power and even anger in two collections of essays edited by the architect Clough Williams-Ellis: *England and the Octopus* of 1928 and the more influential *Britain and the Beast* of 1937.[51] The latter book in particular had a profound impact, being widely reviewed and 'welcomed' by figures as diverse as George Landsbury, J.B. Priestley, Julian Huxley and Baden-Powell. In 1938 it was issued as the monthly choice for February by the Readers' Union.

While the concerns of these rural preservers were widespread and, in many

Plate 11 'A café on the top of every hill . . .' The *bête noire* of the preservationists: a railway carriage turned into a tearoom at Scarborough, Yorkshire *c.*1930. (Reproduced by kind permission of the Rural History Centre, University of Reading.)

cases, entirely laudable, their fixation was with suburban and urban 'sprawl'. Their main enemies were the suburban dweller and the speculative builder who took land out of agriculture and built houses. Their most hated places were the arterial roads out of London with their ribbon development, the shed and old railway carriages which made up proletarian plot land settlements and above all the 'bungalow town' of Peacehaven near Brighton. The inspiration of these mainly urban and mainly middle-class critics was a ruralism and Englishness with which we are already familiar. It is striking that the first photograph in *Britain and the Beast* is of a fox-hunt with the caption 'The only country pageant which is not a revival'.[52] Most of the rest of the 'positive' illustrations are conventional images of rural England (mostly southern), which are set against 'horror' photos of arterial roads, bungalows and urban council developments.

There is little doubt that there was a good deal of sense and real concern behind the sometimes near-hysterical tone of the writing in these books. Unchecked and unmonitored housing development was spreading over large areas of previously wild land. For instance, around Eastbourne, and especially around the satellite villages on its northwest side, huge areas were lost to speculative development in the late 1920s and 1930s. Nearer Brighton, the Cuckmere Valley, the last undeveloped valley running through the Downs to the sea, was constantly under threat of development from the late 1920s.[53] Nationally the figures of land lost to agriculture show just how serious the threat was.[54]

It was at this time, in the absence of any really effective land-use planning controls and with agriculture in a very depressed state and open land cheap to purchase, that the loss of farmland to urban development reached its peak. Over 6,000 acres a year were being taken for the purpose in the 1930s and, if losses to woodlands and other nonagricultural uses are added to this total, the aggregate figure is raised to around 80,000 acres.

In 1932, in response to the growing pressure about building in rural areas, the National Government passed the Town and Country Planning Act, which became law in April 1933. The judgment of the Scott Report of 1942 on the 1932 Act had stood the test of time.[55]

> The story of the 1932 Act is one of high hopes and subsequent disappointment. Many of the powers necessary to put into operation the intentions expressed on behalf of the Government were whittled away as the Bill proceeded through Parliament . . . [and] though the eventual Act was called a Town and Country Planning Act, practical experience quickly proved that it was entirely inadequate for the formulation of country planning schemes.

Although this judgment is substantially correct, and is supported by many historians,[56] there was some change. This mainly involved the use of so-called Section 34 orders, which enabled local councils by paying compensation to reserve an area as 'permanent private open space'. In Sussex this was widely used to protect downland, and despite some planning difficulties, notably the failure to create a 'national park' in the Downs by East Sussex County Council in 1934, by the outbreak of war 85 per cent of the South Downs were 'protected' from development by Section 34 Orders, purchased by local authorities or by private trusts.[57]

The pre-war planning battles and discussions revealed just how changed the rural was and began to show the first signs of arguments about the countryside which were to dominate the second half of the century. A.G. Street, a farmer and writer saw this clearly in his contribution to *Britain and the Beast* – the only contribution from a countryman from the 'traditional' rural world.[58]

> Very definitely, the majority of people in this island have no use for the countryside. . . . Those who do value the countryside as a free playground consider its use for this purpose to be far more important than for farming. . . . Indeed, I doubt whether there are a thousand people in England today, either country folk or townsfolk, who value the countryside for its own sake. Generally speaking, the former value it as a business premise, and the latter as a free playground.

This is not all Street has to say in one of the most interesting pieces in the whole book, but it does have a real prescience about the future of the rural areas — for the first time people were asking the question: what is the countryside for?

Yet, at the end of this section on the years between the wars, we should beware of going too far. Vast areas of England and Wales remained untouched by suburbia or by the 'resident tripper'. The 'visitor' here remained unthreatening and, when she or he came to a village or farm, was even mildly profitable. In the north and west of England and in much of Wales isolated farmsteads saw little change from the late nineteenth century; while even in the south and east, outside the Home Counties a long-lived farmer or farm worker would have recognised much which looked like the 1870s. Even in the Home Counties and especially in the south Midlands there were, despite urban growth, great swathes of land where what were effectively still single occupation, agricultural, village communities still dominated. There were also still closed villages, despite the aristocracy's general lack of interest in the land, and many market towns retained an essentially local social and economic structure. Perhaps above all, partly because of the depression in farming which marked most of the inter-war years, physically the landscape was little changed. Certainly there were barns with broken roofs and fields gone to weeds, but the horse still dominated the arable areas, the southern landscape was still divided into fields whose boundaries were normally, at their most recent coming up for 200 years old. Nor, despite the criticisms of the tiny proto-organic movement, was there much use of artificial manures and practically none of chemical insecticides or herbicides. In many ways the actual attraction to the countryside was that the rambler, the cyclist, the motorist or even those who bought a house in 'Hassocks Village', a select development at the foot of the Downs near Ditchling, were going back into a landscape which appeared unchanged and unchanging.

Part III

The second agricultural revolution, 1937–90

7 War and state agriculture, 1937–45

Throughout the 1920s and early 1930s successive administrations had refused to use a wartime threat to Britain's food supplies as a reason for aiding agriculture. As Murray writes:[1]

> The decision not to anticipate the outbreak of war in agricultural policy had been accepted by the Committee of Imperial Defence as early as June 1924. In 1926 the Government had announced its decision that no case had been made out on defence grounds which would justify the expenditure necessary to induce farmers in times of peace to produce more than economic considerations dictated.

This view was reinforced as late as July 1938 when Chamberlain, in a speech to farmers at Kettering, stated that there was 'no need to encourage the greatest output of food at home' since ample supplies would continue from overseas in the event of war.[2] In this he was supported, at least in part, even by radical critics of government policy. In the same year Lord Addison could write, 'we cannot plan the course of agriculture, which should be developed in the ordinary life of the nation in terms of the emergencies that might confront us in war.'[3]

However, contingency plans had been laid, in secret, from as early as 1933, 'when a body of officials reporting to the Committee on Imperial Defence was contemplating a high degree of control over prices, wages, and profits, from the outset of a major war.'[4] In 1935, the Ministry of Agriculture set up a parallel committee with its sister bodies from Scotland and Northern Ireland to prepare the outlines of an agricultural policy to be followed in the event of war. It reported to the newly appointed Food Supply Sub-Committee of the Committee of Imperial Defence in May 1936, and this report laid down the main features of what was to become Government policy on the outbreak of war in 1939.[5] The central thrust of the committee's arguments was based on the lessons of 1914–18, and especially the period of intense state intervention after 1916. It argued for:[6]

firstly, a policy of achieving a high degree of soil fertility in peace-time by maintaining livestock production and secondly, a plan for the immediate ploughing up of grasslands upon the outbreak of war for the increased output of human foodstuffs and of feeding stuffs, pending a planned reduction in livestock numbers if wartime requirement dictated this.

In addition it was proposed that local War Agricultural Emergency Committees be appointed for every county to oversee wartime need and plans, again on the model of the Great War. Indeed Chairmen, Officers and Secretaries had been selected although they themselves did not know this.[7]

At a practical and public level, plans for war were given two major forms before September 1939. The first of these was the Agriculture Act of 1937. The purposes of this Act were to address the first part of the 1936 recommendations by increasing the fertility of the land in preparation for war. This was done by grants for drainage and a subsidy on fertilisers. In addition the wheat subsidy, discussed at the end of Chapter 3, was extended to oats and barley, primarily to encourage the home production of foodstuffs. The second key piece of legislation was the Agricultural Development Act of 1939. This enabled the Ministry of Agriculture to buy and store fertilisers, to buy tractors and tractor machinery, to increase grants for drainage and, more importantly, to offer a payment of £2 per acre for every acre of permanent grass ploughed up between May and September 1939.[8]

By the outbreak of war then the machinery of agricultural administration was in place.[9] Targets were also set for production and labour. In 1936 it had been proposed that 10 per cent of permanent grass should be brought into cultivation in the first year of war. This meant in total about 2 million acres by 1939. The power to order ploughing up was given to the War Agricultural Executive Committees, and they also had power over farming standards and cropping. Labour was protected by reserving key occupations and by instructions to enrol and train the Women's Land Army. In these respects Britain's agriculture was relatively well prepared, certainly better than it had been in 1914.

However, there were problems. Government had refused to allow the stockpiling of foodstuff and fertilisers, let alone human food, and fertilisers particularly were to cause problems later, especially to smaller farmers and growers. A fruit grower in Worcestershire told a worker for the organisation Mass-Observation in July 1940, 'we get a bit of trouble with potash. It nearly all came from France and Germany. . . . There's also the bird fertilisers, which came from South America.'[10] Most serious of all was the general state of farming. As we saw earlier the worst of the inter-war depression had begun to lift but there were still huge problems for many if not most farmers. Despite government intervention and signs of recovery in some areas,[11] much land was in a bad state, especially arable land that had been let go back to pasture. Hedges and ditches were over-

grown and drainage systems blocked and broken. Farms were also undercapit-
alised and farm buildings and equipment antiquated and in a bad state of repair.
As a result, as Murray writes:[12]

> Many parts of the country were ill equipped for the expansion of food pro-
> duction from our own soil, which the curtailment of imported supplies of
> foodstuffs and of feeding stuff would necessitate. It was the failure to appre-
> ciate this state of affairs and the consequent need for greater financial
> resources to turn farming from its peacetime economy to a wartime footing
> that was one of the most serious deficiencies of pre-war planning.

The acceptance of that failure was not only to guide wartime agricultural policy,
but also to shape the post-war world.

The onset of war, however, was not only a matter of planning for wartime
production; it was also, overwhelmingly, a matter of how those in the rural areas
took the outbreak of war. Unlike 1914, there was little surprise at the outbreak
of war even among ordinary people since its 'coming' had been heralded for so
long. The extent to which the inhabitants of the country districts, as opposed to
the urban areas, were or were not prepared for war depended, in the first
instance, very much on who and where they were. In country towns, especially
the larger ones, the fears of bombing were similar to those in other urban areas.
In Chelmsford a young trainee journalist wrote on 24 August 1939 that he had a
'most jittery day. Feeling war to be pretty near.'[13] Less than a week later things
had moved further with 'visible precautions in town include[ing] extensive sand-
bagging of hospitals, police stations, all drill halls and military buildings.'[14] In the
rural areas of the east coast, especially the holiday areas, the beginnings of the
crisis at the end of August saw the first signs of war. From Walton-on-the-Naze
in Essex an office worker wrote on 31 August that the town 'which was just
beginning to make up for a bad season, is rapidly emptying of visitors'.[15] In some
rural areas there were signs of panic buying and hoarding. A young married
woman wrote from Little Wilbraham near Cambridge on 29 August 'no sugar
obtainable when the grocer's van called. Village shop sold out.'[16] In north
Norfolk there was a rush to buy petrol in anticipation of rationing. 'All cus-
tomers', wrote a young woman who worked in a garage, 'filling up petrol tanks.
Sales larger quantities than usual [sic].'[17]

For most though, the first impact of war was felt through the arrival of
refugees from the cities. Well before the mass evacuations of school children
from the danger areas on 1 September 1939, numbers, possibly large numbers,
of urban dwellers took to the countryside. This had also been true during the
Munich crisis of the autumn of 1938 when a member of Mass-Observation
reported she had met a friend with her husband who 'has been out in the car . . .
in pelting rain looking for accommodation in the country. Everything was

crowded out. Money was no object – but all they had was a vague possibility of a tiny two-bedroomed cottage which three families hoped to share.'[18] In August 1939 a Norfolk diarist noted a similar reaction in her area when she noted, that families were arriving 'with children to beach bungalows for safety'.[19] Two days earlier, a 'neighbour's wife's mother, father and sister arrive with much baggage from London in panic stricken condition having had pets destroyed.'[20]

In the early months of the war several of those who kept diaries throughout the war for Mass-Observation were in this situation, albeit with less obvious signs of panic. A diarist writing from Port Isaac in Cornwall was on holiday there on the outbreak of war from Tadworth in rural Surrey, but 'thought it would be better to stay down here, where there was little sign of war and try and let the children carry on their lives with as little interruption as possible.'[21] Others went to family, like Mrs McDonald,[22] who went with her children from Croydon to her mother's old house in Great Wilbraham near Cambridge, where she still had an uncle and aunt, in August 1939, to be joined by 'my uncle's eldest brother and his two daughters' from London in September.[23] Both of these women were middle class but not all were. For example, a young married woman from South London who went to Hassocks in Sussex, rented rooms with her children and took up cleaning work.[24]

With war inevitable and fear of bombing of cities, the government put into action its long-term plan for the evacuation of children to safe areas on 1 September 1939.[25] Evacuation was to be voluntary. Children of school age were to go with their schools; those under school age with a parent. They were to be billeted in private homes rather than barracks or camps. The first groups left the cities on the early morning of 1 September and began arriving in the country areas that afternoon and evening. Despite huge problems the exercise was largely successful in that most children were settled, albeit not always happily, within 48 hours. Much of the success was due to real sympathy on the part of country people and enormously hard work by local government officials in the receiving areas. Having said that, the problems were very real and quickly became worse, even if they only ever affected a minority. As a London schoolteacher evacuated to Brighton said: 'We knew that 90 per cent of the children were well behaved and happy. But the only stories regaled [sic] to me were of the horrors of the wild London children.'[26] There were however positive aspects to evacuation, as Emily Baker, a Sussex schoolteacher, saw. The health of many children was enormously improved by country life, while many clearly enjoyed the change, like the 10-year-old girl from Greenwich who a week after evacuation was 'helping to drive cattle, turning out cows to the manner born.'[27]

More importantly a set of evacuee myths began to grow up concerning on the one hand the filth and ill-manners of urban children and their families, and on the other the greed and snobbishness of country people. That both these myths had a basis in reality is less interesting than what they reveal about image and self-image. Crucially they point, as Mass-Observation itself noted in 1940, to the huge differences between town and country, both real and imagined,[28] which were to continue throughout the war. A major complaint by evacuees (or more properly their parents) was the 'backwardness' of the country – a complaint as old as urban life itself. A Norfolk diarist wrote in October 1939 that the evacuees said 'they found the country very quiet and lacked amusement. One woman said: "I'd rather be bombed on me own doorstep than stay here and die of depression."'[29] In return country people found the evacuees coarse, overdressed and 'fast'. Both accounts are in part mythical; as a perceptive Sussex diarist wrote in 1940, 'I begin to think that except in some definite cases those without evacuees do more talk of moaning than those with.'[30] Yet there remains a core of truth in these perceptions. As we have seen the countryside in the immediate pre-war period had suffered badly economically and remained remarkably untouched by many of the popular cultural changes, which are so much part of the 1930s; there was a genuine sense in which it was backward – or at least different. This was spelt out clearly by an observer in Worcester in September 1940.[31]

> During the last fortnight large numbers of refugees have come into Worcester from London, and it is easy to pick them out on the street. They are soon recognised not so much because of the ordeal they have been through [sic] has left its mark on their faces . . . but because of their clothes, their style and their manner in general are so different from the normal citizen of Worcester.

As the war went on this difference was in part exacerbated and subtly changed by a growing belief in the differential 'sufferings' of the civilian population in town and country, and the notion, again growing through the war, that somehow the country districts were 'doing well' out of it. The beginning of these feelings can be seen as evacuation dragged on into the 'phoney war'. Many who had come in fear and even panic in September 1939 were, by the end of the month, drifting back taking with them the beginnings of the urban myths of rural greed, backwardness and aloofness. Equally, in the country areas, their going left a similar residue of bitterness against those who were seen to be better off and ungrateful, and who had exploited country people when it suited them. Both these versions were to pass into the mythology of the war generation as counters to a united idea of a 'people's war'.[32]

The actual declaration of war was a curiously muted and private affair for most people in the rural areas, perhaps even more so than in the towns. There was no repetition of the scenes of 1914, with crowded streets and a 'rush to the colours'. The latter was meaningless since conscription was already in place, the former, given the sense of inevitability around the onset of war, simply inappropriate. The news was also usually received in private over the radio with family, and perhaps a few friends gathered round. The young married woman 'refugee' in Port Isaac wrote on 3 September, 'this morning everyone, barring three of the children, have stayed in to hear the ten o'clock news bulletin.'[33] After the broadcast Emily Baker wrote from Sussex, 'I am thankful there is none of the patriotism blather. I can recall 1914 and the immense excitement and bursting ideals. (I was an impressionable adolescent of 14.)'[34] From rural Northumberland another teacher wrote, 'in spite of the insanity however, it seemed to be (the) only course left open.'[35]

Despite the apparent inevitability of war many, probably most, were still shocked. A customer told Muriel Green, working in her garage in Norfolk, that war had been declared and writes of a 'feeling of hopelessness'.[36] From Cambridgeshire, Mrs MacDonald wrote, 'well it is War! I feel it must all be some horrible nightmare from which I shall presently awake.'[37] For many though war had already had an effect, especially in the areas where evacuees were billeted or where the call up had already started. By 3 September my father, who had been in the Supplementary Reserve since 1933, had left rural Oxfordshire and was in Catterick. By 20 September he was *en route* to France with the British Expeditionary Force (BEF).[38]

However, some country workers escaped immediate conscription even when they were in the reserves. Worries about harvest and about labour requirements for the ploughing-up campaign caused registration to be delayed and numbers of key men were released from the Territorial Army. In addition, soldiers were made available for the harvest, a practice which was to remain common throughout the war. As a result of these measures the harvest of 1939 and the start of the ploughing campaign went satisfactorily, indeed when bad weather came in the winter of 1939–40 it was estimated that there were about 50,000 agricultural workers registered as unemployed.[39]

The problem of unemployment was however short-lived. By March 1940 the Ministry of Agriculture estimated that agriculture had lost some 50,000 workers, of whom about 20,000 had taken advantage of wartime labour demands to move out of farm work to better pay and conditions elsewhere, especially the construction of military installations. In fact the situation was worse than this since the increased acreage envisaged under the plough-up campaign demanded an increase of some 60,000 full-time and 22,000 casual workers over the 1938–9 strength. The short-term solution was to attempt to use substitute workers, for example the urban unemployed, conscientious objectors, refugees, schoolboys and roadmen, but these were simply inadequate. A longer-term solution therefore was to encourage men to stay on the farms by increased wages and/or to prevent them moving by government restriction. Both these methods were used. Wages went up first. By March 1940 all forty-seven County Wage Committees had raised wages and the national average had gone up to 37s 10d. It was a move that

Table 7.1 Indexes of changes in minimum wages and cost of living, 1937–46[41]

	Average minimum wages for basic hours	Cost of living index	
1937–8	34s 2d	100	100
1938–9	34s 8d	101	103
1939–40	39s 5½d	115	116
1940–1	48s 5d	142	129
1941–2	57s 10d	169	137
1942–3	60s 0d	176	142
1943–4	63s 1½d	187	145
1944–5	67s 10½d	199	148
1945–6	72s 2d	211	154

was continued through the war (see Table 7.1). As Armstrong writes, 'the war years are notable for the fact that, in contrast to the late nineteenth century and the inter-war years, real gains were made at a time of rising prices.'[40]

In addition to these wage increases orders were issued in 1940 and 1941 to restrict the movement of labour out of agriculture. Together these measures had some success as the figures in Table 7.2 show.

These figures also illustrate other key factors in dealing with the wartime labour supply: first, the enormous increase in the number of women both full-time and part-time in agriculture. By 1943 the WLA had reached a strength of 87,000 full-time workers, which accounted for all the increase in full-time agricultural employment for women since 1939. On top of this, and outside the official WLA structures, some 66,000 women had taken up casual agricultural employment, meaning that upwards of a third of the farm workforce was composed of women in 1943.

The second source of labour was prisoners of war. It was agreed in January 1941 that Italian prisoners of war should be used on farms, and by harvest that

Table 7.2 Numbers of agricultural workers (United Kingdom) 1939–44 (in thousands)[42]

	Regular workers*			Casual workers			All workers		
	Male	Female	Total	Male	Female	Total	Male	Female	Total
1939	592	71	663	90	50	140	682	121	803
1940	578	78	656	91	59	150	669	137	806
1941	578	89	667	106	77	183	684	166	850
1942	578	130	708	115	92	207	693	222	915
1943	567	157	724	123	108	231	690	265	955
1944	597	173	770	120	85	205	717	258	975

Note
*Including Women's Land Army (WLA) and Prisoners of War.

year some 2,500 were employed. Initially they were employed in gangs, working on drainage schemes as well as the harvest. After February 1942 arrangements were made for them to live-in on individual farms and carry out general farm work. However, the vast majority of 20,000 employed by mid-1942 lived in 'secure' hostels and camps. By the end of the war some 50,000 prisoners were employed.[43] Third, there were miscellaneous groups including conscientious objectors, organised government 'gangs' and school children on farm camps.

A final factor in dealing with the labour problem in wartime was the hugely increased use of machinery. Pre-war, as we have seen, British agriculture was slow to adopt machinery, even tractors which by the 1930s had a proven record of reliability. Government purchase of tractors in 1939 had given the War Agriculture Committees (War Ags) a basic supply, but more importantly had encouraged manufacturers to go into mass production. As a result the relative position of horse and tractor as suppliers of power to Britain's farms was reversed in the war period, while the amount of power available on farms more than trebled (see Table 7.3).

Nevertheless we need some caution here. Brian Short's study of the 1943 Farm Survey shows that only 21 per cent of farms owned one or more tractors in that year, and that these tended to be larger units, both in terms of acreage and workers employed, and to be higher rented – that is better farms in terms of land quality.[45] Against this the 'machinery pools' set up by the War Ags provided tractors and other machinery on loan for key tasks which brought that machinery to many smaller farms and farmers.

However, in the first months of war most of these changes were far in the future. Indeed war itself seemed remote to many in rural areas – and even something of an anti-climax. A young office worker wrote from Walton-on-the-Naze in Essex in November 1939:[46]

> After nearly three months since the outbreak of war the unanimous opinion seems to be, 'This is a funny war'. The contrast between these boring almost uneventful days and the catastrophe, which was expected to come, swiftly and without warning, no doubt accounts for this.

Table 7.3 Changes in farm power supplies in Great Britain 1939–46[44]

	Stationary power (000 hp)	Motor tractors		Horses		Total power (000 hp)	Index
		(No. (000))	(000 hp)	(No. (000))	(000 hp)		
1939	854	56.2	1,075	649	649	1,724	100
1942	871	116.8	2,293	642	642	2,935	170
1944	847	173.4	3,388	577	577	3,965	230
1946	911	203.4	3,935	520	520	4,455	258

Indeed for those left in the country districts there was little real sign of the war. Even on the east coast where, fuelled by endless rumours, there had been initial fears of bombing and invasion, things remained 'normal'. A series of reports, from Hollesley near Woodbridge in Suffolk, by a Mass-Observation worker, Richard Picton, in the spring of 1940 begins: 'The war does not seem to affect the life of the people in the villages around here as much as one would have expected. There is an intensification of agricultural activity and gardening . . . and on Saturday even plump housewives were seen digging their vegetable patch.'[47] From the north Norfolk coast Muriel Green wrote: 'Nothing worth reporting to M-O seems to happen in the country. We receive no AR [air raid] warnings and would not no [sic] a war was on apart from radio, newspapers, and people's conversation.'[48]

In some areas the billeting of soldiers provided a diversion – not always welcome – and like evacuation seem to have fuelled town/country animosity rather than pacifying it. In Suffolk, army occupation of land near the coast caused problems as a farmer told Picton in July 1940: 'A cocky little sergeant no higher than a shillings worth of ha'pence came up the other day and asked me what I was doing. I was in my own bloody field too. I told the little bastard what I thought of him.'[49] In the same district a year later there was continued, and growing, resentment against the billeting of soldiers in the area.[50]

To the young women of these rural areas, though, the arrival of soldiers was often a welcome addition to social life. A land girl told Picton in Hollesley that 'we had a very gay party with the officers at Bawdsey the other night. I didn't get to bed until four. Such a hang over.'[51] Village dances were much enlivened by the arrival of Scottish and Liverpool conscripts in Suffolk and, although there was not the moral panic caused by the Americans 2 years later, there were still problems and doubts expressed by the older generation. 'The soldiers', Picton wrote, were 'welcomed by the shopkeepers but largely ignored by the remainder of the population with the exception of the girls.'[52]

In Shropshire a more material threat to agriculture was posed by RAF commandeering of farmland and buildings. A Mass Observation writer reported that her cousin's farm had been taken over by the RAF and 'the fine farm buildings and home . . . are to be razed to the ground. The family is benumbed. We feel the Germans could not do much worse than this.'[53] The same problem arose in Cambridgeshire.[54]

> My uncle informs me that the farmer who employs him has got to give up about 150 acres of his best land to the Air Ministry for an emergency landing ground. It does seem an anomaly that when one farmer is being urged to plough up grass land to grow corn (which it wouldn't do in the first year anyway) another should have to give up his best wheat-growing land with next year's crop in and already up.

Yet this was a pinprick compared with what was to happen as the war progressed. By 1944 11,547,000 acres, or about 20 per cent of the land area of England and Wales, was under military control. The vast majority of this, some 9,769,000 acres was used for battle training and on some 391,000 acres 'the military occupied the land totally and the civilian presence was removed.'[55] These areas stretched throughout Britain and included sections of the South Downs, parts of Norfolk, Yorkshire and Lincolnshire, and most famously the area around Tyneham in Dorset, which still remains in military 'possession', and the Slapton Sands area of Devon which, at 120,000 acres, were the largest areas taken completely under military control.

As the winter of 1939 turned into the winter and spring of 1940 a number of Mass-Observation rural diarists mentioned ploughing-up orders, and the first wartime problems of shortage of feeds. Ploughing up was not always as simple as it seemed. As Emily Baker wrote from Sussex, as the area was largely a dairying one before the war, some farmers actually had no plough, nor any workers able to do the ploughing. As a result both workers and tools had to be hired in.[56] By March 1940 though things were going apace and she wrote: 'There has been much ploughing lately. Previously we could only see 2 ploughed fields, now 7...'[57] To Tony Harman in the Chilterns ploughing up was the means of extending his cropping into previously closed land.[58]

> In the late spring of 1940 we were ordered to plough out about 66 acres of Shepherds Farm which we had rented for some years as rough grazing land. . . . The owners had previously refused to let us plough them up so we were quite glad when the War Ag over-ruled their objections. I remember I ploughed the land myself. . . . The weather was cold and wet and it was already too late in the Spring to plant a proper crop, so I had to get the work done as quickly as possible in order to get anything growing at all.

The achievement of people like Tony Harman and his workers was impressive. In 1939, when some improvements in productivity had already been gained, there were 8.3 million acres under crops in Britain. By 1945 that figure had reached 13 million acres.[59] In terms of food produced this represented by 1944 increases of 90 per cent in wheat, 87 per cent in potatoes, 45 per cent in vegetables and 19 per cent in sugar beet. Most of this gain was made by ploughing up – by bringing more land into cultivation. As Martin points out, 'the 90 per cent increase in wheat output coincided with a 92 per cent increase in the area of land devoted to it. Similarly, the 87 per cent rise in the tonnage of potatoes was a direct result of a 96 per cent increase in the area grown.'[60] In a situation where, especially early in the war, machinery still played a relatively small role, what this meant was that, as in earlier agricultural revolutions, much of the gain was due to increased use of labour.

Plate 12 Ploughing up. Between 1939 and 1945, about 5 million acres of land were brought into crop production. Here a Caterpillar tractor, a powerful symbol of the new agriculture, clears the last 16 acres of an ancient deer park in Northamptonshire. (Reproduced by kind permission of the Rural History Centre, University of Reading.)

There were also small gains in yields per acre, although these tended to drop as the war progressed and land, which had been under grass and was thus relatively fertile, lost fertility through cropping. This was partly offset by an increased use of artificial fertilisers, although still on a relatively small scale. The quantity of potash and phosphate applied to the fields roughly doubled between 1939 and 1945, while the use of nitrogen in the form of sulphate of ammonia rose from 60,000 tons to 172,000 tons in the same period.[61] However, there were losses. The switch to arable could only be at the cost of pastoral farming. As a result beef and veal production fell by about 8 per cent during the war, mutton and lamb by 28 per cent and pigmeat by 65 per cent. Milk production was, however, maintained at near pre-war levels, which had its costs when small farmers in particular suffered from lack of foodstuffs being diverted away to dairy production. In early 1940, for example, Emily Baker talked to a 60-year-old woman who owned 'a minute pig farm' who was finding it almost impossible to get feed for pigs and poultry.[62]

There were also less obvious changes, but ones which acted directly on the 'alternative agriculture' which had been so successful in inter-war England and

Wales. *Farmers Weekly* noted even in March 1939 that the soft fruit industry was changing, with fruits that could easily be made into jam like raspberries, currants and gooseberries being kept in cultivation, while strawberry beds were grubbed up for wheat. Derelict orchards were grubbed while in the bulb fields of East Anglia production was reduced to 20 per cent the pre-war level – the minimum necessary to maintain stocks.[63] In the Vale of Evesham production of asparagus was reduced by 25 per cent in 1939 and over 50 per cent by 1943. In 1944 the Vale of Evesham Asparagus Growers' Association wrote to the Minister of Agriculture asking for permission to put one chain of land down to seed since production was less than one-third of pre-war levels and asparagus crowns took four years to mature.[64]

In other ways things changed remarkably little. All rural observers noted that even in the middle of the war the 'fortunes' of agriculture remained a central topic of conversation, while the simple seasonality of agricultural production ensured that little changed in the day-to-day sense. For example, Emily Baker noted each year the coming and going of 'hopping'. In October 1942, despite a late start at her school, 'most hop picking chd. [sic] back but not the backward ones. They had to go down to get their money with their parents.'[65] These children's earnings continued central to country budgets as she wrote a year later; 'one of the schoolgirls – an active girl of 13, tells me she has earned £9 in the hop gardens. She has given it to mummy to buy clothes.'[66]

With the fall of France and the Low Countries however, war came to the countryside, or at least the eastern and southern Counties, with renewed fear of invasion. In mid-June 1940 Muriel Green wrote from north Norfolk that a rumour had spread through the village that all coastal areas were to be evacuated, and she and her mother and sister had packed ready. Indeed her mother and she wanted to leave anyway.[67] From Suffolk Richard Picton wrote to Tom Harrisson:[68]

> I think the invasion may quite possibly take place next week. The tides will be right and the military say they expect it from Tuesday onwards. . . . I think it might be a good idea if you were to post my expenses tomorrow as I may need all the money I can get to make my getaway.

However neither Picton or Green left in the short term, although Picton was called up in August 1940 and Green in May 1941. In Sussex Emily Baker, having packed ready to flee in May, decided at the beginning of June that her elderly mother should at least be moved out of the invasion area. (They were about 10 miles from the coast.) 'The news of the plight of refugees on Belgian roads, the various hints that we may expect an attempt at invasion here, make me determined to try and get mother to visit the aunt in Shropshire ... I cd [sic] not bear to think of her a fleeing refugee.'[69] In mid-June others followed when the remaining LCC evacuees were 're-evacuated' to Cornwall and Wales.

'How empty the village is without the evacuees,' wrote Emily Baker in her diary.[70]

In the meantime worries continued, particularly about parachutists who took on almost mythical status after the invasion of Holland.[71] Air raids had also started to affect country districts, again especially on the east coast, although most people's actual experience of raids was very slight outside the country towns. Away from the coast there was even less recognition of war. At the time Hollesley was experiencing its first bombs and parachutist fears, Malvern in Worcestershire seemed 'so far removed that it is indeed difficult even for obs [sic] to realise [war] is still going on. . . . Most of the talk is about the fruit, the gardens, the weather.'[72]

However, as bombing of the cities grew in intensity, news bulletins, new refugees and rumour increased fears even well away from the attacks. By August Worcestershire was worried about invasion, and depression was appearing among some people as a result of bombing. An observer recorded a woman in September 1940 saying about the radio news: 'I can't bear listening, it upsets me too much. I feel nervous, I don't know what's going to happen, I really don't. They can't go on like this, there won't be anything left.'[73] Near London, as an observer reported from Radlett in Hertfordshire, 'the impression that many people have there is that London is razed to the ground, "crucified" as a waiter said.'[74] Emily Baker in Sussex experienced more than most as Burwash was on the direct flight path to London. From early August, first during the day and then at night, scarcely a day passed without bombers overhead, and the inevitable small-scale casualties caused by ditched bombs. By December she hardly commented, except on unusual nights, as on 14 December when 'the stream of planes became unbroken – poor London.'[75]

For most though the end of the 'phoney war' and the blitz marked not a dramatic change, but rather the beginning of adaptation to what many in the country districts, as in the towns, realised was likely to be a long slog. The changes over pre-war agricultural society and farming were perhaps less obvious than popular histories and indeed wartime propaganda would have us believe. Much, indeed most, of day-to-day farm work continued to rely on the horse, and there was a serious shortage of horses; in the early years of the war prices of good stock rose dramatically.[76] Similarly, the number of combines was insignificant and although reaper binders to take the harvest could be pulled by tractors, there was still a huge amount of work in stooking, loading and carting which relied on hand labour. Not for the first time in British history were huge gains in productivity based on an increased labour force working harder – and for not very much more money. Even driving a tractor was no good unless you drove it for longer as a Huntingdonshire labourer remembered:[77]

I started work each morning at 05.00. . . . From then until nightfall; I kept going until I could hardly see the front of the tractor; after 20.30 I kept the engine running. I stopped only to refill the paraffin, to relieve myself, to swig tea from a bottle or to adjust the plough; I ate my sandwiches while ploughing. So in about 14 hours ploughing time I ploughed ten acres, using 30 gallons of paraffin. I did this day after day, so, with only about 200 acres of autumn ploughing, it was finished in three weeks.

Nor did the apparently national control of the Wages Boards do away with regional differences completely. For example, before the establishment of a national minimum wage of 60s a week in 1943, workers in Wales, a traditionally low wage area, were still earning considerably less than workers in Lincolnshire. Furthermore, the difference between total earnings – that is pay including over-time and bonuses – and the minimum remained much lower in areas where there was a smaller workforce based on family labour and where the simple geography of the land made it difficult to plough up. Hence in Wales labour demand remained relatively low and wages followed. In 1943 Welsh farm workers earned about 68s 11d a week on average against 73s 1d in East Anglia.[78]

In the north of England and parts of Wales even traditional hiring remained unchanged in some places. In Cumbria the practice of annual hiring and the hiring fairs continued throughout the war. At the Martinmas hirings in 1939 *Farmers Weekly* reported that wages had gone up considerably, especially for 'lads' aged between 16–18 who were exempt from conscription, who were demanding £28 a year.[79] By the Whitsun hirings at Carlisle in 1942 the same group were getting £55 a year although there were 'few men and no women' at the hirings.[80] By then, though, Carlisle was an anachronism. The great hiring fairs of the East Riding had, according to Caunce, ceased to function as places of wage bargaining in the grim years of the 1930s,[81] while even in lowland Scotland and the Borders Richard Anthony argues that the system was finished before the outbreak of war.[82] The war put the final nails in the coffin of the hiring fair for the vast majority of working men and women.

There were however great changes in the farm workforce, the most obvious of which, as we have already seen, was the reappearance of women on the land. The Women's Land Army began with a meeting at the Ministry of Agriculture in April 1938 when it was decided to set up a Women's Branch under the Director-ship of Lady Denman who had served on a similar committee created during the Great War. However, despite this apparently advanced planning it was not until July 1939 that the Ministry finally accepted Denman's offer of her own house, Balcombe Place in Sussex, for use as national headquarters. The headquarters, run by what was effectively a women-only workforce, remained the core of the WLA throughout the war.[83]

Many of Denman's initial problems were a result of prejudice in the Ministry but to start with, at least, there was even more resistance to women on the land from both the farmers and the farm workers. Although there were 17,000 women enrolled in the WLA at the outbreak of war only 1,000 had been placed by November 1939 and 6,000 by the spring of 1940 — and most of those in the southern counties.[84] In December 1939 a WLA volunteer from Leeds wrote that she couldn't get work in Yorkshire and that 'the farmers in my part of the county don't appear to support us much.'[85] Nor was there much support from the farm workers. The editorial of *The Land Worker* in July 1939 wrote 'the Hon Mrs This, Lady That and the Countess of Something Else are all on the warpath again. The Women's Land Army is here, and they have all got their old jobs back — of bossing people, and of seeing that the farmers find a way out of their labour shortage without having to pay better wages.'[86]

Once on the farms the largely urban women of the WLA found that prejudice did not vanish easily:[87]

> We were sent to a farm near West Bromwich. We had already come across what to us was really unexpected, that the old farm hands really hated us, made life hard in every way they could, had some notion we would take their sons' jobs while they were away . . .

However, prejudice did eventually vanish. Unlike the Great War the numbers involved were very much higher and the general conscription of women in 1942 made women's work in general much more acceptable across all social groups. Most importantly it had become clear by the middle years of the war that not only was women's work essential to agriculture but that most of the women involved were simply very good at it. Sadie Ward quotes a farmer from the Isle of Ely on the work done by 'his' land girl.[88]

1   Drives away a manure cart etc.
2   Harrows in with one horse behind a drill.
3   Loads straw when at litter cart.
4   Holds sacks when putting up corn.
5   When chaff cutting pushes the straw to the feeder.
6   Takes off chaff when threshing.
7   Took up quite a lot of beet, and always earned her money and a little more at £2 an acre.
8   Takes up mangolds very well.

And one could add to that tractor driving, ploughing, forestry, milking, looking after sheep, pigs and chickens, thatching and hedging and ditching. By the end of the war there was no area of farm work that some member of the WLA had not carried out — and all for half the male wage plus board and lodging.

For some who joined the WLA it transformed their lives. Muriel Green, aged 20, and thinking she would be conscripted in the first age group of women in

March 1941, volunteered for the Women's Garden Association, which supplied women workers to replace conscripted gardeners in large houses and market gardens. She quickly took to it, and as early as April she wrote in her diary: 'gardening all day. I love it. I would not have believed it.'[89] Nor was it only the work, although she became increasingly proud of her gardening skills; it was also the recognition of the importance of what she was doing. 'I must say it is pretty great being a land girl here. Every one treats us as heroines, especially the soldiers. Nothing but admiration is forthcoming from the villagers, esp. during the cold weather.'[90]

Not that the work was easy. A few weeks after this entry she wrote: 'hard frost. Work wretched. How many more winters shall I have to stick it?'[91] The following year days of digging from seven in the morning until six at night led her to write: 'I never regret leaving home but sometimes I regret becoming a gardener. . . . It is not particularly encouraging to think of scratching the soil for several more years for 52 hours in the summer and 48 in the winter for the minimum agricultural wage.'[92] On balance though the rewards won out. In June 1942 she was put in charge of her 'own' greenhouse growing tomatoes. By early 1943 she thought of herself as a gardener, and attended the West of England regional conference of the Women's Land and Garden Association. Here, to her surprise, she found herself agreeing with a speaker that while 'returning men from the forces would need first consideration for jobs etc. the women must not be squashed in agric. and horticulture.'[93] In 1943 she and her sister went to set up a garden attached to a war hostel in Somerset. It was a huge success and seemed to transform their lives. Even when she was on holiday at home at Norfolk in September 1943 she wrote: 'I am convinced now that those carefree pre-war days can never come again. Home will never be the same to me. . . . I don't think I could ever settle again in this village.' A week later she added: 'I am looking forward to returning. I can't deny it. My work and my hostel has more attraction for me than my home.'[94]

Other groups moved into the farm workforce as a result of the demands of war. Again, as in the Great War, but again in larger numbers and better organised, schoolchildren were brought into key operations, especially the various harvests. Edward MacKenna, who worked on a farm since he was medically unfit for the services, wrote in his Mass-Observation Diary in 1941: 'We were to have gone potato picking with sixteen boys from Wolverton Secondary School but the rain put this off.' The boys eventually arrived two days later but, he writes, 'I think they are too young for this sort of work. Most of them are between 12 and 14' and they 'just want to play about'. Three days later the boys were replaced by women from the nearby village and the wives of two of the farm workers. The job was done.[95] As the war progressed 'farm camps' were established both for school children and for urban workers with the notion of combining a country holiday with useful farm work. By 1943 there were over 1,335 camps organised throughout Britain attended by 63,000 children of both sexes. Adults were

Plate 13 The People's War in the countryside. A posed and perhaps glamorous picture of London members of the Women's Land Army learning to milk at Church Knowle Farm Training Centre, Dorset. The reality was often much harder and, without the work of women, agriculture would have faced a fatal labour shortage. (Reproduced by kind permission of the Rural History Centre, University of Reading.)

brought in from non-agricultural occupations and from urban areas under the 'Lend a hand on the land' scheme. By 1943 this would-be holiday with pay scheme attracted 20,000 volunteers at 160 adult camps in 25 counties, while between 70–80,000 volunteers worked from home.[96]

Perhaps more striking, however, is the extent to which other aspects of country life remained unchanged by war, to such a degree that some accounts of country life seem more like 1916 than 1943. Despite the fact that various government departments, hospitals, museums and schools commandeered something in the region of 300,000 rural buildings during the war,[97] much of elite life continued. Fox hunting for instance continued throughout the war in many areas. One of the most interesting war diaries in M-O was kept by Caroline Haig, the wife of a retired senior army officer, who lived in rural North Oxfordshire. In the early summer each year she and her family continued to go to Scotland for fishing and through each autumn and winter her husband hunted. In the winter of 1943–4 both her sons, who were in the army, returned home on many weekends to hunt with the Bicester and Warden Hill and Heythrop Hunts – in every way more like Sassoon's army than a 'people's army'.[98]

The social life of Caroline Haig and her peers also seems to have remained much the same, although perhaps on a less grand scale than in pre-war days. They visited London regularly, staying at Claridges where the 'food [was] so good and everything so pretty.'[99] Less obvious, but more significant, is the extent to which she and her family remained a separate class apart, untouched by any notion of a 'people's war'. They visited houses within a narrow circle in the county, and a wider one nationally, which was carefully prescribed by class. They continued to go to the Eton and Harrow match and were delighted by their nephew's success at Eton. In their regular observation of their Angli-can religion they continued to act out Bagheot's 'rituals of deference' untouched by war or democracy. Even when they came into contact with the 'people' it was within carefully prescribed traditional frameworks. I suggest below that in some senses the attitudes of the elite were altered by the war, but the social relationships remained essentially 'traditional'. For example, Caroline Haig took the wife of her son's army servant under her wing when the wife had to go into hospital in the autumn of 1944.[100] Also in 1944 she responded to the 'age-old' problems of rural immorality as generations of ladies of the manor had done. 'I am much distressed over the various girls in the village who have got illegitimate babies, all, as far as one knows, with American fathers.'[101]

In other areas traditional social relationships also remained. The Home Guard in the rural areas was a long way from Tom Wintringham's 'people's army'. A panel member wrote from a Worcestershire village in August 1940:[102]

> There is no conception of a people's war. . . . It is felt that the officers aren't trusting their men, they are not giving them any ammunition. . . . There is distrust, grumbles, a sense of being useless.

Similarly the diary of a bellicose Sussex market gardener, and Great War veteran, is a litany of complaint against the snobbishness and lack of military ability of the Home Guard officers who 'commanded' him.[103]

The continuation of these pre-war attitudes did cause problems and comments by some at least. Emily Baker wrote in her diary in February 1941: 'Mad to talk about weeding out farm workers *and* to plough so much extra. And yet there was an advert for a maid, (in the local paper) "4 in family 13 indoor servants" – let them weed there.'[104] Similarly, unequal access to food, and especially to game, was a source of anger and conflict. Edward MacKenna noted in his diary a fellow worker's comments. 'You hear people say we're all rationed alike. Yet we aren't. They (the boss and his father) can come across the fields with a gun anytime and take a couple of rabbits; but that sort of things [sic] not for the likes of us.'[105] In Sussex the war seems to have made little difference to the traditional views of the game laws.[106]

> The damage done by rabbits is spoken of again. Also the pheasant question. My neighbour counted 32. When there was a shoot in the winter he cd [sic] see they deliberately shot only cocks. Yet the farmer must plough up the land and sow it. . . . He has had a good few [pheasants] on the q.t. [quiet].

Nor were problems simply restricted to the traditional conflicts of the rural areas. Food rationing, although planned from the mid-1930s, did not actually begin until January 1940, when a 'flat' per head ration was introduced for the entire population. This gave equal shares of bacon, ham, butter and sugar. Meat was added in March 1940, and in July tea, margarine and cooking fats; it was finally extended to preserves and cheese in 1941.[107] In addition other foodstuffs, like sweets, canned and processed foods were gradually put on ration on a points system, where the consumer used his or her rationed points to 'buy' other categories of foodstuffs which were in short supply, from the end of 1941.[108] Finally there were was a whole category of foodstuffs, often luxury items, which remained 'off ration'. This was particularly the case of restaurant food, which was to remain a problem throughout the war.

The onset of rationing brought more problems with widespread allegations that the wealthy were doing better out of the system than the poor. An observer wrote from a Worcestershire village early in 1941:[109]

> One aspect of the food shortage has been the distribution of goods in the village. Whilst those living in big country houses have had no difficulty in getting their normal supplies of farm produce . . . the villagers, with only farm workers' incomes, have been discriminated against.

Despite these problems most Mass-Observation writers agreed that food was better in rural areas during the war, a further source of urban resentment. Mass-Observation Directives on rationing done in 1942, 1943 and 1945 show that country people themselves thought they were relatively well off. There are constant references to gardens and allotments, as, for example, from Somerset in 1942:[110]

> The food situation here is fairly good in comparison with other areas known to me. The chief reason lies in the fact that Wellington is in the centre of a very prosperous agricultural area, and the majority of people are able to supplement their rations with their own garden produce and things they can buy direct from the country.

For those who actually farmed, or were closely involved with the farming community, things were even 'better'. A small dairy farmer's son from Leicestershire wrote in answer to the same Directive:[111]

> Most farmers round here do and can make a bit of butter to help with their rations. Some kill their own pigs so the bacon rationing is not noticed. Tin foods are not much used. Eggs being home produced are always available and similarly with milk. . . . Rabbits are vermin here and so are readily available to everyone. . . . There are tons of potatoes in this area, which farmers are trying vainly to sell. Not until bread is rationed will the food situation in this area become a major topic.

Perhaps it was for these reasons that 62 per cent of those living in rural areas said they 'approved' of rationing in 1942–3 as against 53 per cent in the urban.[112]

Where supplying food in this kind of way moved from simply helping a neighbour and became part of the illegal 'black market' in foodstuffs is difficult to decide. The vast majority of prosecutions during the war were for illegal sale of foodstuffs, and the bulk of these offences were committed by retailers. Most of these offences concerned the sale of meat which had been illegally slaughtered. As early as September 1940 the Minister of Food wrote: 'Meat is the only rationed article in which the rationing rules are being persistently evaded.'[113] However there were problems 'on the ground'. The number of 'legal' slaughterhouses was reduced from 16,000 in 1939 to 600 in 1941. As John Martin writes:[114]

> While there is little doubt that animals were occasionally killed in unlicensed premises, it is probable that these activities happened much less than contemporary folklore would have us believe. [War Agriculture Committees] kept a close eye on the number of animals retained on holdings and investigated disappearances or cases where productivity was less than anticipated. The rationing of animal feedingstuffs was directly linked to farm sales, minimising opportunities to participate in black markets.

There were however problems. Many village shops were inadequately stocked and ill equipped to deal with rationing and registration. As one observer wrote from a village near Colchester, 'the shop is an awful muddle and they are gradually being defeated by all the wartime complications of forms, rations etc.'[115] More general were problems associated with 'luxury' foods, like fruit, but above all, fresh meat, which seem to have 'got stuck' in the urban areas. From south Devon in 1942 a panel member wrote: 'The most difficult item is butchers' meat,' as it was in Gloucestershire and many other counties.[116] The problem also spread to larger country towns, and it was written from Worcester that in December 1940, 'there was no meat for nearly a week', a problem which was repeated in the first week of 1941.[117] Other replies mentioned shortages of sweets and cakes, as well as tinned foods.[118]

As the war progressed attitudes to the land and to agriculture seem to have undergone subtle changes. Wartime propaganda around the 'Kitchen Front' and 'Dig for Victory', coupled with the need for rationing and the decline of food imports, brought an awareness of Britain's continuing reliance of home-produced food even to an urban public. In September 1942 Mass-Observation sent out a Directive asking how the problems of agriculture should be dealt with after the war. The replies show a high degree of awareness about agriculture, as well as a more predictable concern about the countryside. However, it must be said, there is little sentimentality about 'rural England' of the kind one might expect in view of some wartime campaigns which stressed idyllic views of the countryside as something 'we' were fighting for.[119]

Many replies to the Directive began from a sense that agriculture had been badly treated before the war, for example a panellist who wrote from urban Lancashire, 'agriculture must never be allowed to fall into the condition into which it had descended prior to the war in this country.'[120] There was, as a result of this feeling, a widespread belief that wartime controls and subsidies should continue after the war – to a remarkable degree foreshadowing the policies of all post-war governments. Similarly, and perhaps more predictably, many of the post- (and pre-) war concerns about conservation and town planning found constant echoes in panel replies. A woman wrote from Newcastle:[121]

> There must of course be careful planning of both urban and rural amenities . . . the National Trust might be put in charge of all land, which it is desired to preserve as national monuments, it could combine with similar bodies or absorb them. The whole coastline of England . . . should be placed under its care together with the Lake District and Snowdonia.

More specifically, and speaking for many, a man wrote from Swindon: 'It should no longer be possible for further encroachments by speculative builders without due regards to the needs of the people.'[122]

However, many (albeit a minority) were critical of aspects both of farming and of government policy. Looking to 'future' concerns there was a high degree of awareness of 'environmental' factors. A clerk wrote from Oswestry in Shropshire:[123]

> I do hope our farmers first, and then our authorities, all the people in general will learn the folly of treating the soil as a medium for growing things in. Such a conception leads to the belief that all we have to do is discover by

laboratory methods what each crop needs for its growth, and then to see to it, merely by adding chemicals to the soil.

Perhaps surprisingly a number were familiar with very specific proposals, especially those of Sir Frank Stapledon, whose work on 'ley-farming' was closely associated with both the pre-war 'organic' movement and with the post-war development of the Soil Association.[124]

Equally interesting is the extent to which 'older' ideas of 'back-to-the-land' and land nationalisation remain a powerful current, running directly against post-war planning; although land nationalisation was part of the 'Reading' resolution carried at the 1944 Labour Party Conference.[125] A panel member from Somerset who described himself as the only non-farmer in a farming family wrote for many when he said that 'the land should be nationalised with only very small compensation to the present owners, and that the state should lease farms to present occupiers at reasonable rents.'[126] For others nationalisation was only part of the process. For a man in Plymouth land nationalisation was to lead to a process which would 'stop towns and industry spreading over our *good* [sic] land. Maintain the agricultural committees (and encourage) smaller farms more intensively farmed, which could absorb more labour.'[127] To a woman from Sherringham in Norfolk it all had a deeply personal edge. 'I wish things could be arranged that my husband and I could have a farm after the war.'[128]

These responses may have been conditioned by and certainly fed into the debate around the publication of the Scott Report on the utilisation of land in rural areas in August 1942.[129] The committee had been appointed to look at issues of building and planning in rural areas in relation to 'the maintenance of agriculture ... [and] the well-being of rural communities and the preservation of rural amenities'.[130] Although Lord Chief Justice Scott gave all appearances of being a rural conservative, steeped in a tradition of Englishness and ruralism, the Vice-Chairman of the Committee, the geographer L. Dudley Stamp, was not. His influence, Matless has argued, was fundamental.[131]

> Stamp was the dominating figure, *The Economist* commenting that the Scott report might 'more properly be called' the 'Stamp report'. Stamp championed the report as 'A New Charter for the Countryside' and advocated 'a *prosperous* and *progressive* agriculture' as the cornerstone of a 'national estate' under a Central Planning Authority.

Scott and Stamp saw the wartime model as the basis for the future. The War Ags were seen as supervising a countryside which had, moved 'from an atmosphere of neglect' to one which 'has assumed an air of busy prosperity'. Government intervention had given to the farmer a fair return and price stability. To the farm worker it had given a living wage and job security. To the townsman it had given

a hugely increased bread basket.[132] Although Scott made no direct recommenda-
tion on these issues – indeed that was outside the remit of the committee – it is
clear that he and his committee believed that wartime planning should form the
basis of post-war agriculture.[133]

What Scott was more directly concerned with was the countryside as a site of
leisure, as a place to live and with the planning issues that controlled the nature of
the countryside. Even here, although much of the rhetoric is of deep England, the
reality of Scott's (or perhaps Stamp's) vision was firmly in accordance with the
progressive ruralism of the pre-war leadership of the CPRE. Planning was essential – indeed the report ends with 'A Five-Year Plan for Britain' – planning which
would begin by zoning land for planning purposes within a year of the end of
war. Zoning was to lead to 'town and country planning schemes which would
cover the whole country'. But this was the first step. To follow was the wholesale
'reconstruction' of rural England and the relationship between town and
country.[134]

But the Scott Report was not simply about planning – it was a rural Beveridge.
Like the Beveridge Report it was shaped both by the locust years of the 1920s and
1930s and by the politics of 'new Liberalism' but, also like Beveridge, it had a
vision of a new Britain. On its second page the report, having presented a conventional, even idyllic picture of rural England, said: 'but we do not want a countryside which behind a smiling face hides much human poverty and misery.'[135] In
the five-year plan, as well as the control of urban building, were to be new
towns, proper housing for rural workers, the reconstruction of villages with
social centres and schools, while electricity, gas and water were to be brought to
the country districts. For the nation (and for the tripper) there were to be
National Parks and nature reserves, with signposted footpaths, clear rights of
access and hostels for those who sought rural England.[136] The Scott Report was to
shape post-war rural England and Wales in the same way that Beveridge was to
shape the welfare state.

Yet in 1942–3 this seemed far away and a general weariness appears in some
of the writing from the country districts. Ruth Child, a university graduate
working for the WLA on a poultry farm near Peterborough, wrote in 1942:[137]

A perfectly lovely day but that didn't seem to help much. The first year of
war the beauty of the countryside used to thrill me even though I was tired
and miserable. That doesn't happen now. That year my feelings were very
intense. Now they seem to be on a dead level. A sort of empty, acquies-
cent calm.

The reasons for this were many, and were common to both town and country.
The Allied campaigns seemed to be going slowly, even after the invasion of North
Africa heard the church bells rung for the first time since 1939. Losses mounted

while at home the simple boredom of 'austerity' and the nagging irritation of rationing wore many down.

In early 1944 the wealthy and normally ebullient 'lady of the manor' Caroline Haig wrote of her niece: 'Eileen went this morning. I can see how all these girls are longing for some fun and frivolity, feeling their young days are passing with so very little.'[138] There was also the almost casual horror of the stray bomb, as near Burwash in Sussex in early August 1943, when a stick of jettisoned anti-personnel bombs killed 'a boy, son of a small holder on his way to work on his bike'.[139] For many there were the constant fears for family members in the forces, especially where, as for many, it was the second time in their lives. As Caroline Haig wrote on hearing her son was in Normandy, 'it is rather over 29 years since I started writing to [my husband] in France in the last War, Jan. 1915, how merciful it is one does not know the future.'[140]

For some though the 'disruption' of wartime created chances to move which were simply not available to country people, especially women, before the war. At a minimal level the demands of war work drew young women away from their usual occupations, much to the delight of Emily Baker who revelled in the opportunities for her girl pupils to do something other than go into service.[141]

Others became country people as a result of war – most notably those drafted onto the land either because they were medically unfit for military service, or because they were conscientious objectors. Edward MacKenna left Cambridge, worked on the land and then joined the Forestry Commission as a forester preferring outdoor life to temporary work as a librarian even though this work was 'approved'.[142] Others shared these feelings. A Mass-Observation report from the 1941 Kent hopping on 'new' wartime hoppers said:[143]

> Most of these people and some of the 'old hands' would like to stay in the country now, or would like to go and live in the country after the war. . . . A new interest in the country has been awakened in a number of London people, women and children being more interested than men.

In 1945 Emily Baker wrote in her diary of the large number of ex-officers looking for farms 'of about 90 acres, with big, convenient, pleasant house. As after the last war, the war and the army life having left them with a longing for an open air life.'[144]

However, not all felt like this. The same account of the 1941 hopping recorded a woman who echoed many urban dwellers, especially evacuees. 'She would most emphatically NOT like to live in the country either now or after the war. . . . "There's not enough to do. And it's too quiet and lonely for my liking."'[145] J.B. Grierson was a London pacifist postman drafted into agriculture in 1941. At first he found it difficult to get work as 'most farms refused to employ COs',[146] but in April 1941 he found work on a farm near West Looe in Cornwall. The work was not as easy as he had thought but it had compensations:[147]

> Work hard. Found my back aching after about two hours. . . . In spite of several blisters and an aching body I did not find the work too distasteful. There is a sense of freedom about it and a delightful stillness – in sharp contrast to town and office life, which is to the good.

Grierson stayed on the land until the end of the war but never really liked it, an attitude shared by another CO in Oxford. 'My job as a market gardener is tolerable but I shall be glad when I can change to something quite different. It is healthy and interesting up to a point, but there is a lot of monotonous drudgery.'[148] In contrast another 'draftee', working as a living in farm servant in Cheshire wrote, 'I like my job and am keen on learning all I can; if it had not been for the war I should never have been able to do farm work but would probably have been on the dole.'[149]

Even in those cases where an individual apparently went through little change in his or her situation as a result of the war there were often concealed, and significant, shifts in emphasis. Caroline Haig, for example, remained in the same house throughout the war and, as we have seen, carried on with aspects of pre-war life to a remarkable degree. Yet within that there were changes. Crucially she adapted the pre-war model of the 'lady-bountiful' to wartime needs, and transferred the peace-time skills and role of local charity work and organisation to wartime voluntary work. In the summer of 1943 she was involved in War-Savings, the Women's Institute, the Women's Voluntary Service (WVS) and the Church of England. She was local contact and organiser for the Women's Land Army; she served on the Invasion Committee, the Salvage Committee and worked with the Child Health Clinic in 'her' village. In addition she had given up part of her house as a first aid post in case of air-raids, and regularly took part in organising 'one-off' campaigns like 'Wings for Victory', while also continuing a good deal of individual 'parish visiting'. She also, like others, regarded her M-O diary as part of the war effort.[150]

Although in a sense this work was simply carrying on the pre-war imperatives of her class and gender, she saw differences in her own feelings about the work, at least while the war continued. In August 1945 she looked back over the war in her diary and wrote rather wistfully:[151]

> I can't begin to think about leading a different sort of life, and I don't suppose there is much choice. (My friend says) how thankful she will be to get rid of those awful jobs – but I feel what would my life be without jobs? What could I put in their place? How empty life would be.

As the war drew towards its end violence returned to southern England at least, in the shape of V1s. Areas like the Kent and Sussex Weald, which had previously been safe apart from odd stray bombs, found themselves seriously threatened either from doodle bugs that fell short, or were forced down *en route* to London. In the summer of 1944 a new 'evacuation' began, this time from the rural areas. As Emily Baker wrote in her diary 'the vicar of Burwash has sent his children away. . . . The working class kids (maybe partly for lack of opportunity) are taking this steadily with chins up – the "national-leaders" skid-addle.'[152] By July instructions came from the East Sussex County Education Committee 'to register all unaccompanied school children for evacuation'. The teachers objected and so did the parents. However, some went to South Wales, returning in December.[153] At the end of July the school in the next village was closed until shelters could be built, and on 6 August all remaining schools were closed on council instruc-tions.[154] In the meantime a number of shelters had been built and many villagers had had 'Morrisons' installed, but real worries of a kind not seen before in rural areas appeared. 'Wherever you go all the conversation is doodles. There is no war in Normandy etc., only doodles. Some of them won't move out of reach of their shelters.'[155] The threat though was relatively short-lived. Emily Baker's school reopened on 6 September with only 25 children present out of 76. The problem though was not 'doodles', but late hopping.[156]

Many historians, following the magisterial work of Angus Calder, have called the Second World War 'the People's War', stressing the commonality of suffer-ing and of triumph.[157] The rural areas fit in some ways into this view, but not in others. Evacuation and rationing were experienced differently in the country dis-tricts than in the towns, which probably tended to highlight the differences rather than the similarities of the urban and rural experience, and may have contributed a widespread idea that 'the country did well' out of the war. Despite this feeling there was widespread sympathy for the problems of agriculture and a belief, even in urban areas, that it needed protection after the war. Similarly, there was a powerful feeling that the countryside needed protection and even 'rebuilding' with the aid of government through 'national parks' and careful planning. The war also gave some new opportunities, especially to younger women, to move away from village life into sometimes rewarding careers. Conversely, it moved others from the towns to the countryside, not always with the same happy results. It is difficult to quantify changes here, but certainly brushes with country life may have counteracted a tendency for other wartime changes to harden rural/urban divisions. Contact with the country almost certainly contributed to the desire of some to live in the countryside, and more to see the rural areas as sites of leisure in the post-war world.

There were however also continuities. Agricultural production could be modi-fied, as it was, but it could not be easily changed. Less obviously, the class struc-ture in rural areas remained much stronger, and traditional roles and class divisions which contemporaries saw as threatened in the towns, especially early in the war, seem to have remained much less of a problem in the countryside.

Much of this was to be tested in the 1945 election. In the country districts, as elsewhere, there was a swing to Labour. However, outside a few regions, especially East Anglia, Labour fared much less well in the country than in the towns. Interestingly there were major gains in M-O's heartlands in the southeast.[158] Caroline Haig, returned from Brighton to Oxfordshire on the day the results were announced convinced that a Conservative victory was certain. Indeed 'her' seat remained Tory, but she 'turned on the wireless at 2. To our horror the Labour Party was leading by heaps . . . lots of cabinet ministers have gone down in the landslide.'[159] But in other areas, even where Labour did not win, there was a different country voice and perhaps one which owed something to the war. Although much recent historiography plays down the 'dramatic' aspect of the 1945 result many M-O writers clearly felt very differently. Muriel Green writing on VJ Day from the war hostel in Somerset where she still lived spoke for them.[160]

At last, at long last! The day we have waited for nearly six long years has come round. A new era has dawned in which it is up to the survivors and the young people to let it not happen again. A new people's parliament has opened and the world is ready for better things.

8 'Tractors plus chemicals'
Agriculture and farming, 1945–90

The end of the Second World War saw British farming standing high in public opinion. The enormous changes in production made by wartime agriculture, and discussed in the last chapter, were widely believed to have saved Britain from starvation. This was clear, as we saw, as early as 1942 when the replies to a Mass-Observation directive on 'post-war problems' strongly supported the farming industry, often seeing a continuation of government support as fair payment for wartime sacrifices. Strikingly, support for agriculture came more strongly and less critically from urban areas than from rural. For example, a social worker from Chiswick wrote: 'Our agriculture must never again be allowed to decline to the pre-war level;'[1] or the suburban housewife quoted in the last chapter who wrote that 'the farmers have done their damdest for the country, it should be seen [sic] that they are not allowed to go back to penury and difficulty.'[2] In contrast, Muriel Green, who was born in the country and who we met in the last chapter working on the land, was keen to stress the hardness of rural life: 'Agricultural workers, particularly the women, work far longer hours and for less pay (than the factory workers). . . . The work is skilled, and any fool cannot do it.'[3] Edward MacKenna, working on the land in Buckinghamshire, also stressed the hard work and, drawing on his own experiences, suggested that the wartime reforms of agriculture had not gone far enough, arguing that, 'the ploughing up policy is still too half-hearted and will have to be developed much more swiftly after the war', and that 'the workers ought to be allowed to have a say about how the farm's to be run.'[4]

In 1945 though these criticism were forgotten or buried – farming and the farmers were among the heroes of the 'people's war'. Yet, as in 1918, the farming community were worried and distrustful of government – memories of the 'Great Betrayal' died hard. Throughout the war farming opinion had stressed time and again that there must be no repeat of 1918–21. In 1939 A.G. Street wrote of the repeal of the Agriculture Act in 1921 in *Farmers Weekly* that 'even today the burden of that piece of political treachery presses hardly on some farmers.'[5] In 1942 in response to an article in *The Economist* arguing that subsidies should cease with the end of the war, *Farmers Weekly* carried an editorial and a large number of letters saying that the continuation of subsidies and, more surprisingly, the War Ags, was essential to peacetime prosperity in agriculture.[6] This feeling may have contributed to the Labour gains in 1945, or at least prevented some farmers voting Conservative. As the 'Editor's Diary' noted just after the elections, 'I have not found a vast enthusiasm among farmers for any party programme' in comparison with 1935 when farmers were overwhelmingly Conservative voters.[7] As a Kent farmer told Mass-Observation in 1947:[8]

> No government's interested in farmers until the plight of the country makes them. You've only got to cast your mind back over the years to appreciate that – they've always glutted the market with imports from abroad at the expense of their own farming; they've shown so little interest in their welfare until a war has cropped up and then made them.

Yet the farmers had done well out of the war, as they had in 1914–18. J.K. Bowers notes that 'by any standards British farmers had a good war'. According to his calculations net farm incomes at constant prices tripled during the war years.[9] This was also a huge comparative increase. As John Martin writes, 'farmers collectively saw significantly greater increases in their disposable income than entrepreneurs or managers outside the agricultural sector.'[10] However, these profits were spread unevenly. In general, incomes rose most during the first years of the war, peaking in 1943–4 and declining slightly thereafter. Farm profits also varied according to cropping and to region, and marked an important change from the pre-war dominance of dairying. As Murray writes:[11]

> After two years of war, returns on all arable land had multiplied many times due largely to the phenomenally high prices of barley and oats and, on average, exceeded those obtained from grassland and mixed farming.

A new geography of agricultural prosperity in which the cereal growing areas, especially in the east of England, were to emerge as dominant, was beginning to appear.

This new prosperity was to be fixed by the immediate post-war changes in government policy towards agriculture, which transformed the 'temporary' demands of potential wartime food shortages into a permanent policy of agricultural support. As early as November 1940 the Government recognised that the creation of a stable and prosperous agriculture should be a central part of post-war policy.[12] As a result in the summer of 1942 'the foundations of post-war policy were laid down by the Government which stipulated:

1   That all reasonably good agricultural land should be maintained in a state of fertility and productivity, and

2   That any policy must secure to the utmost practical extent proper standards of up-keep of the farm and farm buildings, proper standards of
farming, and economic stability for the industry.[13]

In January 1944 the Government announced the Four Year Plan which promised
that 'assured markets' would be maintained for home-produced farm products
based on an annual price review each February.

The Labour administration elected in the summer of 1945 committed the
Government to continued agricultural intervention for reasons, as Martin writes,
which were not simply an ideological commitment to a planned economy.[14]

Food shortages had reached crisis proportions in 1945, threatening mass starvation across large areas of war-torn Europe. . . . The sudden termination of
American lend-lease aid in August 1945 created a dollar shortage in Britain,
which made the acquisition of high priced foodstuffs in the dollar dominated
markets financially undesirable and logistically impractical because of shipping shortages. Expanding domestic production was therefore an essential
prerequisite of the post-war reconstruction process.

In 1947 Tom Williams, the Minister of Agriculture, announced the Agriculture
Act to the House of Commons. The object of the new policy was:[15]

To promote a stable and efficient industry capable of producing such part of
the nation's food as in the national interest it is desirable to produce in the
United Kingdom and to produce it at minimum prices consistent with
proper remuneration and living conditions for farmers and workers in agriculture and an adequate return on the capital invested in the industry.

The 1947 Act was, according to Newby, 'the single most influential piece of legislation which governed post-war agricultural policy'.[16] It had two main areas.
The first, and in the long term the most important, was designed to guarantee a
high and increased level of agricultural production by paying guaranteed prices
for the vast majority of agricultural products. This was done via the annual price
review in which representatives of the farmers, dominated by the National
Farmers' Union, and the Ministry of Agriculture met each February to negotiate
minimum prices for the following year. Since the Government was still purchas-
ing the vast majority of foodstuffs this guaranteed farmers a stable income.
Where market prices fell below the minimum a 'deficiency payment' was made
from general taxation to cover the difference. This enabled the government to
pursue a 'cheap food' policy, while maintaining a stable income for farmers.

The second main part of the Act dealt with 'good husbandry'. It kept the War
Ags under the new name of the County Agricultural Executive Committees

which, in theory, had the same powers to direct and control agricultural production as their wartime counterparts. In fact, as Newby notes, these committees had little real power, and what little they had was rarely used even compared with the relatively soft touch of the War Ags. 'The stick which the Ministry of Agriculture increasingly chose to adopt was the sanction of the market.'[17]

The Agriculture Act was not the only legislation which affected the farmer as a result of the Labour victory. In 1946 the Hill Farming Act, wartime legislation which provided improvement grants to upland farms, was continued and extended and by July 1949 over 2,000 schemes covering nearly 700,000 acres were in place. This Act was extended in 1951 to cover upland but non-mountain areas.[18] Nevertheless hill farming, especially in parts of Wales, remained a precarious living, and as early as 1955 an investigation of mid-Wales argued that many holdings were unable to generate sufficient agricultural income to justify their continued existence as farms.[19]

With high wartime profits and the provisions of the 1947 Act most farmers were able to face the immediate post-war world with a sense of moderate well-being and security. As Tony Harman a Buckinghamshire farmer wrote:[20]

> In 1947 everything changed. It was a year as important in my life as 1921 had been, or 1931 when I took over Grove Farm, or 1934 when I got married. The reason everything changed was because Tom Williams . . . brought in the 1947 Agriculture Act which, for the first time in peace-time, incorporated a system of guaranteed prices into the law of the country. . . . Almost from that moment on the whole aspect of farming in Britain changed and instead of being a country which could only produce a very small percentage of its food requirements, it became able to produce almost all we needed and indeed to export quite a lot too.

Yet other sections of the agricultural community fared less well. As in the Great War agricultural rents had been effectively frozen during hostilities, having risen only about 11 per cent compared with a rise of 129 per cent in farmers' net income. As a result the landlords' part of the social income of agriculture had dropped from 24 per cent in 1939 to 11 per cent in 1945, while the farmers' had increased by almost exactly the same amount – a transfer of about 11 per cent of the fortunes of agriculture away from the owners of land.[21] In the post-war period there was certainly a sense of impending doom. As victory was celebrated in 1945 the Earl of Radnor remarked to his Countess that no matter how bright the dawn for the people, 'now our personal problems begin.'[22] Labour was committed to land nationalisation, a policy which was reiterated in 1946 in *Village Life and the Labour Party Today*, a pamphlet prepared for local government elections. Taxes on income were also increased. Marginal income tax rates were pushing 100 per cent. Normal death duties were to rise to 65 per cent during the war and remained at that level afterwards, while they were raised to 75 per cent on estates of over £1 million. Additionally, ways of avoiding tax and death duties were considerably tightened up in the years immediately after the war.

These changes saw the decline in the country house, which had begun in the inter-war years, continue. During the war, despite all the problems brought about by military and civilian 'occupation', only twenty-eight houses had been lost. Seventy-eight were demolished between 1945 and 1950, and a further 204 in the following 5 years – the peak period of destruction in the twentieth century.[23] Further, the political and social role of the aristocracy seemed set into continued decline. The Labour government of 1945–51 was the least landed ministry in modern British history, and even those few peers and younger sons who supported Labour were often the landed elite's sternest critics. In county government the story seemed similar with the post-war trends continuing:[24]

> The massive legislation of the Welfare State imposed on the localities unprece-
> dented responsibilities concerning health, planning, and education. Between
> the 1930s and the 1960s, the personnel and expenditure of most county coun-
> cils more than trebled. Local government thus became a fully bureaucratised
> profession, in which the experts – the engineers, the planners, the permanent
> officials – were the men who mattered, not the old patrician amateurs.

Yet it remains, as in the post-Great War period, a matter of emphasis. Unlike the period 1918–21 there were few land sales as a result of the war. Partly because at this stage there were no takers – farmers were unwilling to repeat the rush to mortgages that had been so disastrous after the Great War – and partly because, if as landowners the aristocracy and gentry had suffered, as farmers they too had prospered. This aspect was helped by changes in taxes. Although death duties were increased a 45 per cent abatement was given on agricultural land. As Peter Mandler writes:[25]

> Accountants advised owners to take their farms back from tenants and culti-
> vate them personally or through estate offices. Many owners, especially
> younger ones, did take their farms in hand. . . . By becoming farmers,
> younger owners could keep more of their income for themselves and
> improve and prettify their homes and estates in the process.

As a result as late as 1980 about half the families who held great estates in 1880 still held great estates, even if on a reduced scale; while even among the gentry the figures were remarkably similar.[26] However, they now held their estates more often as farmers than *rentiers*.[27] In 1951 a government was returned which was as aristocratic as virtually any other in the twentieth century – and not all those who came from the landed estates were the old and tired.

The farm workers' position was also changed by the war and, to a more limited extent, by the election of a Labour government. Wartime wages had certainly increased, and at a faster rate than the average for all industries. According to Armstrong, farm workers' wages had increased by 170 per cent since 1938 as against 81 per cent in all industries.[28] These gains were due in part to labour shortage, but mainly to the national Agricultural Wages Board fixing a national minimum wage. These increased earnings continued in the immediate post-war period rising to 94s per week in 1949. This put the farm worker at much the same level as a labourer employed on the railways or by local authorities. However, such a comparison is at best confusing and at worst insulting. Much farm work was and still is highly skilled, and on that basis other comparisons might be made. For example in October 1949 average weekly earnings of all industries was 142s 8d a week meaning that farm wages were still in the region of 38 per cent lower than all earnings. The comparison is even worse if compared with all manufacturing industries, where average weekly earnings were 148s at the same point.[29]

However, the relationship between the national minimum and actual earnings was a complex one. Certainly, in some areas workers earned more than the minimum wage, but this was nearly always at the cost of working longer hours. In 1946 the hours of work for the minimum were set at 48 hours a week, already above the national average weekly hours actually worked, but they seldom fell below 50 hours, especially for those working with animals who, even in the 1960s, were still working a 53-hour week. There also continued to be regional variations with more opportunities for overtime on larger arable farms set mainly in the east of England.

The 1947 Agriculture Act gave little to the farm worker, although indirectly he or she could be said to have benefited from the increased stability of the industry as a whole. More directly, also in 1947, the Agricultural Wages Act made the wartime Agricultural Wages Board a permanent feature of post-war agriculture, with its annual round of negotiations on wages sitting alongside the annual price review. Yet much remained undone. Working conditions were still often appalling and the 'Tied Cottage', which meant that many farm workers had a house tied to their job, remained common despite the fact that Labour had been pledged to its abolition since 1906. Many farm workers, especially those in the Union, felt that while agriculture had 'done well' out of the post-war settlement the farm worker had not got his or her fair share. Jack Boddy, later General Secretary of the National Union of Agricultural and Allied Workers (NUAAW), but in 1945 a Norfolk farm worker, remembered the years of the 1945–51 Labour government with mixed feelings.[30]

(The Union executive) felt it had a responsibility to the Labour administration not to rock the boat. . . . Because of this, the Union missed the boat during the war years and to some extent, again in 1945. If wages had been raised to a decent level, tied cottages abolished and working conditions improved, I don't think this would in any way have inhibited the economic revival. . . . All the activities of Tom Williams appeared to be directed towards assisting the farmers, leaving the farm workers to pick up what they could from the increasing prosperity of their employers, which left them at the mercy of the Agricultural Wages Board. . . . Sad to say, I believe Labour felt it could ignore the farm workers because their ability to influence the results of the General Election was numerically low as they had become a relatively small proportion of the rural workers.

Compared with later figures though there were still a very large number of men and women employed in agriculture in 1945. Figures vary according to definitions but Murray[31] suggests that in 1944–5 there were nearly a million men and women part- and full-time workers in agriculture, of whom 770,000 were full-time. Of these about 90,000 were members of the Women's Land Army and about 50,000 were prisoners of war. Both these groups continued in importance in the immediate aftermath of the war, especially the WLA which was still recruiting in the post-war period and which was not disbanded until 1950.

The treatment of the WLA in the post-war period was one of the sad and shameful acts, which are too often hidden by history. WLA members assumed that they would be treated in the same way as other women who had joined the forces since they were a uniformed organisation run directly by government. It was not to be. Unlike women in the armed forces and eventually Civil Defence and other auxiliary workers, WLA members were given no resettlement grants, no post-war training, no 'demob' leave and no extra ration coupons for civilian clothes. Lady Denman fought hard for 'her army' but in the end resigned in protest in February 1945. In the following months members of the WLA took matters into their own hands. Many had joined the Union during the war and they now went on strike, despite the fact that the Union and the WLA leadership refused to support them. In April 1945 representatives of the War Cabinet, including Churchill, met a deputation from the WLA but their demands for a war service gratuity, pensions for sickness or injury and a guarantee of new jobs or training were turned down.

Even with the gradual run-down of the WLA and the return of prisoners of war, the farm workforce in 1949 stood at 648,000 male and female, full- and part-time workers, the highest peace time number since the 1920s. They were better paid than their fathers and mothers and were more regularly employed; yet many had a sense that the New Jerusalem did not have a place for them. In the next 20 years their numbers were to halve as the agriculture of England and Wales became ever more prosperous.

The history of British agriculture from the late 1940s until the 1990s was one of apparent and unproblematic success. That success was based on two quite different foundation stones. First, a growing consumer demand for food, and then more and better food, then more diverse types of food. Second, and perhaps more importantly, a belief held by successive governments that a stable and successful agriculture was vital to national well-being, and that Britain's economy demanded that as much of the nation's food as possible should be produced in Britain. Both of these demands pushed agriculture and agricultural policy down a productionist path for most of the rest of the twentieth century.

Demand was initially a simple matter. As Zweiniger-Bargielowska writes, 'most people had expected rations to be increased after the war;'[32] in fact they were cut as a result of world shortages, the end of lend-lease and the need to conserve Britain's foreign reserves. Worst of all:[33]

> In addition to the ration cuts the post-war period witnessed two highly controversial extensions, viz. bread rationing, operational from July 1946 until July 1948, and the control of potatoes during the winter and spring 1947–8. The entire system of food controls was based on ample supplies of these so-called buffer foods and any restrictions had to be avoided at all costs during the war. Bread rationing represented the height of post-war austerity and the policy dealt a 'symbolic blow to civilian morale'.

Nor was that the end of problems; as late as 1951 the meat ration was reduced again having been raised a year earlier. In this situation the question for agriculture was not demand but supply, and especially supply of the basic goods. However, the gradual decontrol of food from the late 1940s began to shift the equation in favour of demand. As foodstuffs came back onto the market the demand for basics, such as bread and potatoes, and substitutes, such as margarine, began to fall as consumers switched demand to the things they had missed most in the 1940s.[34] When jams and preserves, the first items to be taken off the ration, were decontrolled in December 1948, Sainsbury's branch in Colchester sold 8,575 pounds in a week.[35]

Demand however did not always work in one direction. Potatoes, for example, were grown on about 1.2 million acres at the end of the war but, as Holderness notes, this acreage 'was not likely to be maintained as the economy pulled out of austerity' and by 1960 the acreage had been halved to 660,000 acres. This decrease was largely a result of careful monitoring of consumer demand by the Potato Marketing Board.[36] Even wheat production was subject to consumer vagaries. The English demand for white bread, well established by the 1880s, demanded a high proportion of 'hard wheat' which continued to be imported, so although technically self sufficient in wheat by the 1980s, Britain still imported about 16 per cent of bread wheats.[37] In other areas there was evidence of a plateau in demand. For example egg production increased very rapidly in the 1950s as more and more producers adopted first 'deep-litter' and then battery methods of production. However in the early 1960s 'near saturation of demand' caused a levelling off of production. At the same time, other changes in production, particularly the rapid fattening of broiler fowls in deep litter houses, met a growing public demand for chicken meat which had in the past been seen as a luxury. However, there was again evidence of a plateau in demand and although the broiler flock stood at 60 million birds in 1980, 'the age of expansion had passed by the mid-1970s'.[38]

Consumer demand, especially in the immediate post-war period, provided the impetus for increases in agricultural productivity. The state laid the foundation of growth in the subsidies and price stability following from the 1947 Agriculture Act and as a result the gains in productivity were staggering. The area under wheat increased from 746,000 ha in 1939 to 1,955,000 ha in 1990 and that of barley from 410,000 ha to 1,517,000 ha in the same period. There was also a huge increase in yields per hectare with wheat yields rising from about 2 tonnes per ha. in the 1930s to over 7 tonnes by the early 1990s.[39] The same period saw increases in the scale and productivity of the livestock sector. As we saw in Chapter 3 dairying was the most successful sector of agriculture in the inter-war period. After a slight decline during the war as a result of land switching to arable, the numbers of animals raised on British farms increased rapidly. The dairy herd increased from 2.6 million cows in 1945 to 3 million by the mid-1970s, and the beef herd from 8.6 million cattle in 1945 to 13.5 million by the mid-1970s. Since the 1970s, partly as a result of Milk Quotas which were introduced in 1984 and partly simply because of consumer demand, the numbers first levelled out and then began to decline, and indeed there are fewer dairy cows now than in 1945. The numbers of dairy cattle however conceal the huge increase in milk output, which rose by around 70 per cent in the 30 years after 1945. As a result, certainly until the early 1990s, dairying remained the cornerstone of British agriculture contributing above 20 per cent by value of all agricultural output.

The history of other livestock was more volatile. The numbers of sheep, in common with other livestock, increased in the post-war period; however, as with poultry and egg production the market played a key role. Traditional sheep were multi-purpose being raised for both wool and meat but in the post-war world, as to an extent in the inter-war period, British wool was not of high enough quality for most uses, being mainly used for carpet production. Further, the traditional hill sheep produced large joints of meat, which found a smaller and smaller market in the face of imports of chilled or frozen meat from the Commonwealth. In response sheep farmers turned to a lucrative niche market in younger and smaller lambs which produced sweeter, less fatty and fresher joints, meaning that although only about 50 per cent of lamb eaten in Britain is home-produced it continued, at least until the 1990s, to fetch good prices. Additionally, especially after entry into the EEC in 1978, there was a considerable demand for lamb, particularly from France, where lambs were exported 'on the hoof' and fattened abroad. 'Pig-keeping', as Holderness writes, 'has tended to be the most volatile type of animal husbandry. It has fluctuated more widely than the poultry trade since the war.'[40] Pork was traditionally a mainstay of working-class meat consumption and was as a result one of the main areas into which post-rationing food expenditure went. Government, which recognised that of all meat producing livestock the pig was in many ways the most efficient, since sows litter twice a year, supported this. Furthermore, pigs, like poultry, have a high feed efficiency conversion and growth rate. However, in both cases this only works if cheap concentrates are available, which they increasingly were in the post-war period.[41] In the short term it was also possible to rear pigs with little capital input. As a result the years 1945 to 1960 saw the number of pigs rise from 1.6 million to 5.2 million while domestic demand for pork doubled in the same period. However, as with eggs, a plateau of demand was reached in the 1960s when the British population was eating about 26 lb per head. Thereafter there was no real increase in demand. This levelling of demand was compounded by the inability of the bacon-producing sector to compete with much cheaper imports from Denmark and Ireland, and of the pork and pork products sectors, to export to any great degree.[42]

If consumer demand and government subsidy were the cornerstones of the success of post-war agriculture, science made the success possible by providing 'the tools for the job'.[43] Paul Brassley, looking at the long-term relationship between technical and scientific change and agricultural output, divides the period since 1945 into two parts. One runs from 1945 to 1965 when, in a period of high prices, 'the volume of output rose most rapidly as both arable and livestock sectors expanded'; the second runs from 1965 to 1985 when 'output still expanded, but at a reduced rate, as labour left agriculture rapidly, and much of the extra cereal production was to intensive livestock.'[44] Within these periods scientific and technical change can be divided into two categories: 'the output increasing and the labour saving'.[45]

In the years from the end of the war to the mid-1960s much of the technical and scientific changes, which make up what many think of as a 'second agricultural revolution' were widely adopted. In terms of output gains this was the period which saw the adoption of new varieties of cereals, the widespread use of artificial fertilisers, the increasing use of purchased feedstuffs, the adoption of new breeds of animals selectively bred for increased output, for example the Friesian cow, and the introduction of artificial insemination. Two examples, drawn from Brassley, will serve to illustrate these points. Artificial fertilisers had been used since the mid-nineteenth century and at the outbreak of war something in the region of a million tonnes per annum were being used on British farms. However, between the late 1930s and the 1960s the amount of artificials used increased fourfold to 6.9 million tonnes at the end of that decade.[46] The now ubiquitous Friesian cow came to dominate the British dairy herd in the same period. In 1955 40 per cent of dairy cows in Britain were Friesians, by the late 1980s the breed accounted for 85 per cent. Careful selective breeding using artificial insemination, which was encouraged both by the Milk Marketing Board and the British Friesian Cattle Society, developed the commercial attributes of the breed and was a major contribution to increasing the average yield of the British herd from 2,300 litres in 1945 to 5,055 in 1983.[47]

In terms of labour saving innovations, Brassley highlights combine harvesters, tractors and milking machines as the key technical advances in the period between 1945 and 1965. Again the figures are clear. In technical terms this was the period in which the horse vanished as the main source of motive power on Britain's farms. Even in 1946 there had been twice as many horses as tractors on British farms. Between 1950 and 1960 the numbers were reversed, and after 1960 the number of horses became statistically insignificant. There was a similar transformation in the types of machinery used, particularly at harvest. Before the war cereal harvest operations had been dominated by the reaper-binder, which simply cut the crop and left it in stooks. The reaper binder remained dominant until 1950 when the combine began to appear in substantial numbers. Finally, the milking machine: in 1939 90 per cent of the British dairy herd was milked by hand, but by 1961 85 per cent was milked by machine.[48]

Technical and scientific change after the mid-1960s took a slightly different path. Although output expanded it did so at a much slower rate and was often related to British government or EU grants. For example, new drainage peaked in the 1970s when there were government grants available for 65 per cent of the cost; while the growth of maize was not only related to its uses in silage, another post-1960s innovation, but also to the fact that in the 1990s maize qualified for arable area payments of £320 per hectare.[49]

Probably the most significant scientific change in the period after the mid-1960s was the widespread adoption of pesticides and herbicides. There are no official figures for herbicide and pesticide usage before the 1970s, but the first modern selective herbicide MCPA was developed during the war and marketed from the mid-1940s as Methoxone. The insecticide DDT was developed at the same date.[50] However, take up of pesticides and herbicides seems to have been much slower than with other technical and scientific changes. The main period of research was in the 1950s but Brassley suggests that the period of rapid expansion was in the late 1960s both for home use and for export.[51]

What are striking in all these cases are not only the speed and diversity of scientific and technical change but also the point of its adoption. As Brassley points out, much of this technology and indeed a good part of the scientific knowledge which lay at the core of the second agricultural revolution was in theory available long before the time of its adoption by British farmers. Why

Plate 14 The Second Agricultural Revolution. The notes for this picture, taken in Berkshire in the late 1940s, simply say 'Crouch's new combine' but the banal wording hides the enormous transformation wrought by machinery on English agriculture after the Second World War. (Reproduced by kind permission of the Rural History Centre, University of Reading.)

British farmers took to these new machines, chemicals, crops and techniques in the years between 1945 and 1965 could have many explanations. Certainly the National Agricultural Advisory Service, a by-product of the 1947 Act, played its part by advising farmers about scientific and technical advance but, as Brassley writes, 'something also encouraged farmers to believe that attempts to increase output would not be met with a return to pre-war low price conditions, as they had been after the First World War. The 1947 Act is an obvious candidate.'[52] As with much else in post-war farming, stable, and even rising prices, supported by subsidy, the legacy of a Labour government to profoundly Conservative voters, was the real basis of technical and scientific change.

The great increase in post-war agricultural output also had a profound impact on the broader patterns of English and Welsh farming. Environment meant that the basic divisions between the upland and pastoral north and west (including most of Wales) and the lowland and arable south and east, obvious in the farming of these islands since at least the late Iron Age, remained and still remains unchanged. However, 'tractors plus chemicals' did have some effects on farming practice. As Holderness wrote in the 1980s:[53]

> There is more arable land in the west, especially on the clay lowlands, because technical improvements have extended the potential area in tillage quite considerably. By the same token the revival of dairying in the east has caused some formerly arable ground to be kept in permanent grass. . . . The inherent quality of the land does determine the pattern of agriculture, but where climate, slope and altitude are not unfavourable it has been possible to change the prevailing regime quite successfully.

These changes have often been startling, like the ploughing up of the chalk down lands of southern England or the grubbing up of hedgerows or ancient orchards, and have often been the object of intense criticism in recent years, a subject to which we will return in Chapter 10.

Alongside these changes, and probably more fundamental if less obvious to the outsider, has been the change in farm size and ownership, and the growing specialisation of English and Welsh agriculture. In the 1880s 71 per cent of English farms and 69 per cent of Welsh were less than 50 acres.[54] Even in 1950 over 53 per cent were in this size group. However by the late 1980s holdings[55] of less than 50 acres had fallen to 36 per cent of the total, a decline of some 60 per cent. At the other end of the scale, holdings of more than 450 acres (200 ha) had increased 21 per cent, and those over 550 acres (240 ha) by more than 30 per cent since 1950.[56] Increased farm size has been matched by changes in ownership away from a system dominated by tenant farmers to one dominated by owner-occupiers. As we saw earlier the immediate post-First World War period saw widespread land sales mostly to sitting tenants, which meant that by 1939 around 35 per cent of English and Welsh farmland was in the hands of those who farmed it. During the Second World War there was little change, but in its aftermath the tendency to owner-occupation continued. By the early 1960s the majority of farmers in England and Wales had become owner-occupiers.[57] A local example of this can be seen in Williams' study of 'Ashworthy', a Devon village studied between 1957 and 1960. Here one family had dominated land ownership until the 1920s. In 1922 there were 45 tenant farms on the estate, by 1960 it had dropped to seven.[58] What is interesting here is that the growth in owner-occupation follows a very similar timescale to that outlined by Brassley for technical change, which suggests that the move to owner-occupancy between the late 1940s and the 1970s was, as in 1918–21, a product of perceived price stability.

Growing farm size plus the demands of the market led to increased specialisation on individual agricultural units. Although English and Welsh farms had followed regional patterns of specialised production for centuries, in many ways the 'typical' farm remained mixed until the Second World War. The exception here was, as we saw earlier, that dairy farms tended to become specialised units well before the war. In the post-war period specialist production spread to other parts of the livestock sector with the growth of intensive indoor, 'factory' farming units. The most obvious of these, because it was to attract some of the earliest environmental criticism, was poultry farming. In the nineteenth century poultry had been almost a by-product of the farm. Fowls and, especially, eggs were both the product and the property of the farmyard and the farmer's wife and family. Henry St George Cramp who grew up on a farm in Leicestershire in the 1920s and 1930s writes:[59]

> Perhaps the sound that Mother liked best was that of a cackling hen announc-ing another egg. Since Father provided the hens and the corn, eggs were a net gain to Mother. Not only were there enough for the house, but eggs were Mother's currency. . . . Whenever there were minor debts to settle with local people they were given the choice of cash or eggs. The latter was always the best buy and all the village knew it.

However, even in the inter-war period this was beginning to change. For example, as we saw earlier, in Lancashire the Preston and District Farmers' Trading sold members eggs and acted as wholesaler for feed and equipment for its members; although the trade was unpredictable, especially at the end of the 1920s, by 1939 it had a turnover of over £1.25 million and 3,200 members.[60]

By 1939 many of these poultry farmers were housing their flocks under cover in large deep litter sheds. However in the 1950s and 1960s further technical change, especially battery production, led to further specialisation. Poultry farming, although showing many of the same tendencies as other branches of agri-culture towards larger units, also enabled the relatively small farmer, providing she or he had the necessary capital, to make a reasonable living from three or four, or even one or two intensive units. However, the supply of chicks, the pur-chase of eggs and, especially, poultry meat has tended to move into the hands of fewer companies who are thus to exert considerable control over producers.[61]

Intensive indoor production also spread to other sectors. Like poultry, the pig was originally reared as an extra, near free 'crop' but the huge post-war expan-sion in pigmeat production saw units increase in size and in specialisation. Between 1957 and 1990 the average number of pigs per herd increased from 34 to over 470. By the 1960s *Fream's Agriculture* wrote that 'pig keeping is following the poultry industry into becoming a concrete-based factory enterprise with land required only for the disposal of effluent.'[62]

Less obvious to the non-farming public was the increasing specialisation in field crops. Traditionally even the great cereal farms of the eastern counties had kept sheep or cattle to provide manure, and had grown turnips or mangolds to feed them as part of a rotation. However, according to a 'guide' to East Anglian farming written in 1967 this was a thing of the past.[63]

> In the old days the only means of fertilizing land was by carting out dung made in yards by cattle or keeping sheep on the land eating crops like turnips and Swedes. . . . Though these practices are still sound and persist to a degree, the use of artificial fertilizers has developed to such an extent that the chief method of replenishing the soil . . . is the use of artificial product.

Artificial fertilisers and pesticides also did away with the 'need' to leave arable land fallow, or to plant grass 'leys' restoring its nutrient level 'naturally'. As a result livestock vanished from many areas of eastern England in the 1950s and 1960s.

By the 1970s English and Welsh agriculture was stable, prosperous and by most measures extremely successful. This success was based on continuing subsidy, which guaranteed price stability and encouraged innovation and capital investment. However the nature and, eventually, the source of agricultural subsidy changed significantly in the years between 1945 and 1990. In 1953, with the end of rationing in sight, the government ceased to be the major purchaser of food and farm produce moved back into the free market. In this situation subsidy was continued by deficiency payments paid direct to the farmer. These were determined by the difference between the average world price on the open market and the agreed minimum determined, as in the past, by negotiations between the farmers' representatives and the Ministry of Agriculture. As world prices tended to fall with the adjustment of the post-war economies, and since the British government had no control over these prices, subsidy payments tended both to grow in volume but also to fluctuate. As a result government subsidies to agriculture including monies paid for the research and advisory sector grew from £197.3 million per annum in 1954 to £264 million in 1961. In all this the role of the NFU grew ever more powerful. The annual review, described by Harold Macmillan as 'a debate of Byzantine deviousness' based on 'the Alice in Wonderland method of calculation', brought the NFU into the heart of government. As Tristram Beresford wrote in 1975, the NFU:[64]

> . . . became a bureaucracy that anticipated, interpreted, co-ordinated and amplified the inarticulate aspirations of the majority of farmers. . . . It was too important to offend. The government hobnobbed with it. Placemen touched their caps to it.

But it was not only the annual prices review, as Newby *et al.* observed in 1978:[65]

> . . . there is a close and abiding relationship between those in the top ech-

elons of the civil service in the MAFF and the national officers of the NFU. It would probably be true to say that not a single day passes when someone from the Ministry is not in negotiation with someone from the NFU.

That closeness remained, even under Labour governments, until the end of the century.

However, after 1953, subsidy became much more transparent and thus open to public criticism. Such criticism was as old as the system of subsidies itself. Not all members of the Labour majority from 1945 to 1951 were certain that farm subsidies were an unmitigated blessing. In April 1950 Stanley Evans, Parliamentary Secretary to the Ministry of Food, gave the English language a new phrase when, at a press conference in Manchester, he talked about farmers being 'feather bedded' at the taxpayer's expense. He was dismissed from his post.[66] It was to be the late 1950s before serious criticism began to come from within government. In 1956–7 world food surpluses had pushed annual subsidies up to £288 million and the Conservative government acted to reduce the annual subsidy, but successive balance of payments crises in the 1960s acted to keep home production high, a situation which remained essentially the same until Britain's entry into the European Economic Community (EEC) in 1973.[67]

Britain's entry into the European Economic Community, now the European Union (EU), caused, as Martin says, 'the most significant changes in agricultural policy since 1947'.[68] What was significant though was not that agriculture ceased being subsidised but rather that the method of subsidy was transformed. European agricultural policy in regard to farm price subsidies – the Common Agricultural Policy (CAP) – is complex, has changed over time and a detailed discussion is not really relevant here.[69] At the most basic level the major change was that subsidies switched from a system of deficiency payments to one where individual commodities were given a Europe-wide price. This was then guaranteed by a mixture of intervention, buying and storing – the creation of the notorious 'lakes and mountains' – and export and especially import controls.

Initially this was not a problem, but as food production within the European Community (EC) increased in the 1970s and 1980s, and consumer demand in Europe, especially for basic foodstuffs, appeared satiated, surpluses began to grow, since the EC was compelled to purchase whatever was produced at intervention prices. By 1988, despite some efforts to deal with overproduction, the EC held in storage over 1 million tonnes of butter, 5 million tonnes of wheat, 4 million tonnes of barley and 800,000 tonnes of beef. As a result of uncontrolled growth, by 1990 the CAP was costing at least 60 per cent of the EU total budget, and had risen to more than twice the level of the 1960s.[70]

This in itself would not necessarily have been a problem; however, as Brassley writes, 'overproduction' was seen as benefiting the large farmer at the expense of the environment, the small farmer and the labourer.[71]

In 1992 the Commission estimated that 80 per cent of EC farm spending went to only 20 per cent of farmers and that these were 'generally the bigger and more efficient ones'. Between 1960 and 1990 the numbers of farmers and farm workers in the original six member states of the Community fell from more than 10 million to less than 5 million. The numbers of farms in these countries decreased from 5.9 million in 1970 to 4.7 million in 1987. By the end of the 1970s it was increasingly accepted that the CAP was not meeting its objectives.

As a result the CAP underwent a number of complex changes in the 1980s and early 1990s. The first of these was the introduction, in 1984, of quotas designed to reduce milk production by setting the amount of subsidised milk each farmer could produce. In May 1992 a wider range of reforms known as the MacSharry package after the Commissioner in charge of agriculture at the time was introduced.[72] These aimed at cuts in EC intervention prices, which were to be phased in over 3 years, to directly reduce output. This was supported by payments made to farmers to 'set-aside' land by taking it out of production, thus reducing the area under cereals. In compensation for reduced prices farmers were paid arable area payments, based on their arable acreage. However, both 'set-aside', and the arable area payments clearly benefited larger farmers. In addition MacSharry proposed a number of measures, intended to answer growing European-wide criticism of the environmental effects of agriculture. While aspects of these measures, for example the encouragement of organic farming and environmentally favourable production practices, were driven by worries about damage to the environment, they were also 'clearly designed to limit the output of products in surplus'.[73]

The fortunes of British farming and farmers under the CAP were, until the mid-1990s, generally good, although some sectors, especially the small livestock producers, did less well. In that sense, at the most basic level, entry into the EC continued what had gone before. Intervention prices continued the price stability that had characterised all post-war agriculture, and probably encouraged even higher levels of output. By the mid-1980s the EC had surpluses in all major areas of agricultural production.[74] External factors also helped the farmer. The oil crisis of 1972 led to a rapid rise in world commodity prices, which was followed by bad harvests outside the EC. As a result farm prices rose rapidly between 1970 and 1976, and although they dropped again in the late 1970s and early 1980s crop prices had increased by 204 per cent, and livestock for slaughter prices by 189 per cent in the 10 years before 1983. Again it was the 'larger, progressive arable farmers, particularly owner-occupiers, who were able to exploit economies of scale and increase production', who fared best.[75]

Owner-occupiers and landlords benefited in other ways from the price stability both of the post-war period and the CAP. Land prices rose very rapidly after 1970, which increased the capital value of farm land enormously making farms, especially those in fertile areas, a much more valuable asset. While the difference between wealth and income is obviously crucial for owner-occupiers, in that the value of farmland can only be realised on sale, increasing land values did represent a real gain in most respects. Landlords also gained from the increase in land values not only in terms of wealth, but also in terms of income. Rents remained controlled from 1945–58, but after that date they began to rise again. In 1950 the average rent on farmland was about £2 per acre. By 1980 it had reached £30, although part of that gain was removed by taxes and other statutory charges. Land prices fell in the late 1980s but by the early 1990s farmland had regained most of what it had lost.

Looking back from 1945 to 1939 most historians concluded that agriculture, or sections of it at least, had had a good war. Looking back from 1990 to 1945 much the same thing could be said about the peace. Agricultural output had grown enormously and Britain and Europe were self sufficient in temperate foodstuffs for the first time since the eighteenth century. Farming prospered. In 1995 looking back at an increase in real incomes for cereal farms of about 138 per cent in 5 years, *Farmers Weekly* wrote: 'why should farmers alone be ashamed of making good profits?'[76] Again, that cry might well have been applied to the whole post-war period. Even the landlords, whose immanent demise had been on the lips of every generation since the 1880s, did well. As the *Guardian* wrote in 1994:[77]

> In a century when whole new classes have gained power, and when population growth and immigration have redefined the demographic landscape, land ownership has remained relatively untouched. The club has not bothered to welcome too many newcomers.

Yet there were losers. The number of full-time, non-family farm workers had dropped from nearly a million in 1945 to less than 100,000 by 1990. Those that remain are still some of the worst paid workers in Britain. The land itself, many would argue, has also suffered. In 1945 the landscape would have been recognisable to a farmer of 1880, if not earlier. By 1990 change was everywhere. These changes and others are the matter of the next two chapters where we shall put some figures back in our landscapes.

Part IV

What is the countryside for?

Rural society, 1945–2001

9 A place to work and a place to play

Incomers and outgoers, 1945–90

At the end of the Second World War much of rural England and Wales was still dominated by agriculture and agricultural production. Although the 'new' country men and women who were discussed in Chapter 6 were beginning to make up a substantial part of the population in some, especially southeastern areas, many rural counties remained firmly agricultural. Even in the southeast the new editions of the popular *Little Guides* series prepared between 1946–52 stressed the importance of agriculture in counties like Surrey and Sussex. In both books the persistence of agriculture as an employer and as a shaper of landscapes was given a central place. Of Sussex the *Little Guide* wrote:[1]

> It cannot be denied, of course, that much of the coastal fringe has now lost whatever natural charm it possessed. . . . But when all is said, there remains the larger part of the county which is still unspoiled; and there is comfort in the fact that even Peacehaven is only a short walk from untouched downland.

Even Surrey, a less likely candidate for unspoiled charm, had areas of farmland, and thus beauty, which had escaped 'dingy, dirty, mean, and uninspired suburbia'.[2]

Furthermore, many believed and wished that this situation should continue. In 1946 the Sussex Rural Community Council published a short book, *To-morrow in East Sussex*, which they saw as a contribution to the post-war planning debate. Although the report sees Sussex as a modernising community facing urban growth, it is firmly agricultural in its focus. 'We are convinced that the vast majority in East Sussex will wish their County to continue to be preserved as a County primarily devoted to Agriculture.'[3]

Nevertheless those who worked in agriculture and its associated trades were already under threat by the early 1950s. The increase in numbers employed in agriculture during the war, which was, as we have seen, sustained immediately afterwards, changed to one of declining numbers in the years after 1950.

Between 1946–50 and 1956–60 the number of agricultural workers had fallen from 865,000 to 678,000 – a decline of over 20 per cent. Between the later date and 1981–5 their numbers fell by a further 364,000 to 314,000. By 1991 there were less than 200,000 workers of all kinds employed in agriculture.[4]

Nor was it simply that the numbers employed were declining, but also that other workers were moving into the rural areas. The material is complicated, but the general trends are absolutely clear if we look at the long-term census data from some English and Welsh counties. Beginning after the Great War the population of even the rural counties begins to show a long-term movement towards countryside less of agriculture and agricultural work and more and more as a place to live and spend spare time. This movement, which we have already discussed in the inter-war period, took on a new dimension after the Second World War. As the *General Report* of the 1951 Census noted:[5]

> In the twenty years since 1931 the Southern and Eastern Regions still had the largest percentage increases and Wales and the Northern Region the smallest. . . . The large migration gain by rural areas does not, of course, indicate any return of population to farming but merely a movement of population away from their workplaces in the towns to more residential areas in the surrounding countryside. The almost uniformly outward migration from the conurbations is another indication of this change.

In fact, as we would expect, the change, outside the south and east, although obvious was far from uniform. In Surrey, symbolically at least the most suburban county in England, there were 5,504 male farm workers and 1,749 male farmers in 1931, representing in total 2.4 per cent of the employed population as against a national figure of about 6 per cent. By 1971 the figure had fallen to 1.3 per cent, although the area defined as rural Surrey had substantially decreased as a result of census boundary changes in the intervening period. Interestingly though the story of 'rural' work in Surrey is more complex owing to its important horticultural sector. Although comparisons are difficult to make over time, there were over 16,000 people employed in horticulture in 1931, and although the numbers had dropped by 1971 there were still a substantial number of women workers, meaning that the numbers of women employed in 'agriculture' in Surrey increased in the post-war period from 390 in 1931 to 1,950 in 1971.[6]

Even more obviously 'rural' counties show similar changes. Norfolk, for all of the nineteenth century firmly and proudly the 'bread basket of England' shows, if anything, more startling change. In 1931 44 per cent of the male working population of Norfolk was involved in agriculture in some way or another, the vast majority, 76 per cent, as farm workers or farmers. By 1971 the percentage in agriculture had fallen to 13 per cent although the county retained a relatively high number of 'traditional' workers and farmers. In Devon 29 per cent of the employed male population worked in agriculture in 1931, with 66 per cent farmers or farm workers. By 1971 it had fallen to 9 per cent. Rural Northumberland had a much smaller percentage of the male population employed in agriculture even in 1931 at about 10 per cent, but this had halved to 5 per cent in 1971. Even Montgomeryshire, an overwhelmingly rural county in 1931 with 50 per cent of the workforce in agriculture, saw that number decline to 32 per cent by 1971, although, like many upland Welsh and English counties, it remains 'more' agricultural than most of the land of England and Wales.

During the same period the number of farm holdings also declined. In 1950 there had been 296,000 agricultural holdings in England and Wales, by 1986 this had fallen to 164,000, a decline of 45 per cent.[7] The decline in the numbers of holdings, which was discussed briefly in the last chapter, had a fundamental effect on the social structure of farming in England and Wales. Central to this was the decline in the number of small and medium-sized family farms, and a concurrent growth in the number of larger, consolidated and more specialised units. Although comparisons are difficult this seems to have been regionally differentiated, as Newby *et al.* write, 'trends have been far from uniform from one type of farm and one area to another.'[8] What is clear is that these changes reflect the long-term divisions of England and Wales into the largely pastoral and upland west and north, and the largely lowland and arable south and east. Ironically, although these divisions were modified by the 'second agricultural revolution' this modification in some ways seemed to emphasise the differences in regions as much as ironing them out. For example, within the national picture the consolidation of holdings and their increasing profitability was most obvious in eastern England. By the mid-1970s the average full-time farm in England and Wales was 172 acres. In the predominantly arable counties of Norfolk and Suffolk it was 244 acres and 250 acres respectively. This trend is also clear from the census. In 1951 there were 9,083 farmers in Norfolk in the heart of the arable area, and in 1971 6,770, a decline of 26 per cent, while in Devon, in the upland area, the decline over the same period was 15 per cent, and even in Montgomeryshire it was 17 per cent.[9]

Also, much of the technical change discussed in Chapter 8 was concentrated in the arable areas. While tractors were clearly useful for all farmers, combine harvesters, grain dryers, new seed strains, artificial herbicides, pesticides and fertilisers initially at least had their most obvious impact in the arable areas. This does not mean that there were no technical advances which affected the uplands – machine milking and the intensive rearing of stock were clearly important to many farms – rather that the economies of scale possible on large arable farms were less possible on smaller and less highly capitalised units.

If we look at the different agricultural regions we can begin to see how these changes in farm size and technical change affected the different regions, their farms and farm life in different ways. At one end of the spectrum stand the hill farms of upland England and Wales, at the other the highly mechanised units of the eastern counties of England. We shall look at them in turn.

Between the 1940s and the early 1960s the pastoral and hill farming regions of Britain retained many traditional elements of farming practice, but above all of social and economic organisation. These were areas of small farms dominated, to different degrees, by sheep. Llanfihangel, in Montgomeryshire, studied between 1940 and 1948 by Alwyn Rees,[10] was given almost entirely to sheep grazing with what little arable there was dedicated to fodder crops for sheep and horses. It was also an area of tiny farms, the majority consisting of between a 100 and 150 acres of mostly rough grazing. On this basis most of these farms, in the late 1940s, were barely economic units. Even in the 1960s, after two decades of government support, it was estimated that 45 per cent of Welsh hill farmers received less than a farm worker's wage.[11] Yet Rees' study gives a picture of a community which, although hardly thriving, was surviving if still firmly 'traditional' in its social and economic structure.

The social and economic structure of Llanfihangel, in the years immediately after the Second World War, would still have been recognisable to a farmer or farm worker of the 1850s despite the fact that a major change in landownership had taken place in 1946. Crucially family labour, the hiring of living-in farm servants from among social equals and a high degree on kinship and neighbourhood co-operation remained central to the functioning of Llanfihangel's farms. As Rees writes, the 'ideal' farm unit 'consists of father, mother, one or two unmarried sons in their youth or early manhood and perhaps a daughter.'[12] However, where there were no sons of the right age, for instance when they were too young or when they had left to set up on their own, farm servants continued to be hired, for 6 month terms, to live in the farmhouse. Even in the late 1940s about a quarter of these were the sons of other farmers. This led to a particular class structure in which the difference between master and man were slight since they were often social equals. 'From the point of view of the majority there is nothing degrading in this. They will say the lad learns a lot thereby.'[13] Even where the hired man was the son of a labourer the relatively large number of small farms allowed for a degree of social mobility uncommon elsewhere in England and Wales by the post-Second World War period.[14]

The 'traditional' nature of Llanfihangel was further reinforced by the continued reliance on the labour of neighbours and kin at busy times of the farming year, which also maintained many of the rights and obligations associated with that system.[15]

> Nowadays, the main co-operative tasks are threshing, sheep dipping, shearing, and to a smaller extent, the hay and corn harvests. No one receives payment except those who cannot be repaid with services – and even their reward is often a present of tobacco or farm-produce rather than money.

The co-operative group was determined by locality and, even if a tenant changed on a particular farm, the same co-operative structure was retained, as were the traditional celebrations associated with them.[16]

> In addition to their practical value, these days of co-operative activity are important social events. Elaborate meals are prepared, the best rooms of the house are used, the best cutlery and china are brought out and every effort is made to give the guests a handsome welcome. The prestige of the family is involved in the lavishness of the hospitality . . . and any niggardliness will be criticised among neighbours and ridiculed by the young men.

By the very early 1950s, when Rees finished his study, the traditional nature of Llanfihangel society was already under attack. The number of farm servants was declining, the co-operative tasks were becoming fewer and hence the celebrations associated with them were declining in importance. There was also some evidence of the consolidation of holdings and an increasing use of machinery; this was, even in the immediate post-war period, beginning to open up divisions within the society, which previously had appeared remarkably cohesive. This was reinforced by the declining importance of religious activity in the area which, although it remained high compared with much of England and Wales, had still declined relatively during the twentieth century. Similarly the local infrastructure of shops and trades people was coming under threat from larger nearby villages and even market towns as mobility increased. To the 'outsider' these changes, as Rees noted, may have appeared unimportant but to the insider they were central. 'Judged by urban standards the culture retains many of its old characteristics; judged by its own past it is in full decline.'[17]

Many of these elements were also present in other upland areas into the 1950s. In the 1950s Gosforth in Cumbria retained many traditional features of English and Welsh upland farming communities. For example, Gosforth, like most upland areas, was dominated by living-in farm service certainly until the inter-war period. In Gosforth, as in Llanfihangel, elements of this persisted although not to the same extent. Even so in 1953 there were 'three youths in the parish who are paid half-yearly – at Whitsun and Martinmas – although hiring of labour still takes place at "term-time" on nearly all farms.'[18] This practice conflicted with the regulations of the Agricultural Wages Board but was supported by the non-unionised workforce who agreed to 'tak [sic] things as they come', as well as enabling them to earn well above the minimum wage. This was made easier, as at Llanfihangel, by the fact that 22 per cent of farmers' sons were working as labourers in 1953, and that over half the parishes' farmers had themselves been labourers.[19]

Co-operative working and sharing of equipment was also a characteristic of the social and economic structure of Gosforth as it was of Llanfihangel and on a geographical basis rather than a basis of friendship. As one farmer told Williams: 'Folks have been coming to our threshings from that spot yonder all me life and in me father's time afore me, and I'll not be starting to change it now.' As in Wales shearing and especially threshing were also occasions of social events.[20]

> The amount and quality of food is extremely important as a measure of the farmer's good name. With so many neighbours present no expense must be spared. The best ham has been stored away for this event and it is not unusual for farmers' wives to remark after threshing day that 'We have to scrat along as best we can for many a week.'

By the late 1950s this had begun to change even in the upland areas. The emphasis on production, as we have already noted, worked against the small farmer. Although legislation from the Hill Farming Act of 1946 had sought to aid the small and hill farmer, the effect of this legislation was to progressively under-mine the small farmers' position. This took the form of 'encouraging' amalgama-tion of 'un-economic' units and the direction of support into larger units. As Graham Crow writes, 'the small farm problem was to be combated by reducing the number of small farms.'[21] This move was strengthened by Britain joining the EEC whose policy, certainly since the 1960s, has been to reduce the number of small and 'inefficient' farms. As a result by the 1980s even small farmers in relat-ively prosperous areas like the southeast were seeing this. As a Kent farmer told Graham Crow:[22]

> Family farmers are going to go, they've got to go. These big people are gradually edging small farmers out. They won't push us out in a hurry, but when the old chaps retire the farms go to the bigger farmers. We'll go on until we have to give up. But we'll be the last of (the family) farming line.

Some of these tensions were already in place in the late 1950s when W.M. Williams studied a Devon village he called Ashworthy.[23] Although still largely pastoral, Ashworthy, partly because of the better land and partly because of the timing of the study, looked very different from the 'purer' upland parishes studied in the 1940s and early 1950s. Although still dominated by the family farm, and still reliant largely on family labour, significant changes had taken place. As we noted briefly above, the majority of farmers in Ashworthy, by 1960, were owner-occupiers – only seven farmers out of 99 were tenants.[24] Further, there was evidence of a reduction in the number of farms.

The number of regularly employed farm workers had also declined during the twentieth century and the practice of 'living-in' farm service, which had domin-ated the village in the nineteenth century, had completely vanished. There was also a marked decline in the number of local crafts and trades which serviced the village and agriculture.[25] In place of hired workers farmers relied more and more on 'mechanization, the hire of agricultural contractors and new farming techniques'.[26]

Yet, there was still a high degree of reliance on co-operation among farms, especially the smaller ones. As one farmer put in language, which is almost identical to that used earlier in Llanfihangel or Gosforth. 'There's one thing about Ashworthy. If us be ill, or the tractor breaks down or anything goes wrong, the neighbours are always there to help.'[27] However this account hid real changes. Younger and more 'progressive' farmers were much less likely to rely on neighbours or kin, preferring to hire casual workers on contractors for harvest work or sheep dipping than were older men. Further, the presence of 'new' farmers from outside the village or even the region, who had fewer links with the community and kinship networks further eroded co-operation.

Nevertheless, even in the 1970s small farmers retained a powerful commitment to the ideology of co-operation, even if now it was expressed in terms of the family. As a Kent farmer of 150 acres put it:[28]

> We're better off now than we've ever been, but that's probably because our son worked on the farm for nothing. It's always been hard, it's a question of the family being content. I think family farms are still going to be there, but it depends on what the family is prepared to put up with. The family farm depended on the family.

As Graham Crow writes of these Kent family farms, 'the ideology of the family can be seen to be built around ideas of partnership and co-operation between family members, working together and producing resources for the common good.'[29]

Outside the areas of hill farming the older traditional networks associated with work and community were much further eroded by the 1960s even where they had existed in an earlier period. The parish of Westrigg[30] studied by James Littlejohn between 1949 and 1951 can be seen as a transitional community both in terms of size and socio-economic organisation, standing between Llanfihangel and Gosforth on the one hand and more modern lowland communities on the other. Although strictly in Scotland, Westrigg is most importantly a part of the Borders, a region that has an economic and social character of its own defined more by productive system than by nationality.[31] Westrigg in the early 1950s was still totally dominated by agriculture and agricultural production, with about 60 per cent of heads of households employed in agriculture.[32] As with Llanfihangel, and much of upland England and Wales in the post-Second World War period, the farming of Westrigg was dominated by sheep, although there were also substantial areas of forest and, as in all three parishes discussed so far, some arable.

However, there were crucial differences between Llanfihangel and Westrigg, most notably in farm size and ownership on the one hand and the nature of the farm labour force on the other. Westrigg's farms were large and mostly owner-occupied. Compared with Llanfihangel many of the farms employed relatively large workforces, with the largest farm in the parish employing eleven men in 1949. Kinship was also much less important in Westrigg. As we saw above, Rees argued that in Llanfihangel kinship remained a central part of economic relationships. This was not the case in Westrigg. As Littlejohn writes comparing Westrigg to earlier studies of village communities:[33]

> Westrigg differs from those other communities . . . in the greater importance of its class system; whereas in other communities work-units are largely organised on the basis of kinship ties, in Westrigg they are organised on the basis of employer–employee relationships similar to those which obtain in industrial areas.

This difference was particularly apparent in terms of who worked the farm. As we have seen in Gosforth, which has some similarities with Westrigg, farmers, their families and relatives provided 73 per cent of labour. In contrast in Westrigg all the employees were 'hired' men, with the exception of those of one of the smallest of the fourteen farms in the parish, which was worked by family labour.[34] In short, Westrigg shows many of the characteristics of a capitalist agricultural system, producing primarily for the market and not for subsistence.

Some caution is however needed here. Westrigg existed within a culture of work which was still very different from the highly 'proletarianised' farms of East Anglia, let alone the situation in industry. For example, shepherding was a highly individual calling in which the individual shepherd, especially in the Borders, had as much control over the flock as his 'master'.[35]

> Each shepherd is entirely responsible for his hirstle (an area of land with its sheep at a ration of one sheep to two acres) and guards his independence. Several remarked that if the farmers came 'nosing' around their hirstles they would leave as that would imply lack of trust. All the shepherds speak of 'my hirstle'. Farmers rarely nose, acknowledging that a shepherd who did not know his job better than the farmer would not be worth employing.

In the earlier years of the century and on some farms in the inter-war years this independence had gone further with shepherds owning a 'pack' of sheep which were run with his master's hirstle. In this case the grazing his pack had constituted his wages, although in some areas he also got a cottage, coals and potato ground. In this situation the shepherd was 'a bit of a farmer in a small way' and this 'distinguished him from other farm workers'.[36] This difference was also reflected in the relative unwillingness of the shepherds of Westrigg to join the Union.[37]

Nor however was the situation of the 'ordinary' farm worker in Westrigg a straightforward one in terms of class relationships. Until at least the 1930s the farm workers of Westrigg, in common with many in the northeast as we saw above, hired by the family unit and by the year. They lived in cottages on, or near, the farm, in close relationship with the farmer and his family, while unmarried servants, male and female, lived in the farmhouse or an adjacent building. At times of communal work such as clipping all workers were fed in the farmhouse by the farmer's wife. Although much of this had changed by the early 1950s, elements of it remained in material terms, as well as within the memory and therefore consciousness of those who worked the land of Westrigg. For example, in the 1950s the needs of agriculture as well as parish history meant that most farm workers still lived 'on' the farm on which they worked in cottages owned by the farm. 'The farmhouse and steading is always situated besides the arable fields and near them are one or two cottages in which live those employees whose work lies in the fields and the steading.'[38] Similarly, although hiring by the year at the hiring fairs had stopped before the Second World War, elements of it, especially a notional yearly bond and some payment in kind in addition to a 'cheap' cottage remained.

A similarly 'mixed' socio-economic experience categorised the life of the farmers. Communal or shared work and its associated institutions was much less common in Westrigg than in Llanfihangel or Gosforth yet they still existed to an extent even in the 1950s.[39]

> Each farm is a productive unit on its own, a business from which the farmer tries to make a profit. There is little co-operation among them. The occasions which give rise to most are sheep clipping and threshing. . . . No payment is given but the farmer feeds everyone present.

However, compared with Llanfihangel the social events associated with threshing and sheep clipping were small in scale and divided on class lines, with the preparation and serving of the meal passing away from the farmer's wife and into the hands of the wife of the shepherd.[40]

In the large farms of the arable areas kinship and neighbourliness had never been as important as they were in the peasant farming areas of the north and west. In the early 1970s Howard Newby and others carried out a study of large East Anglian farmers, which shows a situation at the other extreme from the hill farms of the 1940s–1960s.[41] Here there seems to have been no co-operation between farmers and farm units of the kind which was so distinctive even in Ashworthy in the early 1960s. This was mainly of course simply a matter of size – the great farms of the eastern counties all had their own machinery and sufficient labour to work it. As a result there was no need to call on neighbours at harvest. More importantly, the ethos of the big farms was one based much more firmly on class division and competitiveness, as it had been for 200 years.

For the 'wheatocracy' of East Anglia, although family remained important, business needs dominated. Nearly 30 per cent of farmers of over 1,000 acres interviewed by Newby gave market-orientated reasons for judging what made a good farmer. As a Cambridgeshire farmer of 4,500 acres put it:[42]

> A good farmer: a financial success first and foremost. If he's achieving that, the other things follow naturally. He'll look after his land because it is in his financial interest to do so.

Another striking difference was simply how these larger farmers worked. On small farms in the 1970s as in the 1990s the farmer and his family worked the land or, where anyone was employed, they worked alongside their men. However on the large farms, as Newby writes, the farmer seldom did manual work and his contacts with his workers were therefore very different:[43]

> The majority are not so much *farmers* as full-time administrators and managers, who might as easily be working in an office or a factory in any large city. Subjectively, of course nearly all these farmers would regard themselves as being very different from industrial managers; nevertheless, as far as their work situation is concerned, many of the larger farmers do not farm in the general accepted sense, i.e. they do not drive tractors or milk cows.

These attitudes were taken further in relation to their workers. In clear distinction to the hill farm parishes of the 1940s and 1950s the large arable farms hired men, and to a lesser extent women, who were of a different class and treated them as employees. Only a very small farmer's son might go to work on another farm as a labourer or craftsman, although this, as a Kent farmer said, could still be seen as part of training for his own farm. 'My son's away at another farm at the moment, gaining experience. Hopefully he'll come back and work here.'[44]

In all areas in the years since the Second World War one of the most striking aspects of social and economic change has been the continuing and rapid decline in the number of farm workers. Nationally, as we have already seen, absolute numbers employed in the industry declined rapidly after the 1950s, but the national figures conceal the impact of decline in specific areas. In Norfolk, a county which traditionally had large farms with large labour forces, the number of farm workers decreased by 49 per cent between 1951 and 1971. In Devon, an area of small farms, the decrease was 59 per cent in the same period, while Montgomeryshire fell by 69 per cent. However, the number of farm workers also fell relative to the number of farmers. In 1951 in Norfolk there were 2.7 workers for every farmer – a figure which decreased by 1971 to 1.8 and has continued to fall since. In reality, even in East Anglia, 60 per cent of holdings employed no workers at all in the 1970s, relying entirely on family labour plus agricultural contractors and casual workers. In the small farming areas the situation was very different although subject to the same changes. In 1951 in Devon there were equal numbers of farmers and farm workers, by 1971 there were 1.9 farmers for every farm worker, while in Montgomeryshire there were 1.4 farmers per worker in 1951 and 3.8 in 1971.[45]

These changes have subtly but importantly altered the position of the farm worker. In lowland and arable areas, certainly until the beginning of the twentieth century, many of those who worked the land lived in what were, in effect, occupational communities dominated by farm workers. In upland areas the close ties between the family and the workforce created a community which, on the surface at least, was to a remarkable degree, socially homogeneous. In post-war Britain, both these communities were changed by the declining numbers of farm workers and by an influx of new country men and women who had little or nothing to do with agriculture.

The changes were most obvious in the lowland and arable areas. In the counties of East Anglia there had been until the inter-war period a powerful tradition of village self organisation which included the nonconformist chapel, friendly societies and trade unions.[46] As the number of farm workers declined both absolutely and relatively to the number of farmers, this community began to disintegrate. The number of village chapels fell dramatically after the Second World War as the congregations decreased and became increasingly elderly. By the 1990s East Anglia, which had been 'God's heartland' in the 1900s, saw the wayside Bethels, formerly centres of social and intellectual life, turned into desirable residences for newcomers. The village friendly societies, which had hung on until the creation of the welfare state, effectively vanished. Even the trades unions faced serious problems.

In the late 1940s the National Union of Agricultural and Allied Workers had nearly 140,000 members; by 1982, when the NUAAW merged with the Transport and General Workers' Union, it had less than 67,000, and 15–20,000 of those were in factories related to food production rather than 'traditional' farm workers. By 1990 it had fallen to 37,000 members.[47] However, it was not only that membership had declined but also that the place of the union had changed. Although it expanded in a few new areas, especially food processing, the number of village branches declined, the membership was increasingly elderly and many branches were effectively moribund. In 1980, for example, over 2,000 out of 2,500 branches did not recruit a single new member despite a national recruitment campaign.[48] As with the decline in other working-class village institutions the ending of the village union branch was a real blow to the old proletarian culture of the countryside.

It was not that in economic or social terms there was no longer a need for a union. In the 1950s and 1960s wages, as Newby shows, fell relative to those in the industrial sector, after a brief period in the 1940s when the gap between industry and agriculture had begun to close. In fact between 1949 and 1955 real wages actually declined.[49] The tied cottage, where a man's home was linked to his job, not only survived in rural areas but also actually increased. In 1948 34 per cent of farm workers lived in tied housing, but in 1975 the number had risen to 55 per cent. This was in spite of a commitment by the Labour Party to abolish the tied cottage, which had been policy since 1906. For generations farmers had argued that tied cottages were a perk and necessary to keep good workers, yet the reality for literally thousands was very different. Between 1947 and 1979 the union contested 12,482 tied cottage eviction cases for members. Given that union membership never reached even 40 per cent of farm workers, the real figures for evictions must have been very much higher.

The real misery of evictions and the fears they evoked was present time and again in the pages of the union paper, *The Landworker*, until the worst abuses of the system were controlled in 1976. In April 1975 Mrs Watts from Hertfordshire wrote to the paper:[50]

> My husband has worked all his life in farming, the last 20 years as a herds-man. After having been here for 8 years we thought we were settled, and we put a lot of work and money into making the house a permanent home – or so we thought. On March 22 my husband was given redundancy notice and of course along with that, the notice to vacate our cottage on April 8th. The following months were like a nightmare.

The tied cottage was replaced by controlled agricultural tenancies in 1976 and by the 1980s the number of tied cottages had fallen by 45 per cent, yet it remained a real threat even if evictions fell dramatically. As Danzinger wrote in 1988:[51]

> Above all, the tied cottage system runs counter to farm workers' objective interests in the ability to bargain freely for higher wages and better con-ditions of work. By the same token, the tied cottage system satisfies the interests of agricultural employers in keeping labour costs low, while at the same time maintaining peaceful labour relations.

The union was however not entirely powerless in the post-war period even if its gains were slight. The worst abuses of the tied cottage system were removed through tireless lobbying, especially by Joan Maynard MP, who, although she represented an urban seat, was effectively the only farm workers' representative in the Commons in the 1970s. It also fought hard and long on industrial safety. Even so in 1974, after a whole series of legislation, there were still ninety-one fatal accidents on farms in England and Wales, of which twenty-five were chil-dren under 16.[52]

Probably the most successful of the union's campaigns in the post-war period was that against the herbicide 245-T. Using chemicals developed as military defo-liates and used in the Vietnam War, the dangers of 245-T were apparent even in the 1950s. These dangers included death or serious illness as a result of contact and long-term genetic damage. The uses of a form of 245-T in Vietnam led to the payment of $180 million to American Vietnam veterans in 1984. From at least the 1960s 245-T was widely used, in various forms, in British agriculture. Although MAFF continued to insist as late as 1983 that 245-T was 'safe' when used 'properly', from the late 1970s British unions led by the NUAAW began a campaign to ban its use. Despite continued opposition from the Conservative government the campaign grew at the grass roots. The union successfully used its contacts in local government and with countryside organisations, including the Women's Institutes, to pressure local authorities and others to stop using herbi-cides based on 245-T, and by the mid-1980s it had ceased being used in England and Wales.[53]

Less successful were continuing campaigns on wages and conditions. In the mid-1980s average weekly earnings in agriculture were still about 30 per cent lower than those in industry, and the average working week was about 7 hours longer. Each year in the post-war period saw the set piece battle in the Agricul-tural Wages Board to set national rates for the different grades of farm workers, but even these seemed increasingly irrelevant since more and more workers negotiated their own rates of pay. This in turn led more and more workers to see the union as an irrelevance. However, in the 1980s two events did demonstrate that the Union was prepared to attempt to fight back, even if the results were at best mixed. On 15 February 1982, after two months of negotiation, 1,200 workers at the Bernard Mathews poultry processing plants in Norfolk came out on strike over wages and conditions of work. The strike lasted 6 weeks and received widespread support both in Norfolk and elsewhere. The plants were blacked by the Transport and General Workers' Union and a consumer boycott was organised; both activities contributed to what the union saw as a victory. However, it had its costs. Although the strikers were only getting £12 per week strike pay (about a fifth of their normal weekly wage) it cost the union dear at a time when funds nationally were at an all-time low, and indeed it looked towards the end of the strike that the union would simply have to stop supporting their members.[54]

If the Mathews strike was a victory, which in some ways it was, the attempted overtime ban in 1984 showed just how weak the union had become. This was to take place in the last week of August, deliberately chosen not to interfere with harvest, and restricted largely to East Anglia. It was a disaster. It is impossible to know how many members took part but Danzinger, who was in Suffolk during the ban, spoke to twenty-six farm workers of whom only one was supporting the ban. It certainly made little difference to wage negotiations or wage rates. As Danzinger writes:[55]

There was, in general, a sense of powerlessness among farm workers and a consequent unwillingness to participate in the overtime ban. No farm worker believed that he was being paid enough wages, but equally they could not conceive of any means of challenging their situation.

But the sense of powerlessness goes much deeper than the simple strength or weakness of the union and the other institutions of class or community organisation in the village. The changing ratio of farmers to farm workers in the post-war period fundamentally altered the social relations of production on farms, especially those of the arable areas. As Newby writes:[56]

> As the number of workers per farm declined so those who remained were being drawn into a more diffuse, personal relationship with their employers, hardly conducive to a desire for strike action.

By the 1980s and 1990s the average farm worker saw more of his employer during his working time than he did of any fellow worker. This contributed to a growing sense of identity between employer and employee, which found expression in the notion that the farm on which you worked was 'your' farm and that you, the worker, were part of a team. As a Suffolk farm worker put it in the 1970s:[57]

> Every year we're in the competition for the best-kept farm. This year we were in and we won it again. If we were against (the boss) we would say, 'Bugger it', and wouldn't bother. We don't think of ourselves as master and men, we work together.

This attitude could even be found in the pages of the Union's journal where the tied cottage, of all things, found its defenders. Suzanne Morgan, living in a tied cottage near Bristol, praised the farmer who 'spent a good deal of money completely modernising the place and installing central heating';[58] while B. Hunt from Newbury was much more vehement in their defence. 'The farmers are not all bad 'uns – far from it. So why don't you leave the tied cottage alone.'[59]

The third element which changed the position of the farm worker, and indeed that of the farmer, was the changing balance of population in rural areas in favour of those who had nothing at all to do with agriculture. Again this was a long-term trend. As early as 1921, as we saw above, the 'white-collar' worker was well on the way to domination in Surrey. By 1971 this was complete with 35 per cent of the working population of rural areas working in white-collar jobs.[60] Even in less obviously suburban areas similar trends can be seen. In Norfolk, by 1971, 33 per cent of the working population, male and female, living in rural areas were in white-collar occupations. Only in the most remote, upland areas was the increase in the non-agricultural working population much lower. For instance, only about 20 per cent of the working population of Montgomeryshire were in white-collar jobs in 1971, almost exactly the same as the percentage in agriculture.

Although there has been some reallocation of businesses to rural areas, especially in the south and east, since the late 1960s, by definition most of these new countrymen and women would have worked away from their place of residence. This was clear as soon as rebuilding started in the immediate post-war period. The 1951 Census looking at Surrey noted that although the period since the end of hostilities was too short to make real judgements possible as early as 1948, 'the shift back to a peace-time pattern (of population distribution) appears to have been achieved'. From 1948–51 this was clearer still. While 'little growth has taken place in the population of the more crowded areas nearer the centre of London', areas further out in the 'dormitory areas' had increased by over 80 per cent compared with 1931, with something like 20 per cent of that growth taking place since 1945.[61]

While the railways continued to provide the transport infrastructure for growth immediately around London, the growth of private car ownership and the motorway building programme from the 1960s onwards opened up new and more distant areas. Bowers and Cheshire's study of West Berkshire carried out in the 1960s and 1970s showed how motorway building influenced not only the changing nature of the village but the precise ways in which the social composition of the village altered.[62]

> The incomers have arrived in several more or less distinct waves. The first to arrive in the 1960s were the better off local businessmen. The area attracted as a prosperous suburb for Newbury and Wantage. . . . Spurred on by the opening of the M4 (late 1972), there was a large inflow of middle- and upper middle-income executives and professionals. . . . At more or less the same time came an inflow of extremely well-off weekenders (house prices in the area ensured that only the really rich could afford its weekend cottages) and rich retired people.

This pattern was repeated elsewhere in England and, in a different way, Wales in the years from the 1970s until the present day. Little's study of two Wiltshire villages in the 1970s and 1980s points not only to population growth but also the 'disproportionate increase in middle and upper middle class residents'. As with the West Berkshire villages commuting was vital to this. 'In the villages studied daily commuting to London and Bristol was feasible, while some of the intermediate towns such as Swindon, Newbury and Reading were common places of work.'[63] Even in the large and in some ways more plebeian village of Ringmer in East Sussex, studied by Peter Ambrose, a quarter of heads of household were employers, managers or professional workers in 1971.[64]

The situation in rural Wales was different. Here, though there was some similar out-migration to villages in the south around Cardiff and Swansea, it was the movement of retired people and second homeowners into the hill farming districts rather than commuters, which lay at the basis of social and cultural change. From the 1970s the relative cheapness of rural housing in Wales, the obvious beauty of the countryside and its distance from the 'pollution' of the city proved attractive to many English urban dwellers. These factors were especially attractive to those from London who experienced substantial increases in real earnings in the 1980s and sought a cheap second home for weekends and holidays. The peak of this migration appears to have been in the late 1980s, although it was a real factor throughout the decade, and seems to have declined since. However, it may have been replaced by:[65]

> the inward migration of large numbers of new residents, including retired people, those with assets released from the sales of housing in the better off parts of Britain such as the South East, and others who were taking the opportunity to drop out of urban life and conditions.

Elements of this experience were also present in England, but the Welsh experience took on a particular intensity for a variety of reasons. First, Wales, and especially mid and north Wales, remained much more 'rural' both in appearance and in economic structure than did most of England. This increased both the tensions and the attractions of a 'home' in Wales. As Day writes:[66]

> Given the pervading attractiveness of rural locations for many people in Britain, rural Wales is widely perceived as among the more desirable places to live. Whenever people have the ability to act on their preferences, they may opt to move towards such places.

Second, in Wales issues of nationality and, in many areas, language added to the issues of class and urban background, which divided incomers from 'natives' in English rural areas. As a result of these differences opposition to 'incomers', which was a common feature in many rural areas of England, became in Wales a political and cultural issue. The fight over 'affordable housing', for example, was seen in parts of Wales not simply as an issue of class but as part of the centuries-long domination of the English over Wales, made real by rich *Saeson* buying cottages, streets and even whole villages. In fact the reality was more complex; the sale of council housing under the Conservative government between 1980 and 1989 probably did more to reduce cheap housing than English migration, yet the issue remained powerful not least because it became a key political issue for Plaid Cymru.[67]

The erosion of the Welsh language, especially in its rural heartlands, was also blamed on in-migration, and as with housing there was an element of truth in this. As early as the 1950s Emmett's study of the Merionethshire village of 'Llan' noted that English migrants, who were often in economically powerful positions, never learnt Welsh. Further, non-Welsh speakers headed many of the new social organisations like the Youth Club and the Women's Institute.[68] Certainly, before the passing of the Welsh Language Act in 1993, there was official discrimination against Welsh speakers at all levels of civil society, which was made even clearer where there were a number of monoglot English in positions of local economic and social power. Against this the continuing flight from the harsh lands of rural Wales and the perception that Welsh is 'inferior' to English, created by a job market dominated by the English language, is almost certainly as damaging to the Welsh language as 'incomers'.[69]

In the 1980s and early 1990s the campaign against second homes in particular took on a new intensity with the burning of second homes, especially in North Wales, and a campaign of less violent actions like the super-gluing of locks of holiday cottages. Yet, as with other aspects of the Welsh campaigns, what happened was a quantitative not a qualitative difference from much of what was going on in areas of England where resentment against 'incomers' was building up through the decades after the 1960s. All that was different in Wales was the politicised reaction. The arguments in England were identical and centred on the same essential core belief that the 'community' was threatened from outside by those who did not and could not 'understand' its values.

The combination of the declining size of the agricultural workforce and the subsequent virtual collapse of the old plebeian village institution, the changing attitudes on the part of farmers to the land and to farming, together with the changing nature of those who lived in the countryside, created a social transformation in rural areas as great as the economic change produced by 'tractors and chemicals'. By the late 1980s the population of most of rural England had been growing, year on year, for over 30 years. The commuter, once only found in the inner ring suburbs of the conurbations, had spread far out into the countryside. In the more remote areas a second home or a retirement cottage, once the possession of a tiny minority, became a reality for more and more people, especially those working in the affluent areas of the south and east.

In this change the village ceased to be a working, even single occupational community, and became instead a place of leisure where even those who lived there spent only the spare time in the place. Frances Oxford noted the changes in the Essex village of Elmdon, which had been surveyed from the early 1960s to the 1970s by a group of Cambridge anthropologists:[70]

> 'Elmdon isn't really a village at all, it's just a commuting centre.' This view, expressed by an immigrant in 1977, is in plain contrast to the comment of a newcomer in the early 1960s that Elmdon was a 'proper village'. . . .

Whatever other claims are made about Elmdon now that it is a 'freaks paradise', a 'dormitory village', a 'proper working villagers' village', no one thinks of it as either isolated or very rural. Old cottages have been renovated, re-thatched, repainted. The village looks prosperous and vigorous; it is immediately apparent that immigrants are pouring into the village. Virtually none of the buildings are run down or abandoned. Far from being in decline, Elmdon is thriving, changing.

Elmdon's newcomers sought a world which, at one level, had little to do with the realities of rural life and the agricultural economy, except as bit players in an idyllic landscape. Country life was, and is, for the 48 per cent of the urban population who want to move to rural areas,[71] safer, more peaceful and cleaner. The novelist Nicci Gerrard moved, with her young family, to Suffolk in 1999, and wrote about it in the *Observer*.[72]

> I am very glad to be leaving the city. I don't want to be in the swing of things, really, in the grip of fashion and speed and ambition. . . . I love the thought of living among trees, beneath a huge sky. . . . I long to be in the garden, sinking my fingers into the earth, getting my hands dirty at last. I know that tiles will slip off the roof, and the garden will turn to bog in winter, but I also imagine evenings, after work is done, when we can all drive to the coast and walk on shingle beaches. That's happiness.

Mackenzie Thorpe, the artist, his wife and family moved from London to Yorkshire, giving up steady jobs and incomes in what in the fashionable language of the mid-1990s was called 'downsizing'.[73]

> The contrast with London is giant-sized: open spaces, hills and trees. We can go to the beach whenever we want. I don't need to lock my car. The kids can walk to school. It's been so good for them. They're calmer, softer, more polite.

Most new countrymen and women do not have either the financial freedom or the work flexibility of intellectuals and artists. For them it is not a Suffolk farmhouse or a cottage in Yorkshire, rather a 'done-up' farm worker's cottage, an ex-council house, or a house on a new estate in a village setting. Yet the reasons for moving into the country are remarkably similar. One of the earliest studies carried out on 'incomers' done by Ruth Crichton on the Berkshire village of Stratfield Mortimer in the early 1960s wrote of those who had moved there: 'They like the surrounding countryside, the woods and fields. They like the quiet of the country and find it a healthy place to live in.'[74] Nearly 20 years later virtually identical attitudes were expressed in the study of Elmdon.[75]

Families leaving London or the suburbs to live in the country, while continuing to work in the city, often have quite positive ideas about the nature of country life. The pleasures of rural England compensate for the trials of the 8.13 from Audley End to Liverpool Street. Some mothers insist that they cannot bear to bring up children in a town. Many want to be able to have a garden and to live in a larger house than they would otherwise be able to afford.

In the 1960s, the 1970s and the 1990s many who moved to the countryside and to villages were seeking another holy grail – community.[76]

> The romantic model of the village assumes that villages were once self-sufficient, intimate communities. Idealising the cosy community immigrants may seek an 'authentic village'. The expectation is that here the natives will be friendly and, by implication, the immigrant outside will be accepted, if not into the bosom of the family/village, then at least as an integral part of the system.

Yet that community, idealised in popular culture since at least the inter-war period, barely existed, and where it continued it was increasingly hostile to the

Plate 15 'Incomers'. Building Carpenters Close, Stratfield Mortimer, Berkshire in the 1960s. The 1950s and 1960s saw the desire to live in the countryside reverse population decline in many rural areas. Ruth Crichton, who studied this subject in the 1960s, called Stratfield Mortimer a 'commuter's village'. Its experience was duplicated thousands of times in the next 40 years. (Reproduced by kind permission of the Rural History Centre, University of Reading.)

new countrymen and women. The basic reason is not far to seek. In this process those who worked in agriculture, but above all the farm worker, became strangers in their own land. In Elmdon in Essex the number of farm workers fell by 9 per cent in only 6 years between 1964 and 1971, while the number of professionals increased from 13 to 33 per cent.[77]

These change have led to conflicts, of the same kind though of different intensity, as those in rural Wales. Housing in particular became a major issue in rural communities from the 1970s, first in the southeast and then elsewhere. As the numbers employed in agriculture fell, farmers and landlords found themselves with a 'surplus' of cottages on their hands, which were easily turned into ready money, even if the long-term effect has been to deprive villages of affordable rented accommodation. In Elmdon,[78]

> ownership of houses has passed out of the hands of the farming landowners and into the hands of the new immigrants. . . . The old houses and cottages are no longer the homes of local people and the local part of the community has made a spatial shift from one end of the village to the other. The 'toffs' live in one part and, although villagers are still 'scattered through' here, it is a 'different world' and the two ends of the village are described as being quite distinct.

This spatial division in many English villages was made even clearer by local authority housing schemes which were inevitably built on the edges of older villages where land was cheaper and, in some cases, former common or waste land already in local authority control. In Ringmer in Sussex, the village studied by Peter Ambrose in the 1970s, this has created what amounts to two or perhaps three socio-economic areas. The 'old' village around the green consists of housing stock built mostly before the 1900s and now almost exclusively occupied by incomers, many of them retired. Around them, but still 'part' of the 'village' are private developments, mainly small and 'exclusive' and some dating back to the inter-war period. Finally, three-quarters of a mile away from the centre, to the northwest, on what had once been common land, was local authority housing. Separated from the old village the council estate became a planned plebeian ghetto.

Nor was housing the only issue. As in Wales the control of local institutions, both formal and informal, seemed to be passing out of the control of the 'locals' into the hands of the 'newcomers'. As a Suffolk farmer said in the 1970s:[79]

> There's been a splitting between the ex-urban dwellers and the local villagers – that is why we formed a parish council at X with the express intention of welcoming and absorbing Ipswich people moving in. But it was totally impossible – they set up an alternative tenants' association to the

parish council, it was a fiasco. Now the parish council is overrun by urban dwellers and the locals have retired behind walls and given up.

This split could provoke real bitterness in some communities where incomers were seen as preventing the 'natives' from making the best of their own property. In 1996 the Somerset village of Kingsbury Episcopi was split between 'incomers' and 'old villagers' over plans to build 'executive homes' and an industrial site in the village. The plan was supported by local landowners (the self styled 'Old Villagers') and opposed by a group of incomers (the Parish Residents Group). Whatever the merits of argument it quickly developed into a war based on who 'owned' the village, its character and country life in general, with the old villagers described as 'Rednecks' and the incomers accused of wanting to protect their bit of countryside by denying it to others.[80]

Behind these squabbles lay real problems of poverty and deprivation in many villages, which, far from going away, may actually have got worse in the last 30 years of the twentieth century. Certainly, the growing affluence of those villages whose population was dominated by incomers with much higher incomes concealed this poverty and made it harder for those on low incomes to tolerate.[81]

One reason for rural deprivation was simply the low level of wages and incomes in the agricultural sector. As we saw earlier farm workers' wages were consistently below those of equivalent industrial workers throughout the twentieth century. Similarly hill farm incomes, especially in Wales, have been little better than the wages of farm workers since the early 1950s. Further, although rural areas contain some of the highest incomes in England and Wales they also contain some of the lowest, even outside agriculture. However, income alone is not the only measure of real deprivation, although it is much more central than many a rural sociologist or planner would make out. After all a village may contain all the best 'services' available – but this makes little difference if a section of those who live there simply do not have the money to use them. Parts of the north Norfolk coast have, since the 1970s, moved from being relatively poor, largely occupational communities to being one of the most fashionable rural areas of Britain, but few of those who still work on the land, the fishing or related sectors can take advantage of the *Good Food Guide* restaurants and specialist food shops which now seem an integral part of the local 'economy'.

Having said that, deprivation is not simply a matter of income. Rural housing has always been worse than those whose picture of the rural idyll is a thatched cottage imagine. In many cases, certainly until the 1950s, there was housing in the rural districts as bad, if not worse than in most urban areas. In 1951 37 per cent of dwellings in Norfolk were without piped water and 40 per cent without a water closet, in Cambridgeshire it was 31 per cent and 41 per cent and in Montgomeryshire 44 per cent and 51 per cent respectively. The national figures were 17 per cent for piped water and 21 per cent for a w.c. However, even these figures are optimistic as, with the exception of Montgomeryshire, they contain figures from the urban areas. Quite how distorting this can be is seen in Northumberland. Here only 19 per cent of dwellings were without piped water, but in the 'rural' districts, for example Bellingham, the figure rose to 44 per cent.[82]

Conditions were eased to some extent and in some areas by building council houses. Even in the immediate post-war period some Rural District Councils began building low-cost rented housing. By 1949, Wimborne and Cranborne RDC in Dorset had built 120 houses since 1945 and had a further 60 under construction. The Isle of Axholme RDC in Lincolnshire had built 154 houses and eight bungalows in the same period.[83] Such records were however unusual. In many counties entrenched interest groups fought against council house building as a potential cost to the rates; nevertheless building continued and was expanded under the Labour governments of the 1960s. By the time Crichton studied her Berkshire village in the early 1960s, about 25 per cent of housing in the village was council owned, while in Elmdon nearly 20 years later 21 per cent of the population lived in council houses.[84] However, even this minority provision was eroded in England and Wales after the 'right-to-buy' legislation introduced by the Conservative government in 1980.

Along with low wages and low access to affordable housing the decline in public and private services has seriously affected the rural poor in the post-war period. The economic and social infrastructure of rural areas had been under threat for most of the twentieth century. As we saw earlier, village shops and trades were in decline in the inter-war period as bus services opened up the country towns to village shoppers on a regular basis. Even in the remote parish of Llanfihangel in the 1940s, although there were two shops selling most of what was needed on a day-to-day basis, many villagers went to nearby larger villages, to Oswestry and even to Liverpool for special purchases.[85] In my own childhood in the 1950s in a rural market town, people from 'the villages' came to Bicester to the Friday market on 'special' buses, which only ran on Fridays for 'big' or special shopping.

However, by that point, these weekly movements were beginning to seriously affect the village shops. J. Martin Shaw's study of Norfolk carried out in the early 1970s shows that the number of village shops fell by 40 per cent between 1950 and 1960, with the loss being most obvious in smaller villages.[86] This decline continued through the 1970s and 1980s with many villages losing half of their remaining shops. Similarly the decline in the number of pubs had an important effect. In the decade after 1961 many north Norfolk villages lost their last remaining pub, saw the numbers reduced or, perhaps even worse, saw its nature fundamentally changed to be more congenial to incomers or those clutching their *Good Food Guide*. As Newby writes of Suffolk:[87]

> Given the importance of the pub in the agricultural worker's pattern of leisure-time sociability . . . these changes do have real as well as symbolic

consequences. The pub is not only the most important – in many villages the only – meeting place outside work where agricultural workers and their friends can come together to meet and exchange gossip, it is also an arena in which the conventional wisdom of local and national affairs is established and transmitted. The demise of the local pub therefore alienates the agricultural worker from his own village much more than many other consequences of the arrival of newcomers, and its closure is regarded as being synonymous with the decay of the local community.

The decay of 'private' economic services had been matched by a simultaneous decline in public service provision in many villages. This was most crucial in the provision of health care and education. Again, as with economic facilities, both these areas have seen significant decline in the last 30 years. In Norfolk the number of surgeries in rural areas fell by nearly 20 per cent between 1961 and 1971, a decline which was not compensated for by a growth in health centres.[88] Lack of a surgery can be dealt with by home visits but nationally the number of such visits declined by 60 per cent between 1949–71.[89] In this situation particular groups suffer, most notably those reliant on public transport, provision of which has also declined in the same period. As a study of Leicestershire carried out in the 1970s showed, 'the greatest hardship is found amongst those without a car, in large households with limited private transport, lower income groups and amongst women.'[90] The closure of village schools is a slightly more mixed picture. Here the arrival of new residents can actually stimulate growth; this was certainly the case in Elmdon. However, this was not the general pattern. In Norfolk fifty village schools were closed between 1952 and the 1970s leaving more than half of villages without a school. More closures followed in the 1980s and 1990s despite local battles.

This 'hidden deprivation' has created a new rural underclass composed mainly of those on low incomes and the elderly – in many cases the 'traditional villagers' – which remains central to current discussion. Against that is the undoubted prosperity of many rural areas shown by rising house prices and higher than average earnings. It is interesting that an article published in the *Observer* in 1996 on 'downsizing' described a couple who had moved out of London to Devon, and were living on £25,000 a year when 'friends in the London ad world earn four times as much.'[91] At that point over a third of all workers in rural Devon were earning less than £10,000 a year.

These changes have, in the last 20 years in particular, completed a series of social changes which began in the 1900s. As the number of farm workers has declined relative both to farmers and incomers, new divisions and new solidarities have developed in many English and Welsh rural communities. The closeness of employer and employee in the workplace, which has already been discussed, was reproduced in the village with those employed in agriculture setting themselves against those outside it. That this unity was spurious in most respects, certainly in terms of socio-economic relationships, for most of England if not Wales, does not diminish its real power, for most of the time at least. In this worldview the countryside has been taken over by hostile outsiders who do not understand agriculture or the countryside and want to change it to their own image. The language used by farmers interviewed by Newby in the 1970s is very striking here. Time and again those who work on the land are described as 'the village' or 'the villagers' or even, 'the natives', while those who have moved in are 'strangers', 'town dwellers', 'invaders' and even 'aliens'.[92] This division linked farmer and farm worker in a new solidarity against the outsider. As attacks on agriculture became more and more common in the late 1980s and 1990s this 'unity', as we shall see in the next chapters, became more and more central.

10 Defending the natural order?

Environment and conservation,
1945–90

The changes in the rural areas of England and Wales, both in terms of agricultural production and social and economic structure, which have been discussed in the last two chapters, had effects well outside the country districts. As the countryside became more and more a site of leisure and of living rather than simply working, the nature of the countryside, its appearance and the relationship of farming to the 'natural world' became more central for the urban world as much as the rural. Also, the use of the country as a place of leisure raised questions about access to the countryside. All these problems had, as we saw in Chapter 6, been present in the inter-war period. However, in the years after 1945 they took on a new importance and intensity, which was to move from relatively small-scale actions, like the Mass Trespasses and the eccentric and marginal practices of a few 'humus' farmers, to the centre stage of rural and urban life.

As we saw above, the wartime government had, in the Scott Report, almost unwittingly, laid down a post-war blueprint for the rural areas. Central to the Scott Report, as we have already seen, was the notion of access to the countryside, which grew out of the inter-war movements and particularly out of the campaigns by the Ramblers' Association. Also central was the notion of National Parks and Nature Reserves, which would preserve the 'best' of rural England and Wales from development. A key group here was the Standing Committee on National Parks, which had, as early as 1938, produced a pamphlet *The Case for National Parks*.[1] In 1942 the author of that pamphlet, John Dower, by then a temporary wartime civil servant, persuaded Lord Reith, the Minister for Town and County Planning, who had also commissioned the Scott Report, to allow him to produce a report on National Parks for England and Wales which was laid before Parliament in 1945.

Dower defined a National Park as:[2]

An extensive area of beautiful and relatively wild country in which for the nation's benefit and by appropriate national decision and action, (i) the characteristic landscape beauty is strictly preserved, (ii) access and facilities for

Plate 16 Urban invaders. Youth hostellers at Bala in the Snowdonia National Park, late 1960s. The post-war period saw ever more recreational use of the countryside. What had begun in the inter-war period as a trickle had become a flood by the middle of the twentieth century. (Reproduced by kind permission of the Rural History Centre, University of Reading.)

public open-air enjoyment, including particularly cross-country and foot-path walking, are amply provided, and (iii) wild life and places and buildings of historic, architectural or scientific interest are suitably protected.

Alongside Dower others had been working to create a national system of Nature Reserves buying sites of special interest and preserving them in their natural state.[3]

In the aftermath of the Labour victory of 1945 both these aims were to be recognised. In July 1945 a committee was set up under the Chairmanship of Sir Arthur Hobhouse to investigate and make a proposal on the creation of National Parks for England and Wales. It presented its report in 1947. In the same year the Huxley Committee also reported on Nature Reserves. The proposals of Huxley were seen as relatively uncontentious, mainly because they cost relatively little and infringed few established interests. Although they had to wait until 1949 for implementation of the creation of the Nature Conservancy, most of the recommendations of Huxley were implemented.

The situation was different with the National Parks. Here the key issues were of control and of finance, centring on planning in the parks and who should control that planning. The 1947 Town and Country Planning Act, another inter-war dream, had given control of planning decisions to Local Authorities. It also left agricultural units outside planning controls. Both these elements threatened the initial vision of Hobhouse that a new National Parks Commission should have control over planning in the parks. Finally, the Treasury was worried about the costs of a separate National Parks Commission. As a result the Bill, which was passed into law in 1949 as the National Parks and Access to Countryside Act, gave many less powers to the National Parks Commission than either the Hobhouse Report had envisaged, or the Minister Lewis Silkin had wished.[4] Barbara Castle, who like many Labour MPs felt that the Bill did not follow the full wishes of the Hobhouse Committee, wrote in her autobiography,[5]

> This unsatisfactory arrangement has had its inevitable result. The development of National Parks has been uneven, according to the strength of local interests. In some of them rights of access are still being resisted by local landowners. In others tourism is being promoted by local revenue-hungry councillors at the expense of John Dower's vision. . . . The Minister's reserve powers atrophied in the Thatcher decade, when the rights of wealth, private property and profit making were enthroned again.

Nevertheless the passing of the Act was a minor triumph both for those who had fought in the inter-war period for access to the countryside, and for the personal commitment of Silkin whose own support for a more open countryside also dated from the 1930s. It also was a step towards a recognition that the countryside was to be something more than the site of agricultural production and that urban as well as rural voices were demanding a say in rural England and Wales. As Silkin said at the beginning of the Bill's Second Reading in March 1949:[6]

> This Bill is a people's charter – a people's charter for the open air, for the hikers and the ramblers, for everyone who loves to get out into the open air and enjoy the countryside. Without it they are fettered, deprived of their powers of access and facilities needed to make holidays enjoyable. With it the countryside is theirs to preserve, to cherish, to enjoy and to make their own.

Although Silkin was widely supported on both sides of the House of Commons and indeed the Lords, there were those who in opposition to him suggested that the way forward might not be all plain sailing. A number of Conservative members spoke against the Bill on the grounds that countryside visitors would damage farming, while even some Labour members insisted that food production should remain paramount. In the Lords this view was, not surprisingly, put more strongly still:[7]

> Lord Winster was adamant that the Bill should not publicise National Parks, some of the probable sites, which had already been damaged by visitor pressure, whilst Lord Cranworth envisaged an 'orgy' of destruction could result from legislation that encouraged visitors to the countryside.

Some sense of the power of this opposition can be sensed in the fact that although the Hobhouse Committee recommended twelve National Parks, in the event only nine were in place by 1956, with the Norfolk Broads added in 1989. The final one of the twelve, the South Downs, along with a thirteenth, the New Forest, began the process of designation in 1999. The initial reasons for the exclusion of the South Downs were agricultural – it was seen as too highly farmed. The Broads were excluded largely on grounds of cost, despite strong evidence that the area was degenerating.

The first operational National Parks, the Lakes and the Peak District, both established in 1951, were, in the event, the only ones to have full boards with executive powers. The remainder fell firmly into the category of Barbara Castle's 'unsatisfactory arrangement' in which local interests often dominated national concerns. In the 1980s, for example, 30 per cent of the members of the Welsh National Park authorities were either farmers or landowners, while the figure for England was nearer 40 per cent. While it might be argued that this represents in some way the 'local' interest, it was striking, as Marion Shoard argues, that the tourist industry, a great deal more important in most parks than agriculture, has hardly any representation. Further, 'even the Ministerial nominees rarely included people living outside the park area let alone in the urban areas whose populations might be expected to look to the parks concerned for recreation.'[8] This 'local' representation wielded most power in relation to agricultural change within the parks. Although Snowdonia, the Lakes and the Peak District were given special protection against 'unsuitable' agricultural building in 1950 these powers were not extended to the other parks until the 1980s. More fundamentally, landscape change was never really covered. The inter-war conservationists, the Scott Report, and most government publications since 1945, up to and including the 1995 and 2000 White Papers on rural areas, have seen farming as protecting the countryside. In fact the opposite has often been the case. As David Evans writes, 'the worst developments in the countryside

Plate 17 Crummock Water, Lake District National Park. One of the first two National Parks, the Lakes held a special place in the mythology of romantic Britain which protected them better than many other areas. (Reproduced by kind permission of the Rural History Centre, University of Reading.)

since the 1940s have related not to buildings but to land use.' He continues, quoting Richard Mabey:[9]

> It is . . . hard to see what essential difference there is between, say, planting up a stretch of heath land with conifers and building a small factory on it, or for that matter between felling an ancient wood and demolishing a listed historic building.

Nor have the so-called 'closed' sites fared much better. National nature reserves, also created by the 1949 Act, are well protected, not least because many of them are in public ownership or are leased. Indeed, they have expanded their numbers and importance mainly through years of fine husbandry by Nature Conservancy and its successor English Nature. In contrast Sites of Special Scientific Interest (SSSI) have fared badly. Despite their imposing title they had no statutory protection and frequently fell victims to farmers and farming paid subsidies to plough up land. Between 1959 and 1975 113 SSSIs lost their status and a further 87 were reduced in size owing to farming damage.[10]

The other area where government intervened in the immediate post-war period to open up the countryside was in relation to access and particularly to the protection of public rights of way.[11] The 1949 Act laid on local authorities a statutory duty to produce definitive maps showing public rights of way, particularly bridleways and footpaths. This caused problems from the start. As many as 20 per cent of all English and Welsh villages had no parish councils, and it was on the parish councils that much of the unpaid labour of drawing up the definitive maps fell. In the 1940s and 1950s the idea of a footpath or bridleway was also much more utilitarian, and was less concerned with recreation than with getting from a to b. As a result many recreational footpaths simply went unmarked or unrecorded. Finally there was, and indeed still is, much opposition from local landowners to paths and bridleways. This takes many forms. From the start many landowners objected to particular footpaths being included on the definitive map and in the local context, especially a context where food production and agricultural modernisation was seen as central, such objections were seldom challenged. More common was simply destroying the footpath by ploughing or by closing it with gates. Although both these acts are technically illegal it was the 1960s and 1970s before organisations like the Ramblers' Association were strong enough, or indeed had sufficient funds, to bring cases to court.

The 1949 Act also gave powers to create new footpaths, but these have remained substantially unused. As Marion Shoard writes:[12]

> In England and Wales as a whole, few new paths have been created and of these hardly any have penetrated hitherto inaccessible areas. Instead, new paths have usually been created to provide access to new housing estates, to fill in missing links in Countryside Commission long-distance paths or to replace other paths lost in diversion or rationalisation schemes.

One way of creating new paths, and one made much of by landowners, was the provision in the 1949 Act which enabled county councils and National Park authorities to negotiate access agreements to open land with individual landowners. This involves complicated negotiations and the payment of compensation. It is also of little use in lowland or arable areas since there is a relatively small area of 'open land' in these regions. There can be little doubt that in some areas, for example the Peak District National Park, this has had some success. In fact, of the 34,000 hectares of land covered by open access agreements in 1989, 20,000 hectares were in the Peak. However, even this came under threat at the end of the 1980s. As Roland Smith, Head of Information Services in the Peak wrote in 1989:[13]

> The evidence of our existing agreements is that for the board, the 1949 Act worked quite well and provided a basis for successful negotiation of access agreements in the 1950s and 1960s. In recent years most owners who have

been approached have received any attempts at negotiation far less favourably.

The central problem here is that, year by year, demand for access to the country-side is growing, and growing particularly fast outside the traditional areas for hill walking in the uplands. By 1984, according to Countryside Commission figures, 12.5 million trips were made into the countryside in winter, a figure which rises to over 18 million on a typical summer Sunday. This generalised 'going to the country' was far more popular than going to the sea, visiting country houses or taking part in or even watching sport.[14] By 1998 the Countryside Agency esti-mated that 1,343 million 'day visits' were made to the country, 15 times more trips than were made to the seaside. Twenty-five per cent of those trips were made in the southeast where there was least access to open or walking country.[15] Put simply, more and more people are aware of the countryside as a site of leisure and are finding that access to the country is getting more difficult if only because of numbers. Perhaps because of the 1949 Act and its bold hopes and real achievements, the demand for a bit of the country, for a day out or a longer holiday, has been, like the demand to live in rural England, a central fact of urban life, and urban/rural relations in the post-war world.

One of the central problems of planning in the National Parks was, as we saw above, the inability of local and park authorities to control agricultural develop-ments. After the 1960s the notion that agriculture was beyond control became, for an increasingly large number of people, a real concern that began to alter public views of the countryside and of the agricultural industry.

As we argued in Chapter 8, at the end of the Second World War British agri-culture stood at a high point in public esteem. Britain's farmers had more than helped to win the war – they had in the view of their own organisation and, more importantly in public opinion, been absolutely fundamental to victory. In the 'Conclusion' to his 'official' history of wartime agriculture Keith Murray writes, 'this history should be, without question, a "success story" – successful far beyond the calculations and estimates of the pre-war planners.'[16]

That success was achieved, as we argued above, by mechanisation and the widespread use of artificial fertilisers, herbicides and pesticides; these inputs grew in importance in the 1950s and 1960s. This created what was, in the view of most contemporaries, one of the most successful agricultural systems in the world. Initially at least this was not a problem. From at least the early 1930s, as we have already suggested, most writers on the countryside saw a modernising and progressive agriculture as an essential part of the protection and regeneration of rural England and Wales. Planning, eventually enshrined in the 1947 Town and Country Planning Act, would ensure that the urban world was kept at bay, while machinery or improved farming techniques would increase productivity and profits thus regenerating the English village.

However, to others this very system threatened the existence not only of an 'older and better' rural England but the very land itself.[17] As with the groups who began the arguments about access to the countryside for recreation, those who saw modern farming, and especially farming based on chemicals and machinery, as destructive have their origins in the nineteenth century but their modern genesis in the inter-war period. From at least the 1920s, individuals and groups began to emerge who argued that modern agriculture, based entirely on productionist imperatives, was destroying both the land and the 'organic' and 'natural' communities of the rural areas, which it supported. Many of those involved in this movement were of the extreme political right who linked the urban areas with both capitalism and socialism as the twin evils of the degenerate twentieth century. Most notable among these were two southern English landowners Rolf Gardiner and Gerard Vernon Wallop, Viscount Lymington and after 1943 the Earl of Portsmouth. Both men, and many of those associated with them, were pro-Hitler and admired the 'achievements' of the NSDAP regime in Germany. Through the 1930s Gardiner and Lymington used their estates in Dorset and Hampshire as models of rural regeneration combining 'organic' husbandry with a totally invented notion of 'English' culture involving Morris dancing, communal work, singing and invented festivals drawn from all over 'Saxon' Europe.[18] Many of these associations – 'muck and mystery' to the critics of the organic movement – remained with the movement in the post-war period, as indeed did Lymington and Gardiner as well as many other figures.

More seriously though there was a small, but powerful, core of scientific interest and knowledge within the pre-war organic farming movement. Sir George Stapledon, for example, who is credited with creating the subject of grassland agronomy, and had a major influence on aspects of post-1945 agriculture, was a lifetime supporter of aspects of the organic movement.[19] Stapledon, as Conford writes, 'was admired by both the organic and the orthodox school of agriculture, and belonged to both camps while having reservations about both.'[20] John Boyd-Orr, the pioneering nutritionist was also associated with the organic movement, although rather more than Stapledon he was ambiguous about a 'pure' organic farming.

Agriculturalists like Stapledon gave the pre-war 'humus' movement, as it was popularly called, a modicum of scientific respectability among the crowds of mystics. This was reinforced by Stapledon's appearance both on 'The Brain's Trust' and on mainstream farming programmes during the war. Scientific support was also given to organic farming by the attempts from 1939 by Lady Eve Balfour to 'prove' the success of organic farming on two farms in Suffolk under the name of the Haughley Research Trust. Balfour, although converted to organic farming by Lymington's book *Famine in England*, was largely untainted by the far-right politics of the pre-war organic movement, and had both a conventional agricultural education at Reading and twenty years of farming experience by 1939. In

1943 she published *The Living Soil*, which was to become the founding text of the post-war organic movement and of the Soil Association, which Balfour was instrumental in setting up in June 1945.[21]

As with many such organisations unity among diverse opinions was not easily achieved but in May 1946 it finally drew up its agreed aims. These were:[22]

1   To bring together all those working for a fuller understanding of the vital relationship between soil, plant, animal and man;
2   To initiate, co-ordinate and assist research in this field;
3   To collect and distribute the knowledge gained so as to create a body of informed public opinion.

From the late 1940s until the 1970s the Soil Association (SA) dominated what became known as organic farming. By 1953 it had 3,000 members, mostly working agriculturalists and was worldwide. However, those who dominated the movement throughout the immediate post-war period remained those who had been active in the 1930s and retained many of the 'muck and mystery' elements of the pre-war world. Lymington and Gardiner, for instance, remained on the Council of the SA, while the editor of its journal *Mother Earth* until 1963 was Jorian Jenks who had been interned as a fascist during the war and continued active in the Mosleyite cause in the late 1940s.[23]

As a result the SA was seen as marginal in the face of the huge changes taking place in British farming. As Tracy Clunies-Ross writes in her study of post-war organic farming, 'during the 1950s and 1960s they (organic producers) became a discredited group who were considered to have nothing serious to offer.'[24] Nevertheless serious work was done. In 1954 Lawrence Hills, a gardener and nurseryman who was also a member of the SA, established the Henry Doubleday Research Association in Essex. This subsequently developed into the National Centre of Organic Gardening at Ryton-on-Dunsmore near Coventry and, as well as carrying out research, has become 'one of the largest and most successful societies of organic growers'.[25]

From the 1960s the rosy view of post-war agriculture came under increasing criticism. The criticism came, initially at least, not from organic growers or theorists but from a new 'environmental' concern. A key text here was Rachel Carson's American study *Silent Spring*, published in 1962. Carson's concern as a scientist was essentially to produce a case for modifying the use of pesticides, especially DDT, which she argued destroyed not only 'harmful pests' but, by destroying food for birds in particular, did widespread environmental damage. However, she herself constantly distanced herself from any wider organic arguments insisting:[26]

> that she was not arguing against the use of all chemicals, she did not want to turn the clock back, she merely wanted more careful consideration to be

given to the harm that could be caused by the indiscriminate use of ever more lethal chemicals, especially where they combined to form a cocktail effect.

Whatever Carson wished, the effect was to alert pressure groups in Britain, especially those connected with bird life, to the dangers of chemical agriculture. By the 1960s about 200 pesticides were in common use in Britain. These played a vital role, as we have already suggested, in the increases both in quality and quantity of post-war agricultural production. As Sheail writes:[27]

> Herbicides were particularly welcome at a time when labour costs had made hand hoeing so expensive, and when the farmer wanted to concentrate more and more on cereal production. It was a time when housewives were also demanding better-quality produce. . . . Although the relationship could not be measured precisely, there was little doubt that pesticides made a major contribution to the post-war increases in efficiency and productivity in farming.

However, from *Silent Spring* onwards environmental awareness began to grow. This was not primarily in the form of an organised 'green' politics but rather in a generalised sense that something was going wrong with agriculture and the countryside. A good deal of this general sense is certainly based on an essentially misguided view of the rural past. This fact is not lost on the big farming lobby, as *Farmers Weekly* wrote in February 1994, 'most consumers romanticise a British countryside that never was, yet they are wholly reliant on modern farming for low-cost, high quality food.'[28] Nevertheless from the mid-1960s onwards there were real concerns which could not be dismissed as simple golden ageism. The most striking of these, because it was visually so powerful, was the loss of hedgerows. Between 1946 and 1974 farmers removed a quarter of the hedgerows in England and Wales – some 120,000 miles in all. In some areas it was worse; in Norfolk 45 per cent of hedgerows were removed in the same period, mainly for increased barley production, and in Cambridgeshire 40 per cent were removed.[29]

Removal of hedgerows had a gradual, but in the end, massive, public response. In a survey carried out in 1995 through the organisation Mass-Observation, which sought to find public perceptions of changes in the countryside, the removal of hedgerows was the largest single 'bad' change that the group thought had taken place since the war.[30]

Frequently hedgerow loss was equated, largely correctly, with the introduction of large-scale machine farming. A man from Surrey writes, 'undoubtedly the countryside has changed dramatically over time as more and more machinery is introduced and hedges get ripped out to make way for more intensive forms of farming.'[31] More specifically a retired librarian from a Norfolk village writes: 'My admittedly rather jaundiced view of Norfolk's countryside is reinforced by the money-grubbing vandalism which resulted [in] the grubbing up of the lovely hedgerows which sustained so much wildlife.'[32] Or a working-class man who grew up in the London suburbs remembering cycling in Sussex and Surrey just after the war:[33]

> Further out in the country we used to see patchworks of small fields each being used for a different crop or grazing. Now all the hedgerows have been grubbed up and larger fields made for easier management with agricultural machines.

These quotations point to why the loss of hedgerows is seen as so central to the notions of a changing countryside. First, they are believed to be haunts of wildlife which when destroyed in turn destroys flora and fauna. Again the evidence here overwhelmingly supports this view. The British Trust for Ornithology annual monitoring has revealed,[34]

> a dramatic fall in population numbers for a whole range of farmland (birds) over the past twenty-five years – the tree sparrow down 89 per cent; the bullfinch down 76 per cent; the song thrush down 73 per cent; the spotted flycatcher down 73 per cent; lapwings down 62 per cent; sky larks down 58 per cent; linnets down 52 per cent. Population numbers of the corn bunting are now too low to be routinely monitored.

But it is not only the destruction of animal and bird life but also most importantly the interpretation of those physical changes which is so important. Paul Brassley has argued that changes in what he calls the 'ephemeral landscape' – for example, field boundaries like hedges and walls – as well as cropping, are central to our perceptions of the countryside. It is they, as much as the great subjects of space and vista, which so influence artistic theory, which affect how we respond to the countryside. He concludes:[35]

> the ephemeral components of the landscape have a major, and hitherto unrecognised, influence on the way in which it is perceived and valued. Moreover, many of the ephemeral components of the agricultural landscape have been subject to extensive changes over the last sixty years. Consequently, when ordinary people articulate concerns of the rapidity of agricultural change, it may be the changes to the ephemeral landscape, which are the root cause of their concerns.

Again this is borne out clearly in the survey replies. Changes in meadowland were often noticed. A woman who grew up on a Dorset farm before the Second

World War writes of 'the meadows in June like Swiss Meadows, full of a variety of flowers, herbs and grasses so good for the cows when made into hay',[36] but the sense of visual change extended much further, 'thatched barns replaced by silos and battery chicken houses, different crops – we never used to see bright yellow fields of oil seed rape and now blue ones of flax – even the pigs have changed their shape.'[37]

Both the increased use of machinery and pesticides and herbicides were also widely blamed for the deterioration of country life. A woman writes from the outskirts of Norwich, 'the land between our house and the bypass is farmland. Intensively farmed unfortunately. During the summer potatoes get drenched in chemicals every 7 days or so. . . . The lapwings have long gone since all insects both good and bad have been zapped out of existence.'[38] Machinery was also linked to the destruction of hedgerows as we have already seen, and to larger fields.

Perceptions of landscape change here are less related to large cultural theories of, for example, national identity and identity, but to 'real' changes in the countless small elements which constitute a landscape within, or perhaps alongside, the broader brush strokes of the theoretical construction. We might for a moment think of the statement made by one woman Mass-Observer that 'now' all the cows were black and white whereas in her childhood they were 'different' colours. This is certainly true. The domination of the British dairy herd by the ubiquitous Friesian is, as we saw above, a post-war phenomenon. It marks in a profound, personal and real way for the observer, the standardisation of landscape under the influence of agri-business, which is concealed by the continuities within, say, the landscapes of the South Downs. Here, although change is real enough, two things hide it. First, the ideology of the landscape of the south lands stresses its continuities in the face of change. Second, the simple fact that the landscape shape and contours remain the same as long as they remain un-built up – but the cows are black and white, the pigs are a different shape and the hedgerows have gone.

These changes are perceived to be the result of farming practice, as were the majority of reasons given for deterioration in country life by those who wrote in reply to the Mass-Observation directive. The prime movers in this change were, if only by implication, those who worked the land. A small number of those responding blamed pressure from the Government, or the EU/CAP. An eloquent example of this comes from a woman born in Norfolk in 1932 who spent much of her life until the late 1950s overseas.[39]

> On returning from overseas in the late 1950s I was amazed at the destruction of hedgerows, grubbing out has continued ever since, starting during WW2 [World War II] to increase food production acreage govt. [sic] funded and since the late '60s CAP funded. Now 'setaside' is with us, hedges being replanted, golf courses laid out, land rescheduled for road building – all subsidised by the taxpayer.

More, 10 per cent of women and 16 per cent of men showed a positive hostility to farmers. This is fairly low but in total only 28 per cent of men and 12 per cent of women were prepared to 'blame' anybody, which means farmers were easily the largest group identified as 'blameworthy'. This is increased if one considers that all the 'worst' problems of the countryside were associated with farming practice. At the most extreme farmers were seen as fat cats, cushioned by subsidies and destroying the countryside because of greed:

> I think the farmers have been cushioned too long by subsidies and it is about time they suffered financially as the rest of the working population have had to recently.[40]

> Sadly, though the chief change I have seen in my life is that farmers are no longer in sympathy with the land. Their activities have been dominated by politics and economics.[41]

> My views on farming changed many years ago when the prariefication of East Anglia started, and agri-business was born. Once the cost accountants come in, morality, compassion and tradition go out of the window.[42]

> It is all big business now, not a farmer making a living for him and his family in a small way. . . . Personally I think it is only the farmers who have benefited from being in the Common Market, in fact I would go as far as to say that the farmers have got very rich at the expense of the rest of us. I have no sympathy with them at all.[43]

The Mass-Observation directive revealed that those who wrote believed that there were more general changes in country life which were not directly attributable to farming, and which suggest a general deterioration in the rural areas. The most obvious change stressed by the group is continued urbanisation. One particularly striking example comes from a woman living on a post-war estate built in the countryside on the outskirts of Leeds. When she moved there, she writes there were 'several patches of woodland left to grow, dotted across the estate and grassy areas too.' But since the 1960s, 'our countryside has been pushed further and further away from us, over the years the green land has been taken for private housing estates and businesses. Some of our grassy areas on the estate are now covered with a Sainsbury complex. . . . So I'm back to feeling a "townie" again.'[44]

Linked to this was a sense among some that government had failed here, especially in relation to road building and to green belt legislation. 'Green belt protection,' writes a man from Nottingham, 'which seems to have been progressively watered-down and withdrawn by the government over the past years is essential if we are to avoid further urban development at the expense of the countryside and everyone's quality of life.'[45]

Another key area, much more difficult to quantify in any real sense, was the perceived deterioration in village life. This came mainly from people living in villages or suburbs. The complaints are already familiar enough and are mainly about services. However, there is a real sense of the 'local/incomer' battles that were discussed in the last chapter. A woman born in Polegate in Sussex and still living there writes: 'In the early sixties when people started to build new estates the village began to expand. I remember feeling a bit resentful of the people who moved in. They were mainly people who had retired from London. They were different to the local people I knew.'[46] Equally familiar is the anger from a north Lincolnshire village at incomers pushing up prices and forcing out 'locals'. 'The small hamlet that was once lived in by farm workers is now inhabited by wealthy middle-class professionals . . . my friend's parents who had retired (who had lived in a semi-tied cottage) ended up in a council flat in town.'[47]

These reactions to the perceived degeneration of the countryside and country life since the Second World War began, in the late 1960 and 1970s, to feed into a growing environmental movement. Unlike the experience of continental Europe this has not, to any great extent, resulted in the growth of a large party political 'green' movement rather, as we have already suggested, it fed into existing organisations, especially those connected with animal welfare and, more spectacularly into the counter culture of youth which developed in the 1960s.

Organisations to protect animals from cruelty have a longer history in England and Wales than in any other European country, although the fight against cruelty to animals was by no means easy. However, in 1824 the Society for the Prevention of Cruelty to Animals was founded and in 1840 the young Queen Victoria added her name to the list of supporters to enable it to become the Royal Society for the Prevention of Cruelty to Animals (RSPCA).[48] Its initial campaigns, and indeed successes, were against cruel sports, like bull baiting, but also against the cruel treatment of farm animals, both of which areas were legislated against in 1835. Through the nineteenth century it extended its campaigns by prosecutions of those guilty of cruelty to domestic and farm animals and by 'public education'. By the beginning of the twentieth century the RSPCA was one of the most powerful charities in Britain, and one that commanded near universal support for its aims. Another nineteenth-century campaign, that against the killing of birds for their feathers, created in 1891 what was to become one of the key environmental pressure groups in the years after 1970, the Society for the Protection of Birds which was given a Royal Charter in 1904 (RSPB).[49] As with the RSPCA the RSPB saw itself as having both a law enforcement role – by initiating prosecutions under the 1896 Wild Birds Protection Act – and a role in educating public opinion.[50]

By the post-Second World War period both of these organisations had mass memberships. In 1971 the RSPB had less than 100,000 members, by 1994 it had

870,000. The RSPCA has grown in the same period. More importantly, wittingly and unwittingly, both organisations changed in the post-war years. The involvement of the RSPB in monitoring the effects of pesticides and herbicides on the wild bird population, and the link made between DDT and that decline, brought the organisation into environmental politics in the early and mid-1960s.[51] More openly the RSPCA began in the 1970s and 1980s to adopt a much more radical stance, moving from a straight concern with animal welfare to a more problematic notion of animal rights. Although the most 'extreme' radicals were ultimately defeated the RSPCA entered the 1990s a very different organisation from the rather fuddy-duddy organisation of the 1950s and 1960s. This is clear from the RSPCA's adoption of the 'Declaration of Animal Rights' as well as their education pamphlets on the same subject.[52] Growing out of that the RSPCA's opposition to hunting with dogs has brought them into conflict with many of their more traditional country supporters.

A similar trajectory might be traced in relation to the National Trust. Although the intentions of many of the Trust's founders was to preserve the landscape from the late 1930s the 'country house scheme' had diverted the interest of many members and most of the Trust's finances into the preservation of the supposedly dwindling stocks of great country houses. In the post-war period country house visiting became a national pastime of all classes. While a few 'great' country houses like Woburn (with its zoo park) or Beaulieu (with its motor museum) had 'extra' attractions, most country houses simply opened on their own terms. As Peter Mandler writes:[53]

> Just below (the level of Woburn) stood houses that drew large numbers of tourists without much extra promotion: great historic houses in extensive parks, such as Blenheim, . . . Chatsworth, Berkely Castle, Haddon Hall and Hatfield House. Owners of properties such as these could benefit from the tourist business without having to remodel themselves or their homes.

The reasons for this growth in visiting country houses were complex. As Mandler points out, despite the National Parks the countryside still remained closed to most people. In the 1950s and 1960s:[54]

> Strong growth in personal consumption gave families spending money, leisure and private motor-transport. The do-it-yourself motor holiday began to undermine the popularity of the all-in seaside resort. In default of public recreational provision, the beneficiaries were private sector providers; teashops in the Cotswolds, county inns, the stately-home business and the National Trust.

Yet it was not simply money or a wish to see how the other half lived that prompted stately home visiting. In the era of the Welfare State the privilege of the past became a national treasure to be viewed and celebrated in the popular media. 'Human interest', as Mandler argues, was a central part of country house visiting, an interest that began with the lifestyle of the rich and great but rapidly expanded to life 'below stairs'. A parallel growth in interests in gardens and gardening was another attraction, and gardens were often at least as interesting to visitors as the Van Dyck portrait hanging in the stately hall.[55]

Nationally the main beneficiary of the growth in visiting 'stately homes' was the National Trust. In 1945 it had about 7,000 members, mostly among the 'artistic middle classes'. By the mid-1960s it had grown to 150,000, but the real increase in size took place in the 20 years after 1970 when it increased to over 2 million. This huge influx of members began to change the nature of the Trust. Although few of them took an active interest in the running of the organisation an increasingly vocal minority did. As with the RSPCA and the RSPB, this gradually pushed the Trust to a more campaigning role, which increasingly focused on the environment rather than simply 'country houses'.

The first rumblings of change came in the early 1960s and centred on ideas to get the Trust to take a more active interest in acquiring 'natural' landscapes and to recruit more and younger people to an active role in the organisation. The crunch came over 'Project Neptune', a plan to save 900 miles of unspoilt coastline. Neptune was organised by the 'energetic but irascible Commander Conrad Rawnsley, grandson of the Canon Rawnsley whose passion for the Lake District led to the founding of the Trust in 1895.'[56] Rawnsley was enormously successful. In less than a year Project Neptune raised £700,000, including substantial government grants. By the mid-1990s it had raised over £18 million, acquired 500 miles of coastline and had, to an extent, involved young people as volunteers. Yet it nearly split the Trust. Rawnsley's style was aggressive. He opposed aspects of the sacred country house scheme and like his grandfather wanted to use the Trust to make the countryside more accessible. In October 1966 he was dismissed but, instead of going quietly, he attempted to mobilise within the Trust to replace its current leadership with one which would be committed to 'the leisure pursuits of the people as a whole'. This involved not only more emphasis on open country but also 'downgrading' many country houses:[57]

> Should all the great country houses be shown as museums or should some of them play a more active part in the life of the community? There is little merit in some of the furniture and pictures. Would it not be better to take the best of both and make a few really worthwhile collections and use the other houses for public assemblies, dances and other activities?

At the annual meeting in 1967 Rawnsley's plans for reform were defeated, yet the criticisms he voiced and the method he used, the appeal to the membership, would not go away. Gradually the Trust's policies changed and while not moving

Plate 18 What is the countryside for? By the late 1960s and early 1970s, motor traffic had become a major problem in many rural areas as tens of thousands went in search of the countryside. The 'Goyt Valley traffic experiment, 1973'. (Reproduced by kind permission of the Rural History Centre, University of Reading.)

away from the 'country house' its focus has been more and more on the acquisition of land and public access, while aspects of its land management have come more and more under hostile scrutiny from its members. In the early 1980s the Trust made land available at Bradenham in the Chilterns for the Ministry of Defence to extend a command centre for RAF Strike Command. In November 1982 Sir Richard Acland found sufficient support to call an Extraordinary General Meeting to discuss the issue. Again the dissidents were defeated but with nothing like the ease with which Rawnsley had been routed 15 years earlier.[58]

The question of hunting on National Trust land had first been raised in the 1930s, but again it was not until the late 1980s that it came up in a substantial way at the Trust's AGM. Hunting with dogs was to be a major break point for the Trust, as it was to be for the RSPCA. Hunting held a particular place in the countryside ideal and as such it was untouched by early defenders of the countryside. The 'authenticity' of hunting, and its apparently key part in rural society, made it attractive to both 'country people' and incomers. This again began to change in the 1970s and 1980s when it became clear that the huge majority of people in Britain were against hunting with dogs. Although the Trust successfully fought off calls for a complete ban in 1989, 1991 and 1993 the question was to return to haunt them again and again in the 1990s.

The move of well established animal protectionist organisations to an active involvement in environmental politics, and even challenges within the National Trust, was matched in the years after 1970 by a growth in newer environmental movements many of whose criticisms were either directly or indirectly highly critical of modern agricultural practices, and whose opposition to these brought them more and more into conflict with the farmer and the state.

The origins of many of these new or second-wave environmental movements lies in the counter culture of the 1960s.[59] Although few of the movements of that period, for example the campaign against the Vietnam War, were directly concerned with the environment, most had an anti-technocratic side. In the 1970s, as the more left-wing organisations returned to traditional issues, like trade unionism and more traditional organisations of the 'old left', this anti-technocratic strand began to find outlets elsewhere. Two elements in this concern us here – the idea of going back to nature and the idea, sometimes linked to it and sometimes not, of non-violent direct action in defence of the environment and the natural world. What they shared was a distrust of older organisations which sought to defend the environment. As Emma Must, one of the campaigners against building the M3 through Twyford Down put it, 'there have been 146 public inquiries into trunk roads and on only five occasions has the inspector found against the government. So it is no wonder that people end up in trees.'[60] They also shared a mystic sense of the natural world. This was, and is, not infrequently linked to what John Lowerson has called a 'mystic geography' of Britain. In this a confused sense of pagan belief, pre-historic sites, ley-lines and magic places underpins a deep and very real commitment to a version of the rural which is frequently at odds with modern society.[61]

Dropping out of modern society and going back to the land has a long history and we have already touched upon aspects of it. One could argue that it has characterised all radical movements in the last 400 years. In the 1970s and 1980 it took the form of attempted communal living. Initially, as David Pepper writes, these communes were not necessarily ecologist or environmentalist in an explicit way, rather they combined an anti-urbanism with a mixture of mystic ideas about the unity of 'man' and nature which led to what he calls a 'green critique'.[62] However, it was not always clear where this critique might go apart, that is, from a small-scale refusal to have anything to do with society. Tipi Valley in Dyfed was established in 1976 as a long term eco-friendly community living in tipis modelled on those of native Americans and incorporating aspects of their social and cultural practice. By the 1990s it seems to have made little difference to those outside the community, and even here there are problems.[63] The Centre for Alternative Technology (CAT), set up as a commune in 1974, had a much more 'outgoing' vision right from the start. This was to test out new forms of technology and, by showing that they worked, make them widely acceptable. In most respects this has been very successful, although some within the CAT have been critical and suggested that the original purity of the commune ideal has been sacrificed.[64]

The trajectory of the non-violent direct action movement, which was to have a fundamental place in the environmental protests of the 1990s, is more complex. Beginning both in the Peace movement of the 1960s and 1970s and the counter culture of the Free Festivals, its most obvious and, to the authorities at least, threatening aspect was the Peace Convoy, so called because of its presence at the Greenham Common Peace Camp in 1982. However, potential and real clashes with the police culminating in the attack on the 'Peace Convoy' on its way to the banned Free Festival at Stonehenge in 1985 changed the movement. What followed, 'the Battle of the Beanfield', was not so much a battle – more a massacre. Over 500 travellers were arrested amidst signs of police violence that shocked not only the liberal press but also the Earl of Cardigan, who subsequently gave the remnants of the convoy refuge on his own land.[65] Although the convoy was ultimately dispersed, its ghost lived on in the 1990s with the emergence of those who opposed road building, especially in the form of the 'Tribes'. We shall come back to them in the final chapter.

Between the counter culture and the National Trust was a whole range of new organisations that sought to defend the rural (as *they* saw it) against the ravages of modern society. As Jordan and Maloney show these organisations have grown not only in number but also hugely in membership since the 1960s. In 1992 it was estimated that UK environment groups had a membership of about 5 million people.[66] Probably the most powerful of these was (and possibly still is) is Friends of the Earth (FoE). Friends of the Earth came to Britain in 1971 and by the mid-1990s it had over 100,000 members. Unlike the older mainstream environmental groups FoE is openly political and local branches and supporters have taken part in environmental protests. Compassion in World Farming was organised in 1967 to campaign against the factory farming of animals. By the 1990s it had become a major force both in its own right and as a pressure group on the more traditional animal welfare organisations.

Governments and government organisations have, since the early 1970s, begun to respond to some of these arguments and pressure groups, as well as to disasters like the sinking of the *Torrey Canyon* in 1967. 1970 was declared 'European Conservation Year' and was marked by a white paper on pollution. In February the First Report of the Royal Commission on Environmental Pollution was published. Working from what figures are available John Sheail has made a strong case that not only are fewer new pesticides being developed, but those that are are much safer than in the past. Further it is possible that pesticide use has declined since the 1980s. Much of this is due to government intervention and research.[67] At a more banal level Britain has gradually changed the way it eats. In

1983 Fine Fare became the first supermarket chain to sell organic foods. They were followed by Safeways and Sainsbury's in 1986 and Waitrose in 1987. Although still very much a minority interest in the late 1980s this move began to take organic produce out of the ghetto of 'muck and mystery' to the much stronger position it enjoyed 10 years later. There were also signs of change within the farming establishment. As Clunies-Ross writes:[68]

> By 1990, the attitude towards organic farming had changed considerably throughout the agricultural community. Leaders of the organic movement had by this time developed personal contacts with policy makers, government advisors, research scientists and those with influence in the NFU. . . . It would thus appear that within the decade of the 1980s not only has organic farming achieved agenda status, but organic groups have come to be considered a relevant part of the now rapidly changing policy community.

The history of post-war agriculture has been seen in economic terms as one of success, albeit occasionally qualified success. Such accounts stress increases in output and labour productivity, wider variety of crops while persisting in the arguments of stewardship of the countryside. However, it is clear that the experiences of at least some of those who have lived through this transformation suggest a very different view. At its most simple it is clearly widely felt that the costs of these changes have been too high in terms of the 'quality' of life. Sixty-eight per cent of women and 57 per cent of men who wrote in reply to the Mass-Observation directive felt unequivocally that rural life had got 'worse' in their lifetimes. Seen like this the history of agriculture since the Second World War was far from successful. That in turn has been reflected in the growth of new generalised environmental groups and the radicalisation of older ones. Much of the criticism of these groups has been directed against farming.

The battles over the countryside represented both by the growing power of the 'incomers' and worries over the environmental impact of farming seemed fairly evenly matched at the end of the 1980s. Although many were unhappy with what they saw as environmental damage or cruelty to animals the overwhelming success of British agriculture seemed to guarantee its continuing popularity, even if the battle-lines, in public relations terms at least, seemed a little more evenly drawn than before. That was all to change in the last decade of the twentieth century.

11 The countryside in crisis, 1990–2001

At the beginning of the 1990s, despite the problems we have discussed in the last two chapters, to most people in England and Wales the rural areas seemed prosperous and settled. Although farm incomes fell in the early 1980s, by 1990 they were picking up again and between 1989–90 and 1995–6 they increased from about £2.5 billion to over £7 billion per annum, their highest level since Britain had joined the EEC.[1] Also by 1995–6 the net income of cereal farmers had risen by 13 per cent in 4 years.[2] There were a number of reasons for this rise in farm incomes, some long term, some short term. Long-term factors included the continued concentration and enlargement of farm units, which produced undoubted production gains and hence increased profits. By the mid-1990s less than 30,000 farmers produced 60 per cent of UK cereal production, 60 per cent of milk and 60 per cent of beef and sheep. Continued farm subsidies were a central part of these income gains. Ironically the so-called 'MacSharry Reforms', which were designed to reduce subsidies in the long term, and to change the nature of farm support towards more socially and environmentally conscious agricultural production, had a major short-term effect on profits of large and, in some terms, environmentally more damaging farm units. As we saw earlier part of the MacSharry reforms included a fixed arable area payment made direct to the producer and set each year. Alongside this was to be compulsory 'set aside' in which a certain percentage of arable land was to come out of production in order to reduce surpluses. Farmers were to be 'compensated' for set aside by a fixed payment per acre. In 1995 these payments totalled over £200,000 per year on a 2,000-acre arable farm in Cambridgeshire.[3] Also, short-term falls in the value of the pound after Britain's withdrawal from the European Exchange Rate Mechanism in September 1992 led to higher payments to British farmers at exactly the time when world wheat prices were rising, reflecting an international grain shortage. As a result the MacSharry reforms turned from being compensation for price cuts into a bonus.[4]

The optimism of the mid-1990s was reflected in the farming press. In February 1996 *Farmers Weekly* wrote, after the MAFF announcements that UK farm incomes had increased by 22 per cent:[5]

> No doubt many media pundits will tell only half the story and the spotlight will fall on the role of subsidies and their cost to the taxpayer. Arable and dairy farmers have undeniably had a good year. A number of factors came together to make last year a vintage year for farm profits [and] . . . gave many farmers an income fillip few could have hoped for.

In June and July 1996 fears about pressure within the Conservative Party to quit Europe led *Farmers Weekly* to give an account of the effects of membership of the EU on British farming – and society as a whole – which reflected agriculture's continuing success.[6]

> For 25 years, membership of the European Community has supplied secure markets, social stability and undreamt of prosperity for most UK farmers. The CAP is far from flawless. . . . But it has kept farmers on the land, guaranteed the supply of high quality products and helped maintain a beautiful and viable countryside.

A booming agriculture was reflected in an apparently increasingly wealthy countryside. The value of land, which had fallen in the late 1980s and early 1990s, went up sharply in the mid-1990s. In the 12 months up to June 1994 the value of high quality arable land in Lincolnshire increased by 76 per cent according to the estate agents Savills.[7] House prices followed a similar trend, falling in the late 1980s and early 1990s only to rise again in the middle of the decade. It was said in the City, in the booms of the mid-1980s and the mid-1990s, that every time the annual bonuses came in, 'cottage' prices in the southeast doubled. Whatever the truth of this story the reality is clear enough. Demand both for 'first' and 'second' homes in the rural areas continued to grow throughout the 1990s. The 1991 Census showed that the trend towards living in the countryside was continuing. The fastest growing areas were Cambridgeshire and Buckinghamshire both of which had grown by 10–12 per cent since 1981.[8] Although out-migration from the cities had slowed since the decade 1971–81, the biggest gains in population were in the South West, the South East and East Anglia, all predominantly rural areas.[9] This movement increased the value of rural property so that by the late 1990s housing was on average about 12 per cent more expensive in rural areas than in urban.[10] In the same period second home ownership grew, although in the mid-1990s it still only accounted for about 2.5 per cent of all rural housing stock. However, this reassuring figure, which the Conservative governments of the period up to 1997 used to argue that there was no need for legislation on second home ownership, became a great deal more startling in regional terms.[11] By the mid-1990s 60 per cent of all second homes were situated in the West Country, and by 2001 40 per cent of houses in some Exmoor villages were second homes.[12]

However, the question of second homes points to the problems that were hidden by this prosperity. The other side of rising house prices was, as we saw in Chapter 9, the virtual exclusion of low-income families from many areas of rural England and Wales. Further council house sales reduced the amount of local authority housing available for rent, while increasing house prices encouraged private landlords to sell properties rather than leave them on the market for rent. More problems were caused by the failure of private capital or government to build low-cost housing. By the turn of the century 14.7 per cent of households in rural areas lived in local authority housing, as against 22.1 per cent in urban. As a result the Countryside Agency in 2001 regarded substantial areas of southern and eastern England as suffering from real problems with access to housing.[13]

Nor was the story of farming quite so rosy, even in the mid-1990s, as simple statistics might suggest – a fact not lost on the NFU or the farming press. In February 1996 *Farmers Weekly*, having admitted that there had been an exceptional year for agriculture, went on to say:[14]

> [But] a little investigation reveals that the industry is divided into the haves and the have-nots. Ask an upland livestock producer or an intensive poultry man how he fared last year and the reply will paint a different picture. Fodder shortages, rising feed costs and falling product prices have taken their toll . . . for many groups, and for many farmers within those groups, farming remains a precarious business.

In the 5 years after 1995–6 these divisions were to become more and more apparent until they were to threaten the very future of upland farming.

For the declining agricultural workforce the picture was grimmer still. The 1990s saw the numbers working in agriculture and horticulture continue the unbroken fall which had marked the industry since the Second World War. In the years between the mid-1980s and the end of the twentieth century something like 100,000 men and women left agriculture. However, this decline, as in the whole of the twentieth century, was not evenly spread across the sector. In the first year of the new century 6 per cent of all workers in agriculture left the industry but only 0.6 per cent of these were farmers – 13 per cent were regular full-time workers, 13 per cent were regular part-time workers and 12 per cent were casual workers. Agricultural contractors replaced them, as they had been since the 1950s. By the late 1990s 90 per cent of farms employed outside contractors for at least one farming operation every year.[15] The traditional farm worker appeared, by 2000, to be even nearer extinction than the traditional hill farmer.

Yet the first threats to this prosperous agriculture and to a 'modernising' vision of rural England came not from within agriculture but from outside it and were directed, at least in part, as much against the images of rural England as their 'realities'. From 1993–4 onwards the disparate groups which made up the environmental movement in England and Wales found a focus in two long campaigns, which seem to have marked a major shift in their power and influence. The first of these, the campaign against road building, had little to do with farming but a great deal to do with the countryside. The second, the campaign against the live export of farm animals, centrally concerned modern farming, its practices and, above all, its public image.

The building of new roads, especially by-passes and motorways had been a central feature both of Britain's economic 'modernisation' from the late 1950s onwards and a reflection of the huge growth in the ownership of private cars from the mid-1960s. Initially there had been little opposition, indeed the opening of the first motorway, the M1, was signalled as an economic and engineering triumph; while many a small, and even large town, thanked the planners for an inner ring road or by-pass even if, as say in Colchester or Ipswich, it cut a swathe through historic townscapes. Indeed, it was the defence of townscapes, largely by local civic societies, which marked the first anti-road building protests. Large sections of the city and University of Oxford united in the early 1960s to oppose the building of an inner ring road across Christ Church Meadows, an area of open space on the edge of the city centre. A strange continuity was provided by a key figure in the defence of the Meadows, Edmund Blunden, a founder of Kinship in Husbandry in the 1940s, and associate of some of the less savoury members of the organic movement. A similar campaign in Lewes in Sussex prevented an elevated 'motorway' passing across allotments and open space within a few hundred metres of Lewes Castle.

However, even in the 1960s there were worries about the impact of rural road building, particularly in the National Parks and in areas of outstanding beauty. Control of road building was excluded from the powers given to the National Parks' councils. In 1964 the Friends of the Lake District pointed out in a pamphlet that while planning permission was needed to erect even a porch on a cottage, the National Parks planning authority 'has no right even to comment on the proposal to carry a ruthless road widening all the way up Langdale, which can change completely and for ever the character of the valley.'[16] Similar points were made in relation to the construction of the new A66, also in the Lakes, and the Okehampton by-pass in Devon in the 1980s. By this date though things were beginning to change.

As we saw in Chapter 10 the environmental movement began to grow in power and influence in the late 1980s, presenting a much more coherent and increasingly effective argument about environmental degradation across many different areas. Alongside this, as we also argued above, elements which grew out of the counter culture were becoming increasingly active in the area of environmental protest and using tactics used in the anti-Poll Tax Campaigns of the early 1990s. These groups came together in the protest against the extension of the M3 over Twyford Down near Winchester. The land at Twyford Down was owned by Winchester College and was 'an extremely well protected landscape by official designation: one Site of Special Scientific Interest, an Area of Outstanding Natural Beauty, two Scheduled Ancient Monuments.'[17]

In February the bulldozers moved in to be met by protest groups led by the local Twyford Down Association and Friends of the Earth. But it was the emergence in March 1992 of a group calling themselves the Dongas Tribe, whose origins lay in the late 1980s travellers' movement, which marked a really decisive change.[18]

> A group of people arrived in ones and twos on Twyford Down near Winchester and stayed on to defend it from being destroyed. . . . While most of us were already keen environmentalists, craft workers and herbalists, living full time outdoors in a communal situation, cooking on fires, building simple but snug shelters was new.

The 'tribes' identified themselves as the 'nomadic indigenous peoples of Britain' and drew on a complex of mystical and 'pagan' ideas, which gave a central importance to the land and all natural life. Added to this was a decent dose of anti-capitalism which, largely correctly, identified much that had gone wrong with the landscape and the environment as a result of economic policies and pressures in the post-Second World War world.

Initially the protests were peaceful with the tribes camped on the site, but on Wednesday 9 December (Yellow Wednesday) private security guards of Group 4 Security moved in to clear the land. The violence of their actions was widely reported, shown on television and drew considerable support from the liberal press. For example, John Vidal wrote in the *Guardian*:[19]

> The powerful image of private money hand in hand with the machinery of the state together rolling over the economically weakest to appropriate common resources was given perfect expression. The subtext for environmentally aware youth was obvious; to the list of oppressed people in Latin America, Indonesia and elsewhere, add the English.

'Yellow Wednesday' and the following day ('Black Thursday') when the police moved in to clear the protestors marked the beginning of the end for Twyford, yet the tribes in particular held on for the best part of another year developing guerrilla tactics to slow down the road building, including the spectacular capture of a temporary bridge which was to be laid across the cutting. These tactics, intended to delay progress and increase costs, had the added advantage of drawing public interest and support as well as 'politicising' those involved.

The legacy of Twyford Down was to be considerable. Despite the fact that the road was built (and is now regularly jammed at rush hour) and that many were arrested and seven jailed, it had two major outcomes. First, it gave new tactics and a new inspiration to the growing environmental movement. As one of those on Twyford Down, Donga Alex writes:[20]

> The actions of the Donga Tribe at Twyford Down established direct action against roads as part of protest culture, and inspired action against many forms of destructive development, from logging firms to quarries. Our peaceful protest, and the establishment's violent reaction to it have triggered a response from a broad section of society.

Second, the Dongas (and other groups) built on the notion of temporary and shifting alliances with almost anyone willing to work together in the common cause. Such a framework also enabled the movement to break free from an older and much more rigid notion of protest.[21]

> The answer (is) to move from (one) definition/classification to another . . . or to try to avoid total definition altogether, leaving room for growth and movement of thought and the possibility of unity and cooperation with other groups, ideologies etc. (This happened in the roads protest movement, with interactivity between establishment environmental groups and direct activists such as Earth Firsters, between Travellers and 'NIMBY' Tories etc.)

This combination of peaceful direct action with a broad church approach to allies was to prove extraordinary successful in creating what many in the media began to describe as a 'new age of protest'.[22] In the mid-1990s these mixed and often very confused movements had a key effect on environmental consciousness in general and factory farming in particular, on the continuing roads campaign, especially that against the Newbury by-pass, and on the campaign around live export of farm animals. These campaigns brought together a mixture of 'middle-aged and middle-class' protestors with the much more radical sections of the counter culture like the Dongas, and later the 'Hunt Sabs' and the Animal Liberation Front. The rural impact of this was clear. Road protest put a high value on the land and, in denying the 'right' to develop it, protestors 'took' the land as a common heritage based often on quasi-mystical beliefs which had little or no place for modern agriculture. The campaign on live animals exports took this further, generating a detailed and angry critique of factory farming methods. These movements began in the late 1990s to produce a wholesale critique of post-war British farming and farming practices which was profoundly dangerous to the industry which, by-and-large, initially ignored it as the work of cranks and lefty townies. It was dangerous because, at a time when farming was about to go into crisis, it needed all the friends it could get, urban more than rural.

These tensions are clear in the campaign against the transport of live farm animals from the summer of 1994 to the spring of 1995.[23] Opposition to the transport of live animals has a long history. The Humanitarian League ran campaigns between 1897 and certainly 1903 if not later on the transport of cattle across the Irish Sea.[24] More emotional in appeal, and getting wider support, were campaigns between the 1900s and the 1960s to stop the shipping of live horses to continental Europe for meat. In the 1950s this campaign was widened to include farm animals shipped for slaughter in Europe and extended in turn by the involvement of first the RSPCA and then Compassion in World Farming (CIWF) in the 1970s. As a result there was a temporary ban on live animal exports in 1972, but it was lifted in the early spring of 1975; this was followed, in the 1980s, by a huge increase in the export of live animals. In 1963 the UK exported a total of 655,000 live animals. By 1993 the figure had reached nearly 2.5 million animals per annum.[25]

In January 1993, with the creation of a Single European Market the regulations governing the transportation of live animals were relaxed. In the aftermath of this a 'compromise' was patched up which allowed farm animals to be transported for up to 24 hours without stopping to rest, feed and water them.[26] In the wake of this the RSPCA and CIWF began a publicity campaign to end the live export trade totally. As CIWF wrote in the autumn of 1993:[27]

> CIWF believes that the time has now come for a radical change in policy. The trade in live animals must be stopped. Live exports from the UK should be halted and there should be an end to the trade in Europe as a whole.

To this end they pursued a mixed policy, entirely peaceful, of applying pressure initially on government and the EU and then on organisations concerned with the transport of live animals. Between the autumn of 1993 and the summer of 1994 three petitions were organised. One with half a million signatures was sent to Gillian Shepherd at MAFF in September 1993, one with a million signatures to the European Commission in April 1994 and an organised write-in produced more than 50,000 postcards, again to Shepherd, in July 1994. In addition the CIWF video, 'For a few Pennies More', formed the basis of a *World in Action* report on live exports which was televised in the spring of 1994 and was watched by an estimated 5.8 million viewers.

The most important change though was to bring 'consumer' pressure on the ferry companies and on airlines involved in the live export trade. The main groups involved were CIWF and the RSPCA. Also involved, although a much smaller organisation, was Respect for Animals, founded by Mark Glover, a former Greenpeace activist and founder of LYNX, the highly successful campaign against the use of fur in fashion.[28]

On 18 August 1994 the first success was claimed when British Airways

which really brought the campaign into the national news with the television scenes of a young person with a Balaclava helmet on the roof of a lorry smashing the windscreen. Incidentally the lorry belonged to A. Nicholay b.v., the Dutch company prosecuted in October 1995 and fined £10,000 for inflicting suffering on calves being moved from Northern Ireland to Spain.[33]

The following night 1,300 police were brought in, lorries were taken through another entrance, and what the local press called 'the siege of Shoreham' began. For the next 3 weeks, at the cost of some £2 million, the port was kept more or less open, although the demonstrations continued. Locally the demonstrators were widely supported: Adur District Council (Lib/Dem controlled) and Hove Borough Council (Labour/Independent) who had minority interests in the port, were both opposed to the trade as was Brighton's Labour-controlled council. Further, one of Brighton's MPs, the Conservative Sir Andrew Bowden, was an animal rights campaigner and, with the usual disclaimers about violence, he gave the campaign his full support.[34] Perhaps most importantly so did the daily evening paper the *Evening Argus* not, it should be said, a paper famous for its liberal politics. It is interesting this was also the case at Brightlingsea in Essex, at least initially, where the Colchester *Evening Gazette* ran a series of articles under the headline 'Cargo of Shame'.[35]

What was striking from the start of the mass campaigns in Shoreham and also Brightlingsea was the nature of those protesting. From very early on in both cases the local and national press stressed that these were 'new' protesters, even given the changing nature of public campaigns during the late 1980s and early 1990s. On 8 January *The Times*, which was studiously opposed to the protests, wrote: 'A former fashion model turned animal rights activist stands beside a former Tory councillor. Nearby, a dreadlocked hippie yells abuse next to a well-dressed woman antiques dealer.'[36] Other reports stressed the differences of those involved, but increasingly stressed the 'middle-class' and 'normal' appearance and status of most of protesters. On 7 January the *Guardian* noted 'a middle aged language teacher' and his daughter, a woman accountant and a nurse.[37] Later in the month the Brighton *Evening Argus* wrote:[38]

> It was the last place you would expect to see a rebellion against authority. But Shoreham Port became the venue for a particularly middle-class protest. The last eighteen days have seen pensioners with walking sticks standing alongside mums with toddlers playing on the pavement beside hardened campaigners.

The Colchester *Evening Gazette* produced similar lists, although here 'residents' were stressed along with pensioners, 'young mums', the 'wife and daughter' of a magistrate, and a Churchwarden.[39] The middle-class nature of the protest became a watchword of the subsequent analysis, whether pompously sarcastic as from

Plate 19 Brightlingsea, February 1995. In the short term at least, the blockades of Brightlingsea in Essex and Shoreham in Sussex were some of the most successful of any animal welfare protests. In the longer term, they were part of the growing alienation between the urban middle class and the farming community caused by modern farming practices.

Margot Norman in *The Times* on 16 January[40] or metropolitan patronising as from Peter Hillmore in the *Observer*.[41] This view was also picked up in the 'weeklies'.

At the height of the Shoreham and Brightlingsea demonstrations, in February 1995, I sent out a 'directive' through Mass-Observation on changes in country life and included a question about live-animal exports. The responses to this directive show just how widespread and emotional support for the campaign was among the largely middle-aged and middle respondents to M-O. A retired policeman from Brighton wrote, 'I have the greatest admiration for those brave souls who protest at the export of live animals, making me wish I had their courage.'[42] At least in part this support came from the recognition that those who were protesting were like 'them' – ordinary, middle-class and even middle-aged: 'It's amazing seeing middle-class women more or less creating an affray', wrote a 61-year-old woman from Sheffield.[43] A librarian from Watford was 'so proud of the ordinary people, who have taken part in the protests,'[44] while a secretary from Warwick went further.[45]

> What has made an impression on me is that so many ordinary people of all ages, from all professions and even now different religious denominations have spoken out and physically demonstrated against this trade.

Or a 74-year-old man from Peacehaven, 'this looks like a new form of protests, elderly people getting angry, there's go in the old ones yet and there is [sic] a lot of them. Watch this in future.'[46] Some made a link between Britishness and protest, like this classroom assistant from Lancing in Sussex: 'I am proud of the British – not the bomb brigade, but the steady protesters, standing out in the rain and risking their health and possible injury.'

In general terms the response of the M-O group, of the campaign leading up to the ferry ban and the subsequent demonstrations, does suggest that in the short term the groups involved made a very successful job of mobilising middle-class opinion both as consumers and as protesters. This was given the ultimate compliment in the editorial of *Farmers Weekly* on 13 January 1995. Under the headline, 'No longer enough to defend veal exports from legal position' the editorial concluded:[47]

> Meanwhile, now is the time for farmers and those who claim to represent them to add their voices to what has become a one-sided debate. Defending livestock exports – simply on the basis that it is a legal trade – is no longer sufficient. Farmers, animal welfarists and, indeed, consumers need and deserve more positive guidance.

This was a sharp contrast to the anodyne defence of the trade over a period of years.

In contrast to these arguments it is clear that many of those who took part in the demonstrations took animal rights arguments on board. The attitudes of those involved at Shoreham, even the 'moderates', as expressed in their writing and in press comment do appear to show a recognition of arguments about the 'nature' of animals. Similarly this group, or part of it, was willing to carry on the campaign even in the face of defeat, which came in the summer of 1995.

More serious in some ways were the attitudes towards farmers and farming revealed by the demonstrations. A large part of the M-O group, though still probably a minority, said that the whole issue had affected their attitudes to farming and the countryside. Farmers were often seen as heartless and driven by profit, 'farmers only see animals as objects which provide an income – they don't see them as having feelings' wrote a woman from Preston with an awareness of some of the animal rights issues.[48] Nor did the free enterprise pirates help. A retired typesetter wrote from Surrey:[49]

> The main item, which maddened me about this, was the clever dicks who tried to make a fast buck when the legitimate ferries and road haulers [sic] refused to transport the animals. Their only concern was their pockets and it was sickening to see some of them quoting their rights and saying they were not breaking any laws.

Most central was the evidence from this group in relation to general changes in the environment, which were discussed earlier. This is clearer in answer to other questions on the directive but it was also explicitly linked by many to live animal exports.

However, in the short term the 'farmers' won. Live exports were revived, although not on passenger ferries, and all the breast-beating was forgotten. But it was a hollow victory. The campaign against live animal exports seriously questioned the nature of English farming in a public and emotional way that dominated the press for many weeks – and worse was to come.

Until March 1996 Bovine Spongiform Encephalopathy (BSE or 'Mad Cow Disease') was a problem largely contained within the farming community, although the tragic pictures of animals suffering from the disease and their subsequent destruction regularly made second feature on the television news both locally and nationally. BSE was first diagnosed in cattle in 1984. It now seems likely the disease originated in the 1970s in a single cow which 'developed a mutation of the prion gene that turned the protein products of that cow into the BSE agent.'[50] The first case identified was in Sussex in December 1984. However, how the disease spread is in a way more important. As the Phillips Report, published in October 2000, said, the BSE epidemic was 'a consequence of an intensive farming practice – the recycling of animal protein in ruminant feed. This practice, unchallenged over decades, proved a recipe for disaster.'[51] However, it was 2 years before the source was recognised, the use of sheep and cattle remains as food for sheep and cattle banned, and the slaughter of infected cattle begun. Even with the ban in place there were problems.[52]

> Ignorance about the scale of infection and the amount of material needed to transmit the disease led to thousands of animals being infected after the ban. The feed trade was given a period of grace of five weeks to clear their stocks. 'Some members of the feed trade being given an inch, felt free to take a yard and continued to clear stocks after the ban came into force.'

Alongside the ban the Government introduced, in August 1988, a slaughter policy for all infected cattle which was one of the interim recommendations of the Southwood Committee, which had been set up in April 1988 to assess the significance of BSE. In November 1989 a ban was introduced on the use of cattle offals in human food.

By July 1997, when the outbreak was virtually over, 170,000 cases of BSE had been discovered in the national herd. However, as many as 1 million cattle had probably been infected:[53]

> with the majority being slaughtered before becoming visibly sick. . . .
> Roughly one half of these infected animals will have entered the human food

chain before the specified bovine offal ban was put in place at the end of 1989.

For the farming community, in the early stage at least, the central facts were personal loss and compensation, which was agreed in July 1988, but, to the public at large, there was the much more central problem of infected food. Although there was no hard evidence that BSE could pass to humans, at least until the mid-1990s, the 'common sense' view was that a disease that killed cattle so unpleasantly 'must' somehow infect the meat and milk those cattle produced, especially since the disease took some 5 years to incubate.[54] As the number of cases continued to grow rapidly in the early 1990s these concerns grew and became a regular, if intermittent, news item in the print and broadcast media.

Throughout this period, mainstream scientific opinion, the farming lobby and the Government continued to insist that there was no danger of the disease passing from animals to humans. In February 1989 the Southwood Committee reported its central findings that 'from present evidence . . . that BSE will not have any implications for human health'. A government that was increasingly nervous about public reaction to 'the beef crisis' trumpeted these findings. However, what was less widely reported was the next sentence. 'Nevertheless, if our assessments of these likelihoods are incorrect, the implications would be extremely serious.'[55] There had been even earlier warnings. In December 1986 Ray Bradley, head of pathology at the Central Veterinary Laboratory, wrote to senior civil servants:[56]

If the disease turned out to be bovine scrapie [which it of course did] it would have severe repercussions for the export trade in cattle and possibly for humans, for example, humans with spongiform encephalopathies had close association with cattle. . . . It is for this reason I have classified this document confidential.

Bradley's warnings were not lost on the Government. As Kevin Toolis wrote in the *Guardian Weekend* in 2001:[57]

Bradley's memo set the tone for the Government's official response for the next decade as civil servants and ministers waged a propaganda war to convince themselves and an increasingly sceptical population that British beef was safe to eat.

And, one might add, safe to export.

The central problem was that by 1990 other scientific voices were beginning to argue that British beef was unsafe to eat. Most famous, or initially infamous, was Professor Richard Lacey from the University of Leeds. In 1990

Plate 20 'It is quite clear to me that our beef is safe. My own family eats beef and I have no worry about that.' An image few that saw it will ever forget. John Gummer, Minister of Agriculture demonstrates his confidence in British beef. The photo was taken before any link had been 'proved' between BSE and vCJD as part of the Government's campaign to discredit those scientists who were arguing for such a link.

Lacey predicted that BSE would spread to humans and argued that 6 million cattle should be slaughtered to halt the spread of the disease. He was vilified in Parliament, where his attackers were protected by parliamentary privilege, his house was covered in slogans by farmers, and the Government dismissed him as a left-wing loony with a political axe to grind.[58] Lacey was a high-profile figure who had some public clout; nevertheless, his professional reputation was severely damaged in the short-term at least. Other less senior figures risked more. Harash Narang working in the Public Health Laboratory in Newcastle was a world expert in the field of spongiform encephalopathies. In 1988 he began to believe that BSE could be transmitted to humans. His research support was withdrawn since he refused to accept MAFF controls despite the fact that he appeared to have developed a test to detect BSE. He was made redundant in 1994. Dr Stephen Dealler, who had been working on the relationship between BSE and humans since 1988, wrote to the Government committee set up to survey the progress of BSE (SEAC) in 1993 that eating the meat of infected cattle posed 'a risk to humans' that was 'unacceptably high'. His warning was ignored.[59]

Despite attacks from government and 'scientific' opinion both the tabloid and broadsheet press picked up on these stories, leading to more or less complacent or bizarre reactions from the Government. The most famous of these was the 'forced feeding', with a hamburger, of his daughter Cordelia, by John Gummer, then Minister of Agriculture, at an agricultural show in Suffolk in May 1990. The gesture was supposed to show his public confidence in beef – in fact, it made him a laughing stock. As Minister of Agriculture Gummer had fronted the attack on the growing body of opinion that linked BSE and human disease. In January 1990, for instance, he said: 'It is quite clear to me our beef is safe. My own family eats beef and I have no worry about that. There is no evidence anywhere in the world of BSE passing from animals to humans.' His successor Douglas Hogg took exactly the same position.[60] They found vocal and public support from the Prime Minister John Major who said in December 1995: 'There is currently no scientific evidence that BSE can be transmitted to humans. . . . I am advised that beef is a safe and wholesome product.'[61]

By December 1995 speeches like that took on an increasing Canute-like quality for the simple reason that a new human form of spongiform encephalopathies, new variant Creutzfeldt-Jakob Disease (vCJD) had been identified and was being increasingly linked to BSE. It had also claimed its first known victim, Stephen Churchill aged 19, in May 1995. It was increasingly clear that the public simply no longer trusted the Government and its scientists. Beef consumption in Britain and exports to continental Europe fell from the mid-1980s; despite periods of recovery by 1995 beef produced on British farms had fallen from 1,200,000 tonnes per annum to 900,000.[62] In the last months of 1995 a number of British education authorities removed beef from the school dinner table. By December 1995, at the time of Major and Hogg's reassuring speeches, one school in five had stopped serving beef, 'following concerns from parents'.[63]

According to the Phillips Report in January and February 1996 the scientists of SEAC were finally convinced that there was a link between vCJD and BSE, but the civil servants on the committee still seem to have failed to inform the Government. This was finally done in March and on 20 March 1996 the Government announced that there were now 10 patients whose average age was 27, suffering from vCJD and that there was a probable link between vCJD and exposure to BSE infected meat. The reaction over the next week was to all but destroy confidence in British farming, and beef in particular, and to seriously undermine the Tory Party.

Within a week the EU had imposed a worldwide ban on the export of British beef, but it was at home that the problem took on its most spectacular dimensions. The press from the broadsheets to the tabloids went into free fall on the issue. Figures like Richard Lacey who only weeks before had been vilified now became almost folk heroes. The *Sun* offered its readers tokens to collect for a beef-free British breakfast, while its political editor, Trevor Kavanagh warned that BSE could 'wipe out the Tories'.[64] Even the *Observer* speculated on the Sunday following the announcement with a doomsday scenario that saw the Channel tunnel closed by the French, the health service in crisis as a result of 2 million patients suffering from vCJD and 'the fabric of the nation torn apart'.[65] Public reaction to the announcement was also spectacular. Within days of the announcement all the major supermarket chains announced that beef sales had fallen dramatically and by Saturday 23 March most had reduced beef prices by 50 per cent, but were still unable to sell their stock. More significantly all also announced they were seeking other sources for beef.[66] By the middle of the following week beef sales had fallen by over a third. Most spectacular, in publicity terms at least, was the announcement over the weekend of 23–24 March by McDonald's and Burger King that they were withdrawing all hamburgers made from British beef. Then, on Thursday 28 March McDonald's placed full page ads in all national British papers to announce that from that day onwards all their beef products were made from 'new supplies of non-British beef which come only from established McDonald's suppliers'.[67]

Initially, the Government did little, clearly hoping that the EU ban would quickly be lifted. The ban also provoked the usual anti-EU statements from sections of the Conservative Party, and even after the announcement of the link to vCJD the Government attempted to play down the crisis. However, despite the Government's attempts in May 1996 to force the EU to end the ban by refusing to co-operate with 'normal' EU business, it remained in force for another 2 years.[68] The French maintained their 'illegal' ban until September 2001.

The cost to British farming was huge. By the time the EU beef ban was lifted in November 1998 more than 4 million cattle had been slaughtered. But the costs were much higher than that. When the Phillips Report was published the *Guardian* estimated that the total costs of the epidemic, including compensation, lost exports and estimates of medical costs for known victims was in the region of £6 billion.[69] But the losses incurred by farming were not simply matters of livestock. Although precise figures are difficult to come by it is clear that the large drop in the number of both dairy and beef producing units in the 1990s had a great deal to do with BSE. Even where farmers kept going, the costs, especially to smaller units, was huge. A 220-acre farm in Devon with both beef and dairy cattle, which had been affected by BSE, saw profits fall from about £20,000 to about £7,600 in the 3 years from 1996–9.[70]

This long-term fall in profits was not only due to BSE but was indicative of growing consumer doubts about a whole range of farm products. By the late 1990s the humanitarian critique of farming methods had come together with BSE to effect what seems to be a shift in consumer attitudes to food. The number of people who described themselves as vegetarians has increased enormously in the

1990s. As with the ecological movement in general the growth of modern vegetarianism was closely associated with the counter culture of the 1960s. Cranks,
the first of London's new vegetarian restaurants opened near Carnaby Street by
David and Kay Cantor the in 1960s, laid the foundations of what was to become a
familiar nationwide cuisine and style of eating in the 1970s and 1980s:[71]

> Supplies were as pure as possible – free-range eggs, organically grown fruit
> and vegetables, Losely yoghurts and ice creams. It was also important to the
> Cantors that the restaurant's furniture, fittings and utensils should be made
> from natural materials. There were pine tables and pottery. . . . Cranks set
> the style for the next three decades of vegetarianism – hominy pie, celery,
> nut and carrot salad and courgette and cheese wedges eaten to a background
> of Bach and Vivaldi.

Vegetarian food was also closely associated with youth. The Brighton based Infin-
ity Wholefoods, now a considerable wholesaler of organic and vegetarian foodstuffs, was begun by a student from Sussex University and her partner who found
themselves catering for the first Glastonbury Festival.[72] However, as this generation grew older it seems not to have abandoned its vegetarianism along with its
long hair and loon pants. The concerns about animal welfare generated by factory
farming and issues like the live export of farm animals fed into increasing worries
about the quality of food and especially meat, and led to ever larger numbers
becoming vegetarians. By 2000 the Vegetarian Society estimated that there were
3.5. million vegetarians in the United Kingdom.

Alongside this, although initially at a much slower rate, organic farming continued to move from the cranky minority to the mainstream. The demand for
organic produce quadrupled between 1990 and 1995–6, with the largest
increases coming after the confirmation of the link between BSE and vCJD.[73] As
John Humphries has written, this had a fundamental and apparently continuing
effect on the diet of England and Wales.[74]

> Nothing sounds louder to the ear of a supermarket executive than a cus-
> tomer's threat to take her [sic] business to a competitor. Now the sound of
> customers demanding organic food was becoming deafening. All those
> supermarkets, which had so recently scorned the idea of the so-called beard-
> and-sandal brigade, were suddenly fighting each other for every organic
> carrot and tomato they could lay their hands on.

By 2000 Sainsbury's and Waitrose were stocking close to a thousand organic lines
and Tesco and ASDA were catching up fast. In the same year sales of organic
produce were worth £605 million, an increase of over £400 million since 1996.
In the last 2 years of the twentieth century the percentage of families buying

some organic produce rose from 37 per cent to 67 per cent. By 2001 the Soil Association, the 'purest' of the British organic farming organisations, had about 30,000 members and supporters compared with the handful that founded the association immediately after the war.

The impact of this on British farming remains small. In 2001 less than 0.5 per cent of land was farmed organically despite the Organic Aid Scheme introduced in 1995 to help conversion to organic farming, and a growth of 72 per cent in the organic area between 1998–2000. As a result of the very small area farmed by organic methods 70 per cent of organic food is currently imported, a figure which seems set to remain the same in the foreseeable future.[75] Nevertheless organic farming has gradually become accepted by at least some sections of the farming community, and indeed both the Countryside Agency and DEFRA accept that it has a central contribution to make to the future of English and Welsh farming.[76]

However, in the years after 1995–6 the fortunes of farming and indeed of rural areas suffered reverse after reverse. BSE and the European ban had reverberations far outside beef production, while the huge short-term profits made by the first set aside payments and the value of the green pound, were destroyed by strong sterling. Then the cereal shortages of the mid-1990s disappeared in the second half of the decade returning Europe to the position of a surplus producer. Continued distrust of British livestock seems to have led to the collapse of the lucrative export of lamb as well as veal which had caused so much difficulty in the mid-1990s, while exports of British beef have effectively vanished. As a result total income from farming fell from a peak of around about £6 billion per annum in 1995–6 to £1.8 billion in 2000. In the same period farming's contribution to the UK national income fell to below 1 per cent. However, as the Countryside Agency reported in 2001, 'public expenditure on agriculture has continued to exceed the industries contribution (to national income)', a public support which, according to an anonymous MAFF spokesman in 2001, was costing every British family £4 per week.[77]

In this crisis the general (and overwhelmingly urban) public had little sympathy for the farming community. The destruction of the landscape, live animal exports, BSE and countless other food scares, were laid at farming's door, while the intransigence of many industry spokesmen in the face of criticism often made the farmers and landowners their own worst enemies. Even in the late 1990s continued subsidies bolstered the idea of 'fat cat' farmers despite the growing plight of a section of the industry, especially the hill farmers of England and Wales. In this situation the industry and the countryside began to fight back in the battle for public support.

In November 1995 Sir David Steel, former leader of the Liberal Party, announced the foundation of a new rural pressure group, the Countryside Movement. The movement's charter made its objects clear enough. According to *The*

Times, its aims were 'to protect country life from its detractors and to promote good practice in all aspects of countryside management'.[78] However, *Farmers Weekly* stressed rather different aspects.[79]

> The charter says country people need a Countryside Movement because their way of life is now under siege. Opponents of country ways and values take issue with all aspects of the countryside's management of animals including live animal transport, hunting, livestock husbandry, shooting, fishing and national hunt racing.

The notion that the countryside was 'under siege' from an essentially antagonistic urban world which did not 'understand' country life was not a new one. However, it began to take on new force as it became clear in the mid-1990s that the election of a Labour government, which was seen by many in rural organisations as anti-countryside, was increasingly likely. This enabled the Countryside Movement to draw on a range of wealthy private and industry backers. The first advertising campaign for the movement for instance cost £3.5 million, while a reported unsecured loan of £1 million by the Duke of Westminster helped it through a difficult patch. The cynical might suggest such sums might well have been better used in many of the declining rural communities that the movement claimed to defend.

Yet, it cannot be denied that, in some respects, the Countryside Movement was able to articulate a wide agenda concerned with rural problems as diverse as the collapse of hill farming, the decline of rural services, and the issue of 'incomers', as well as the defence of field sports. Additionally its policy of no subscriptions and no fees helped build up a supporter base of about 100,000 by 1997. Whether these were 'country people' or even more the 'indigenous country folk' so beloved by Countryside Movement propaganda is more of a problem. Although there may have been farm workers in the movement, and some were certainly present on the two great demonstrations in 1997 and 1998, their organisations have strongly resisted any links with the Countryside Movement or its successor the Countryside Alliance. Even more of a problem was the fact that a MORI poll carried out on the 1998 Countryside March showed that 'barely half those who travelled to London claimed to live "in the middle of the countryside".' Of the remainder 22 per cent said they lived 'on the edge' while 5 per cent lived 'in the suburbs'.[80] All this is neatly summed up by a Range Rover seen parked in London's Pimlico soon after the 1998 march with a sticker in the rear window urging all and sundry to 'Resist the urban jackboot', while in the front window was a City of Westminster resident's parking permit.

Nor did some of the corporate sponsors give much credence to the movement's claim to speak for all the inhabitants of the countryside. Holland and Holland, the London gun makers, played a key role in the early days of the movement, while as Nick Cohen pointed out in the *Observer* in October 2000 Britain's biggest builders, Robert McAlpine, Sunley Holdings and Persimmon Homes, all of whom were seeking an end to 'restrictive' building controls in rural areas, were among its biggest supporters.[81]

At the end of 1996 the Countryside Movement was in difficulties. Despite its backers and its membership, its hoped for massive impact and support seemed to be vanishing. With the threat of a Labour electoral victory now all too real, in March 1997 the essentially defunct movement joined with The British Field Sports Society and the Countryside Business Group to form the Countryside Alliance. The Alliance's agenda, while remaining publicly the same, was clearly much more directed at the defence of field sports, and especially hunting with dogs, which seemed likely to come under attack either from a Labour government or from a private member's bill which would get massive support in a Labour dominated House of Commons. These fears were realised when in June 1997 Michael Foster, the new Labour MP for Worcester City, used his first place in the ballot for private member's bills to promote a bill to ban hunting with dogs.

This gave the first 'Countryside March', organised in London on 10 July 1997 a particular urgency. Its impact was enormous. Over 100,000 supporters marched in London to almost universal support. Despite the fact that the majority of the British population were opposed to hunting with dogs in 1997, as they continue to be, a sense of a general crisis in the countryside overrode the issue. Even the *Guardian*'s Environment Editor, John Vidal, who had a long history of critical journalism on country problems was impressed.[82]

> Among (the marchers) will be thousands who depend completely on field sports and who rightly feel threatened. . . . Joining them will be weekenders, pony riders, hill and cereal farmers, country sportsmen and a rag bag of romantics and people who feel that they, too, want a say in how they live today. . . . The great majority will be ill-paid and penalised in terms of education, welfare and housing services. . . . Underpinning the rally is a genuine sense of resentment and betrayal of the countryside by policymakers, and a sense that there is a nasty streak of moralising intolerance abroad in the new establishment.

Vidal's views were clearly shared by the new established of New Labour, or least the Alliance raised sufficient worries about the newly important middle-class and rural vote, which had been central to the electoral landslide of 1997. Suddenly government was concerned about the countryside and even backtracked on fox hunting by refusing the Foster Bill sufficient parliamentary time and eventually appointing the Burns Committee to look at the whole question of hunting with dogs.

The second Countryside March, in March 1998, although it preceded the collapse of the Forster Bill and caused what the *Daily Telegraph* called 'a radical shift in the Government's approach to rural issues'[83] seems in retrospect to have been less successful, certainly with liberal opinion. Although it attracted over 250,000 people its aggressive pro-hunting stance and its fatuous 'Resist the urban jackboot' slogan, with its tasteless attempt to link the problems of the horsy community (it came from *Horse and Hound*) to the dire state of Britain fighting fascism, alienated many potential supporters in urban areas. Further the same MORI poll, which showed that a substantial minority of the marchers had little contact with the countryside, also showed that 79 per cent of those on the march were Conservative voters, thus confirming what many had thought all along.

Despite continued support in the rural areas, and a number of spectacular demonstrations, including one at the Labour Party Conference of 1999, the claim by Alliance supporters that they have changed the direction of the Government rings increasingly hollow. Blair's much vaunted turn to the countryside in February 2000 seemed more concerned with winning a non-agricultural vote in the country districts than making concessions to the farming community. In a speech to the NFU conference in the same month he offered little more than the same message on the need to diversify which the farming community had listened to, and sometimes heeded, for the previous decade.[84]

Further, the involvement of Alliance members in the fuel protests of the autumn of 2000 led many to share the view of Nick Cohen who, writing in the *Observer* in the aftermath of the crisis, said:[85]

> The Alliance's fight to save hunting is no longer being waged with vaguely rational arguments. Enter its collective mind and you are in a war of national liberation against an alien and depraved dictatorship.

Interestingly the Government White Paper on the rural areas, *Our Countryside: the future*, of 2000 makes only one mention of hunting where it says: 'The Government is to bring before Parliament, for a free vote, proposals on a range of options for the future of hunting with dogs.'[86] The anti-blood sports lobby may see this as backtracking, and in a sense it is, but the same document gives seven pages to questions of access to the countryside.

Whatever plans the Government had for the rural areas it was clear they were increasingly shaped by consumers – either of food or of the countryside – rather than agriculture. The long flagged 'end' to the Ministry of Agriculture, for years seen as simply a farmers' poodle, and its replacement with the Department of Environment, Food and Rural Affairs was one indication of this, although it had to wait until another Labour victory in 2001 to come true. By then the game had changed again and, perhaps, forever.

Foot-and-mouth disease has a long history. It was first recorded in 1839 although it certainly existed before that date. There were major outbreaks in Britain 1870–1 and 1878–84. In 1892 a policy of compulsory slaughter of infected and possibly infected animals was introduced which reduced the incidence of the disease until another major outbreak in 1922. From the 1920s to the 1950s the disease appeared to be endemic rather than epidemic with an average of 129 cases a year. However, between the mid-1950s and the outbreak in 1967–8 there were very few cases and, disastrous as the latter outbreak was, with 2,364 cases and the slaughter of almost 434,000 animals, the slaughter policy seemed to have worked and left the national herd more or less free of the disease.[87]

For that reason the most recent outbreak of foot-and-mouth disease came as a surprise. As the report by Dr Ian Anderson published in July 2002 put it, 'the outbreak of FMD was unexpected. Neither MAFF nor the farming industry was prepared for an outbreak on a large scale.'[88] However, although it was seen, from the start, unlike BSE, as a potential disaster, it was wrongly believed to be a disaster which, on the basis of past experience, could be controlled. It was argued that, although the disease is highly contagious, the policy of sealing off infected farms, and slaughtering all animals which could have come into contact with the disease had controlled and then eradicated it in the past, therefore there was no reason to suppose that this outbreak would be any different. Even the worst case scenario would involve only slaughter and exclusion zones around farms where infection was present. After a time, as in 1967, the disease would be wiped out.

The disease was first detected among pigs at an abattoir belonging to Cheale Meats at Little Warley in Essex on Monday 20 February 2001 and was confirmed by MAFF the following Wednesday. An immediate ban on livestock exports was imposed and MAFF began the work of tracing the origins of the pigs, sealing off suspected farms and slaughtering possible infected stock.[89] It is now clear that this approach, supported by all the major farming organisations as well as MAFF, had serious problems, which only became clear as the outbreak developed. Worse still, as Anderson points out, by that date the disease was 'widespread . . . throughout the country'.[90] Three further problems seem to have emerged. First, the size of individual herds had increased enormously since 1967, which meant that when one animal was infected it put many more at risk. This is borne out by a paper published in the journal *Nature* in October 2001 which shows that 'smaller farms [were] substantially less infectious and less susceptible to infection than larger ones.'[91] Second, it quickly spread into the sheep flock, which meant that a majority of animals had not been on infected premises and were therefore much more difficult to trace. The spread to sheep also caused problems since the majority of sheep graze on open moorland making control virtually impossible. Finally, it is claimed that changes in farming practice contributed to the outbreak. This claim is based on the practice of moving animals from market to market, region to region and abattoir to abattoir, to take advantage of specialist demands for particular kinds of meat but, more importantly, variations in regional prices and fluctuating demand. It seems likely that it was some version of this practice that caused the initial spread of the disease from an animal holding centre in Northumberland, where pigs were brought from a number of farms over a very wide area, to the abattoir in Essex. It was also a key element in the later spread of the disease, as the October 2001 paper in *Nature* says: 'Most transmission probably occurred through the movement of animals, personnel or vehicles, rather than through animal contact or windborne spread.'[92]

MAFF and the Government quickly recognised this and a 'temporary' 7-day ban on the movement of animals and the closure of all cattle markets was imposed on Friday 24 February. At this stage, however, all those involved were optimistic that the outbreak could be brought under control; Nick Brown, the Minister of Agriculture, suggested this was a short-term 'inconvenience' which would enable vets and MAFF 'to isolate and extinguish these outbreaks and get back to normal as quickly as possible'.[93] This optimism was hopelessly misplaced. By the following week the disease had spread to the West Country. As in the case of Essex it had been spread as the result of long-distance movement of animals, from one dealer to another.[94] As the Anderson Report says:[95]

> The first responses to the early cases were not fast enough or effectively coordinated . . . knowledge within government of some changes in farming practices was limited. In particular, the nature and extent of sheep movements which contributed to the wide dispersal of the disease before its identification had not been fully recognised.

In the next few weeks the disease spread over much of upland England and Wales. No one who spent any time in those areas in the black spring of 2001, even if they had nothing to do with farming, will ever forget it. Driving across the A66 and then up through the Lakes to Glasgow on the weekend before Easter there were burning pyres every couple of miles. Near Appleby the air stank of burning. At that point John Vidal's comparison of foot-and-mouth with the Black Death seemed all too real.[96] To those who lived on, and worked the land it was inconceivably worse, especially since those who suffered most were not the great sheep dealers and traders, but the tiny family farmers of upland Britain, who had already borne the brunt of the farming crisis. To them their sheep or their cattle were what remained of a livelihood. To many, if not most, they were also the result of years of work, pride and love of the land. The loss of their flocks was a final blow in what seemed like an unequal fight against an uncaring and non-understanding urban world. That world owes them something.

The slaughter policy, bio-security measures (use of disinfectant on clothing, boots and vehicles and the transport) slowed the spread of the disease. However, they 'were insufficient to reverse it, largely owing to long delays between the

Plate 21 'The Black Death'. Foot-and-mouth, which devastated British upland agriculture in the spring and summer of 2002 following, as it did, on from BSE, was an economic disaster for hill farming in particular. Perhaps equally importantly, it symbolically marked the end of rural England for a generation.

reports of possible FMD, confirmation of infection, and culling of animals on the infected farm.'[97] At the end of March the use of the army and culling of animals on infected farms and those adjoining, without waiting for laboratory confirmation began to slow the spread of the disease, as did the practice in severely affected areas like Cumbria, Dumfries and Galloway of culling sheep within 3 km of an infected farm. By 19 September 2001 these policies had resulted in the culling of some 3.88 million animals.[98] However, aspects of this policy were increasingly unpopular inside and outside the farming community. Much of this criticism arose from the culling of uninfected animals along with the refusal by MAFF (supported by the NFU) to create a disease free zone by ring vaccination.

However, the work of Ferguson and the Anderson Report suggests that the slowness of culling both of infected and contiguous farms helped the spread of the disease, especially in Cumbria and Devon. Indeed, they suggest that had culling moved more quickly in these areas the number of cases could have been reduced by 60 per cent and as a result 45 per cent fewer farms would have to have been culled.[99] This would suggest that the culling of uninfected animals was necessary and the main problem was that it was not done fast enough, both through lack of people to carry out the cull and, in some cases, active opposition from the owners of uninfected animals.

The question of vaccination is more difficult. Vaccination has been available as an option since at least the 1900s and was considered by three of the four government reports on foot-and-mouth published in the twentieth century. Indeed both the Gowers Committee of 1954 and the Northumberland Committee of 1969 felt ring vaccination should be at least planned for in the case of serious outbreaks. From early on in the outbreak animal welfare organisations and some, especially small farmers, argued for vaccination as opposed to slaughter. The opposition was based both on humanitarian and economic grounds. To animal welfare groups the slaughter policy was seen as inflicting unnecessary suffering on animals, while to the small farmer whose flock was uninfected vaccination seemed much preferable to the destruction of a life's work.

On the other side stood most of the scientific establishment, MAFF and the NFU.[100] The arguments against vaccination were, and are, complex, but in the end come down to economics. Foot-and-mouth does not kill animals, unless they are already weak, nor can it be passed to humans, but it does reduce the body weight of infected stock and their productivity thus making them less economic. In a period of narrow profit margins this was seen as crucial. Nor does vaccination eradicate the disease but needs to be repeated about every 6 months – a potentially costly operation. But the biggest problem was one of exports. Since the 1980s Britain had been a foot-and-mouth free zone. Vaccination would remove that status. As Stephen Rossides of the NFU told the *Observer*: 'If you don't slaughter you won't be able to export. Once you vaccinate, you lose your disease-free status. Which has a severe economic impact.'[101] At present, as with so much of modern history, the jury is still out, although as the tail of the disease has dragged on, and the real costs of foot-and-mouth become clear, more and more scientific opinion seems to be moving towards an argument in favour of vaccination. The Anderson Committee reporting in the summer of 2002 supported this view, and this in turn was backed by Margaret Beckett, the Secretary of State for Environment, Food and Rural Affairs in the House of Commons on 22 June 2002.[102]

As the outbreak spread its effects became apparent well outside agriculture. Indeed foot-and-mouth revealed just how 'non-agricultural' rural England had become. Within days of the first outbreak footpaths were closed all over England and Wales, even in areas like the South Downs, which were far away from any outbreaks. They were to remain closed in many areas throughout the summer and autumn. The Anderson Report recognised this as a real problem.[103]

> Although supported by many at the time, with the benefit of hindsight, the widespread closure of footpaths, with no straightforward mechanism for reopening them, was a mistake.

This had a severe effect on rural England's tourist industry. National figures produced in March 2001 by the *Guardian* showed just how serious the situation was. Nationally agriculture generated about 1.5 per cent of Gross Domestic Product, while tourism accounted for about 4 per cent. Rural tourism was worth an estimated £12 billion per annum while livestock farming was worth about £4 billion. In the rural areas only 2 per cent of the population worked in agriculture while 21 per cent worked in leisure and distribution. By March 2001 the English Tourist Council estimated that the tourist trade was losing £250 million a week while farming was losing only £60 million. Regionally, the picture was much worse. Devon, Cumbria and Wales, as well as being some of the worst hit foot-and-mouth areas, were also major tourist centres. In Cumbria alone businesses catering to the tourist trade were losing £8 million and 350 jobs a week.[104] In Wales it was estimated that losses were running at £10 million a week at the end of March and were expected to double over the Easter period.[105]

Drawing up the balance sheet of the foot-and-mouth epidemic of 2001 moved far outside the simple apportioning of blame and the working out of costs. The Anderson Report was rightly critical of the handling of the crisis, especially in its early days, and of the behaviour of Nick Brown, then Minister of Agriculture.[106] The costs were huge, something in the region of £8 billion, but compensation still remained a vexed issue over a year after the outbreak had 'ended'.[107]

> Different sectors of the economy were affected in very different ways. Farmers were compensated for animals that were culled for disease control purposes and for welfare reasons. Rural and tourist businesses however received very little recompense. Farmers whose stock was not culled, but who were subject to strict movement controls, received no compensation at all.

However the most spectacular and lasting effects of foot-and-mouth were felt far outside the farming sector and even within farming well beyond the problems of the disease. As the outbreak worsened, the Prime Minister, Tony Blair, decided to cancel the General Election, which had been planned for 3 May in view of the crisis in farming. However, long before that date, in early March, Blair had made a speech on the environment, which drew potentially distressing lessons for agriculture. The CAP, which had been seen as a major defender of British farming by the NFU in the mid-1990s, was 'seriously outmoded. It distorts global agricultural markets and promotes forms of agriculture that damage the environment.' In the following weeks Nick Brown, the Minister of Agriculture, who argued that BSE and foot-and-mouth showed that farming in general was in need of reform, took some of Blair's points up.[108]

These were not of course new themes but they seemed to take on a new urgency at the height of the foot-and-mouth crisis. Public opinion seemed to be losing patience with the farmers. Blair's announcement of the change of the election date was welcomed only by the *Sun* (who had got the story as an exclusive) and the *Daily Telegraph*. The *Guardian*, the *Mirror*, the *Independent* and the *Daily Mail* all condemned it and none more forcefully than the *Guardian*, whose coverage of the outbreak had been mainly sympathetic:[109]

... foot-and-mouth, a regional and sectoral problem fundamentally to do with the small-scale economics of pastoral farming, is allowed to preoccupy the whole government as if indeed it were a national and general question.

Foot-and-mouth also reopened the whole question of farming and food. Although agriculture continued to have its supporters, more and more sections of the media were seeing the disease as the final condemnation of modern farming practice and farming greed. By the end of March what Stephen Pollard wrote in the *Independent* was finding echoes in most of the left/liberal press:[110]

As ye sow, so shall ye reap – unless you're a farmer . . . there's even a strong case now being made that foot-and-mouth is the result of illegal pigswill. But you can bet whatever the cause; the farmers will be demanding even more compensation and subsidy.

In the autumn of 2001 a subdued Labour Party Conference heard Margaret Beckett, Secretary of State at the Department of Environment, Food and Rural Affairs, say much the same thing. Only now it was policy:[111]

Like the rest of the rural economy agriculture is subject to enormous pressure for change. The EU is committed to review the CAP from next year. And the wider European public will I believe no longer permit farming simply to carry on as before – let alone pay for it. . . . What society as a whole wants from agriculture is changing and probably changing irrevocably. . . . There is no long-term future for an industry which cannot develop in line with market forces. No matter what the industry, its history, or the wider contribution it makes to society.

Beckett's speech marked the end of a gradual but major shift in the agricultural policy of the post-Second World War era. Despite the warning in the speech that change cannot be postponed 'for another year or five years or ten years' change will take time. In January 2002 a further step was taken with the publication of *Farming and Food*, a policy report produced by Sir Donald Curry.[112] This moved from the assumption that.[113]

The familiar countryside environment – originally a product of farming – is damaged by years of intensive production and the social fabric of the countryside (which depends heavily on farming) is being put at risk.

The recommendations of the report, not surprisingly, echoed much of Beckett's speech the previous September. Central to this it argued for the dismantling of the subsidy system, and the reallocation of some CAP resources towards the 'social' or environmental aspect of agriculture. The way forward was thus clearly marked. Change will probably take a decade, and will be marked by compromise and political dealing as has all agricultural policy in the last 100 years – but it has begun.

It is not only agriculture which faces change but the whole of rural society. Foot-and-mouth exposed not only a deep disquiet with farming which, despite the talk of the NFU, spreads far outside the 'chattering classes', but also the extent to which rural England and Wales are no longer truly an agricultural society. As the *Wall Street Journal* wrote on 20 March 2001:[114]

> This is probably the last time farming can get the British government to shut down the countryside for its own sake. Next time foot-and-mouth arrives the economic weight of farming will be too slight. Tourism . . . will be more valuable to country dwellers.

What we have here is perhaps the final moment in the battle between town and country – and the town appears victorious. Yet it is an odd victory – if a victory at all. The majority of the population of England and Wales either live in the country or want to, but in return they increasingly want to dictate the terms of country life, and if agriculture doesn't like it, Margaret Beckett and a substantial part of the media and public opinion have a ready answer.

Notes

1 The countryside in a new century, 1900–14

1 James Caird, *English Agriculture in 1850–51* (London, 1852).
2 For a more detailed description of the farming division in the mid-nineteenth century see Alun Howkins, *Reshaping Rural England 1850–1925* (London, 1992) Ch. 1.
3 See Christopher Taylor, *Village and Farmstead. A History of Rural Settlement in England* (London, 1983).
4 Peter Brandon and Brian Short, *The South East from AD 1000* (London, 1990) Ch. 6.
5 For a good discussion of these kinds of variations see Susanna Wade-Martins and Tom Williamson, *Roots of Change. Farming and the Landscape in East Anglia, c.1700–1870* (Norwich, 1999) pp. 7–9.
6 *Census of England and Wales 1921. General Report* (London, 1927) p. 23.
7 B.R. Mitchell and Phyllis Deane, *Abstract of British Historical Statistics* (Cambridge, 1971) p. 60.
8 For these changes see Edward Higgs, 'Women, Occupation and Work in the Nineteenth Century Censuses', *HWJ*, No. 23 (Spring 1987), pp. 59–80.
9 See Nicola Verdon, 'Changing Patterns of Female Employment in Rural England c.1790–1890', Unpublished Ph.D. thesis, University of Leicester, 1999; Celia Miller, 'The hidden workforce: female fieldworkers in Gloucestershire, 1870–1901', *Southern History*, 6 (1984).
10 Caird, *English Agriculture*, p. 520.
11 B.A. Holderness, 'The Victorian Farmer', in G.E. Mingay (ed.), *The Victorian Countryside*, 2 vols (London, 1981) Vol. 1 p. 227.
12 Henry Rider Haggard, *Rural England*, 2 vols (London, 1902) Vol. II p. 536.
13 For a good introductory discussion to the depression see Richard Perren, *Agriculture in Depression 1870–1940* (Cambridge, 1995). Also Howkins, *Reshaping*, Ch. 6.
14 P.J. Perry, *British Agriculture, 1875–1914* (London, 1973) p. xxxviii.
15 *PP 1893–94 XXXV*, 'Royal Commission on Labour. The Agricultural Labourer. England. The Report of Mr Aubrey Spencer on the Poor Law Union of Maldon (Essex)', p. 699.
16 Perren, *Agriculture*, p. 10.
17 E.M. Ojala, *Agriculture and Economic Progress* (Oxford, 1952) p. 209.
18 Edith H. Whetham, *The Agrarian History of England and Wales, Vol. VII, 1914–1939* (Cambridge, 1978) p. 8.
19 *PP 1895 XVI*, 'Royal Commission on Agricultural Depression . . . Lincolnshire', p. 105.
20 Joan Thirsk, *Alternative Agriculture. A History from the Black Death to the Present Day* (Oxford, 1997) p. 218.
21 T.W. Fletcher, 'The Great Depression in English Agriculture, 1873–96', *EcHR*, 2nd series, XIII (1961).
22 E. Lorraine Smith, *Go East for a Farm. A Study of Rural Migration* (Oxford, 1932).
23 L. Margaret Barnett, *English Food Policy During the First World War* (Manchester, 1987) p. 3.
24 See Perren, *Agriculture*, pp. 17–30.
25 A.D. Hall, *A Pilgrimage of British Farming* (London, 1913) pp. 431–2.

26 John Batemen, *The Great Landowners of Britain and Ireland* (London, 1883). This is the fourth edition of a work which first appeared in 1876.

27 David Cannadine, *The Decline and Fall of the British Aristocracy* (New Haven and London, 1990) p. 23.

28 *PP 1895 XVII*, 'Royal Commission on Agriculture. England. Report of Mr Henry Rew . . . on the County of Norfolk', p. 42.

29 Richard Olney, *Rural Society and County Government in Nineteenth-Century Lincolnshire* (Lincoln, 1979) p. 179.

30 Oscar Wilde, *The Importance of Being Ernest*, Act 1, in Richard Ellman (ed.), *Oscar Wilde: Selected Writings* (Oxford, 1961) pp. 303–4.

31 F.M.L. Thompson, *English Landed Society in the Nineteenth Century* (London, 1963) p. 310.

32 Cannadine, *Decline and Fall*, p. 10.

33 Olney, *Rural Society*, p. 179.

34 Ibid.

35 Wade-Martins and Williamson, *Roots of Change*, pp. 34–6.

36 Veronica Berry, *The Rolfe Papers. The Chronicle of a Norfolk Family 1559–1908* (Brentwood, 1979) p. 94.

37 David Lloyd George, 'The Land and the People', Limehouse, 30 Jul. 1910, *Better Times* (London, 1910) pp. 156–7.

38 Thompson, *Landed Society*, p. 325.

39 Cannadine, *Decline and Fall*, p. 106.

40 *EG*, 15 Oct. 1909.

41 Ibid. 4 Jan. 1913.

42 For these divisions see Alun Howkins, 'Peasants, Servants and Labourers: The Marginal Workforce in British Agriculture, *c.*1870–1914,' *AHR*, Vol. 42 (1994) pp. 49–62.

43 What follows is based on the report published in 1905: *PP 1905 XCVII*, 'Second Report by Mr Wilson Fox on the Wages, Earnings and Conditions of Employment of Agricultural Labourers in the United Kingdom'.

44 Anne Kussmaul, *Servants in Husbandry in Early Modern England* (Cambridge, 1981) p. 133.

45 See Gary Moses, 'Proletarian Labourers? East Riding farm servants, *c.*1850–75', *AHR*, Vol. 47, Pt 1 (1999) pp. 78–94.

46 *PP 1882 XVI*, 'Royal Commission on Agriculture . . . Report on the Agricultural Conditions of Northumberland', p. 6.

47 NRO T/70, Interview with Bob Hepple, shepherd.

48 NRO T/98, NRO 1208, Interview with Mrs J. Brown, farm worker.

49 Judy Gielguid, 'Nineteenth Century Farm Women in Northumberland and Cumbria. The Neglected Workforce', Unpublished Ph.D. thesis, University of Sussex, 1992.

50 For the East Riding see Stephen Caunce, *Amongst Farm Horses. The Horselads of East Yorkshire* (Gloucester, 1991).

51 See Gary Moses, '"Rustic and Rude": Hiring Fairs and their Critics in East Yorkshire *c.*1850–75,' *RH*, Vol. 7, No. 2 (1996) pp. 151–75; Alun Howkins and Linda Merricks, 'The Ploughboy and the Plough Play', *Folk Music Journal*, Vol. 6, No. 2 (1991) pp. 187–208.

52 *PP 1893–4 XXXVI*, 'Royal Commission on Labour. The Agricultural Labourer . . . Report of Mr D. Lleuffer Thomas . . . upon the Poor Law Union of Pwllhelli', p. 147.

53 Ibid.

54 D.J. Perry, *The Rural Revolt that Failed* (Cardiff, 1989) p. 10.

55 *Alnwick and County Gazette*, 12 Nov. 1904, p. 5.

56 NRO 479, 'Farm Diaries of J.W. and J.C. Rutherford, North Masons Farm, Dinnington'.

57 *FW*, 17 Nov. 1939, p. 18.

58 Stephen Caunce, 'Twentieth-Century farm servants. The horselads of the East Riding of Yorkshire', *AHR*, Vol. 39 (1992).

59 *PP 1905 XCVII*, pp. 360–1.

60 For a detailed discussion of this see Alun Howkins, '"In the sweat of thy face": The Labourer and Work', in G.E. Mingay (ed.), *The Victorian Countryside*, 2 vols (London, 1981) Vol. 1, pp. 506–20.

61 For much of what follows see *PP 1905 XCVII*, pp. 369–72.

62 See Nicola Verdon 'Changing Patterns'.

63 *PP 1904 XCVII*, p. 12.

64 NRO T/63, Interview with Mrs Murray, farmer's daughter.

65 *Kelly's Directory of Norfolk, 1896* (London, 1896) p. 175.

66 E.N. Bennet, *Problems of Village Life* (London, 1913) p. 124.

67 Ibid. p. 122.

68 *Eastern Weekly Leader*, 9 Feb. 1895.

69 James Obelkevich, *Religion and Rural Society. South Lindsey, 1825–1875* (Oxford, 1976) p. 324.

70 Cannadine, *Decline and Fall*, p. 40.

71 J.M. Lee, *Social Leaders and Public Persons. A Study of County Government in Cheshire since 1888* (Oxford, 1963) p. 16.

72 Ibid. pp. 18–22.

73 *EWP*, 2 Feb. 1889.

74 Cannadine, *Decline and Fall*, p. 159.

75 *Eastern Weekly Leader*, 1 Dec. 1894.

76 Patricia Hollis, *Ladies Elect. Women in English Local Government, 1865–1914* (Oxford, 1987) pp. 363–4.

77 Ibid. p. 365.

78 See Henry Pelling, *Social Geography of British Elections 1885–1910* (London, 1967).

79 See Reg Groves, *Sharpen the Sickle!* (London, 1949) pp. 140–1 and Alistair Mutch, 'Lancashire's Revolt of the Field: the Ormskirk Farmworkers' Strike of 1913', *North West Labour History Society Bulletin*, 8, 1982–3.

80 See Alun Howkins, *Poor Labouring Men. Rural Radicalism in Norfolk 1870–1923* (London, 1985).

81 There is now a very large literature on this area. For the pre-Great War era one still needs to start with Martin J. Wiener, *English Culture and the Decline of the Industrial Spirit* (Cambridge 1981) and the criticisms of that work by W.D. Rubenstein brought together in his book, *Capitalism, Culture and Decline in Britain, 1750–1990* (London, 1993). For a more 'cultural' view see Robert Colls and Phillip Dodd, *Englishness. Politics and Culture 1880–1920* (London, 1986). Other texts are to be found in the footnotes.

82 Quoted in Henry Rider Haggard, *A Farmer's Year* (London, 1899) and p. 466.

83 Rudyard Kipling, 'The Islanders, 1902', in James Cochrane, *Kipling. A Selection* (Harmondsworth, 1977) pp. 116–17.

84 See Alun Howkins, 'The Discovery of Rural England', in Colls and Dodd, *Englishness*, pp. 66–88.

85 *EWP*, 18 Aug. 1906, p. 6.

2 The Great War and its aftermath, 1914–21

1 Quoted in L. Margaret Barrett, *English Food Policy during the First World War* (London, 1985) p. 17.

2 Quoted in Edith Whetham, *The Agrarian History of England and Wales, Vol. VIII 1914–39* (Cambridge, 1978) p. 70.

3 For much of what follows see Barnett, *English Food Policy*, Ch. 2 and P. Dewey, *British Agriculture in the First World War* (London, 1989) Ch. 3.

4 Dewey, *British Agriculture*, p. 10.

5 Interview, AJH/William 'Billa' Dixon, Trunch, Norfolk, farm worker/horseman.

6 Keith Grieves, '"Lowther's Lambs": Rural Paternalism and Voluntary Recruitment in the First World War', *RH*, Vol. 4, No. 1 (1993) p. 68.

7 Peter Simkins, *Kitchener's Army. The Making of the New Armies 1914–1916* (Manchester, 1988) p. 76.

8 *EWP*, 19 Sept. 1914.

9 Grieves, *RH* (1993) p. 57.

10 Ibid.

11 Siegfried Sasson, *The War Poems*, arranged and edited by Rupert Hart Davies (London, 1983) p. 76.

12 See Clive Hughes, 'The New Armies', in Ian F. Beckett and Keith Simpson (eds), *A Nation in Arms. A Social Study of the British Army in the First World War* (Manchester, 1985) p. 101.

13 Simkins, *Kitchener's Army*, p. 187.

14   Angel Hewins (ed.), *The Dillen. Memoirs of a Man of Stratford-upon-Avon* (London, 1981) p. 132.

15   Hughes, 'The New Armies', p. 107.

16   Keith Simpson, 'The Officers', in Beckett and Simpson (eds), *A Nation in Arms*, p. 68.

17   For much of what follows see Pamela Horn, *Rural Life in England During the First World War* (Dublin and New York, 1984) Ch. 6. Still the best basic account of rural women's experience in the Great War.

18   Quoted in Horn, *Rural Life*, p. 114.

19   *EWP*, 15 Apr. 1916.

20   Horn, *Rural Life*, pp. 118–20; Dewey, *British Agriculture*, p. 53.

21   For a detailed account of this see Anne Meredith, 'Middle-Class Women and Horticultural Education, 1890–1939,' Unpublished Ph.D. thesis, University of Sussex, 2001.

22   For an essentially popular account of the WFGU see Peter King, *Women Rule the Plot* (London, 1999).

23   Ibid. p. 56.

24   Susan R. Grayzel, 'Nostalgia, Gender and the Countryside: Placing the "Land Girl" in First World War Britain', *RH*, Vol. 10, No. 2 (1999) pp. 157–8.

25   Ibid. p. 159.

26   Ibid. p. 168.

27   Maggie Morgan, 'Jam Making, Cuthbert Rabbit and Cakes: Redefining Domestic Labour in the Women's Institutes, 1915–60', *RH*, Vol. 7, No. 2 p. 218. See also Maggie Andrews, *The Acceptable Face of Feminism. The Women's Institute as a Social Movement* (London, 1997).

28   Sheila Stewart, *Lifting the Latch. A Life on the Land* (Oxford, 1987) pp. 82–3.

29   Quoted in Pamela Horn, *Ladies of the Manor. Wives and Daughters in Country-house Society 1830–1918* (Stroud, 1991) p. 195. Much of what follows is based on this account.

30   Ibid. p. 211.

31   Ibid. p. 203.

32   Thea Thompson, *Edwardian Childhoods* (London, 1981) p. 229.

33   Dewey, *British Agriculture*, p. 179.

34   Richard Perren, *Agriculture in Depression, 1870–1940* (Cambridge, 1995) p. 32.

35   Dewey, *British Agriculture*, pp. 225–6.

36   Interview, AJH/Jack Leeder b. 1901 Happisburgh, Norfolk, team-man.

37   See Alun Howkins, *Poor Labouring Men. Rural Radicalism in Norfolk 1870–1923* (London, 1985) Chs 6 and 7.

38   See David Cannadine, *The Decline and Fall of the British Aristocracy* (New Haven and London, 1990) Ch. 3 and F.M.L. Thompson, *English Landed Society in the Nineteeth Century* (London, 1963) Ch. XII.

39   Thompson, p. 330.

40   Ibid. p. 332.

41   See 'Review of the year 1919', in *EG*, 3 Jan. 1920, pp. 12ff.

42   See Robert Skidelsky, *Oswald Mosley* (London, pb. edn, 1981) p. 43.

43   Jonathan Brown, *Agriculture in England. A Survey of Farming, 1870–1947* (Manchester, 1987) p. 72.

44   See Dewey, *British Agriculture*, pp. 213–6.

45   Alec Douet, 'Norfolk Agriculture 1914–1972', Unpublished D.Phil. thesis, University of East Anglia, 1989, pp. 49–52.

46   See Whetham, *Agrarian History*, pp. 115–17.

47   Dewey, *British Agriculture*, p. 236.

48   A.G. Street, *Farmer's Glory* (London, 1932) p. 223.

49   Report of Broadwell and Son, estate agents, Nottingham quoted in S.G. Sturmey, 'Owner-Farming in England and Wales, 1900–1950', in W.E. Minchinton (ed.), *Essays in Agrarian History, Vol. II* (Newton Abbot, 1969) p. 291.

50   Sturmey, 'Owner-Farming', p. 294.

51   *PP 1917–1918 XVIII*, 'Reconstruction Committee. Part I of the Report of the Agricultural Policy Sub-Committee', p. 193ff.

52   Ibid. p. 299.

53   *PP 1919 VIII*, 'Royal Commission on Agriculture. Interim Report of His Majesty's Commissioners . . . into the Economic Prospects of Agriculture', pp. 6–7.

54 See Whetham, *Agrarian History*, pp. 120–3, also Richard Perren, *Agriculture in Depression*, pp. 37–9.
55 Interview, AJH/Harold Hicks, Trunch, Norfolk, farmer.
56 *PP 1919 VIII*, p. 68.
57 Sturmey, 'Owner-Farming', p. 298.
58 John Davies, 'The End of the Great Estates and the Rise of Freehold Farming in Wales', *The Welsh Historical Review*, Vol. 7, No. 2, Dec. 1974, p. 192.
59 Ibid. p. 194.
60 Douet, 'Norfolk Agriculture', p. 72.
61 Davies, 'Freehold Farming', p. 201.
62 A.G. Street, *The Gentleman of the Party* (London, 1936) pp. 174–5.
63 Douet, 'Norfolk Agriculture', pp. 82–3.
64 A.W. Ashby, and I.L. Evans, *The Agriculture of Wales and Monmouthshire* (Cardiff, 1944) p. 92.
65 The Rt. Hon. Lord Addison of Stallingborough, *A Policy for British Agriculture* (London, Left Book Club, 1939) pp. 31–2.
66 R.R. Enfield, *The Agricultural Crisis, 1920–23* (London, 1924) p. 9.
67 Kenneth O. Morgan, *Rebirth of a Nation. Wales 1880–1980* (Oxford, pb. edn, 1982) p. 187.
68 *EG*, 4 Aug. 1917.
69 Dewey, *British Agriculture*, pp. 110–11.
70 See Paul Fussell, *The Great War and Modern Memory* (Oxford, 1975) pp. 157–69 and Ch. VII, *passim*.
71 See Barry Webb, *Edmund Blunden. A Biography* (New Haven and London, 1990) pp. 84–5.
72 Siegfried Sassoon, *Diaries 1915–18*, ed. Rupert Hart Davies (London, 1983) p. 147.
73 George L. Mosse, *Fallen Soldiers. Reshaping the Memory of the World Wars* (New York and Oxford, 1990), especially Chs 5 and 6; J.L. Carr, *A Month in the Country* (Harmondsworth, 1980) p. 15.
74 Denis Hardy and Colin Ward, *Arcadia for All* (London, 1984) p. 190.
75 *Census of England and Wales, 1921 General Report* p. 21, *BPP*, 1921.
76 Peter Mandler, *The Fall and Rise of the Stately Home* (New Haven and London, 1997) p. 229.
77 *NN*, 12 Feb. 1921, p. 3.
78 Ibid.

3 The misfortunes of agriculture, 1921–37

1 Adrian Bell, *Silver Ley* (London, 1936) p. 183.
2 There is some disagreement over the repeal of the act. For a brief recent summary see Richard Perren, *Agriculture in Depression 1870–1940* (Cambridge, 1995).
3 *NN*, 11 Jun. 1921.
4 *Mark Lane Express*, 4 Jul. 1921.
5 A. Douet, 'Norfolk Agriculture, 1914–1972', Unpublished Ph.D. thesis, University of East Anglia, 1989, pp. 146–7.
6 Ibid. p. 159.
7 Ministry of Agriculture and Fisheries, *Report of the Sugar Beet Industry at Home and Abroad* (London, 1931).
8 S.L. Bensusan, *Latter Day Rural England* (London, 1927) p. 65.
9 Jonathan Brown, *Agriculture in England: A Survey of Farming 1870–1947* (Manchester, 1987) p. 86.
10 David Taylor, 'Growth and Structural Change in the English Dairy Industry, c. 1860–1930', *AHR*, Vol. 35, Pt 1 (1987) p. 62.
11 Brown, *Agriculture*, p. 93.
12 M. Messer, *The Agricultural Crisis of 1931* (Oxford, 1937) p. 13.
13 Douet, 'Norfolk', p. 114.
14 J.M. Lee, *Social Leaders and Public Persons. A Study of County Government in Cheshire since 1888* (Oxford, 1963) p. 96.
15 Simon Moore, 'The Real Great Betrayal? Britain and the Canadian Cattle Crisis of 1922', *AHR*, Vol. 41, Pt II (1993) pp. 155–68. Moore is the source for much of the next paragraph.

16 Mary Bouquet, *Family, Servants and Visitors. The Farm Household in Nineteenth and Twentieth Century Devon* (Norwich, 1985) p. 65.

17 RHC, PF-CR PFL AD1/2 Minutes of AGM Preston and District Farmers' Trading Society, 14 Feb. 1931.

18 Quoted in Douet, 'Norfolk', p. 164.

19 Bensusan, *Latter Day*, p. 156.

20 RHC, Preston Farmers PFL AD1/2, 5 Feb. 1916.

21 Ibid. 31 Jan. 1924.

22 See Christine Hallas, 'The Social and Economic Impact of a Rural Railway: the Wensleydale Line', *AHR*, Vol. 34, Pt 1 (1986) and David Hey, *Yorkshire from AD 1000* (London, 1986) p. 310.

23 *The Times*, 19 Mar. 1923, p. 18.

24 Clare Griffiths, 'Labour and the Countryside: rural strands in the British Labour movement 1900–1939', Unpublished D.Phil. thesis, University of Oxford, 1997, p. 61.

25 Quoted in Griffiths, ibid. p. 224.

26 Bensusan, *Latter Day*, p. 67.

27 Brown, *Agriculture*, pp. 107–10.

28 Whetham, *Agrarian History*, p. 238.

29 Brown, *Agriculture*, p. 113. See also Whetham, *Agrarian History*, pp. 243–6 and for an interesting and near contemporary account Viscount Astor and B. Seebohm Rowntree, *British Agriculture* (Harmondsworth, 1939). The book was written in 1936–7.

30 K.A.H. Murray, *Agriculture. History of the Second World War, United Kingdom Civil Series* (London, 1955) p. 38.

31 Andrew Fenton Cooper, *British Agricultural Policy 1912–1936* (Manchester, 1989) pp. 94–7.

32 J.A. Venn, *The Foundations of Agricultural Economics*, 2nd edn (Cambridge, 1933) pp. 402–3.

33 Howard Newby, *Country Life. A Social History of Rural England* (London, 1987) p. 173.

34 *Agricultural Statistics, 1939* (London, 1939) p. 63.

35 Brown, *Agriculture*, p. 122.

36 Quoted in Murray, *Agriculture*, p. 53.

4 Landowners and farmers

1 David Cannadine, *The Decline and Fall of the British Aristocracy* (New Haven and London, 1990) p. 83.

2 F.M.L. Thompson, *English Landed Society in the Nineteenth Century* (London, 1963) p. 331.

3 On Derbyshire see Heather A. Clemenson, 'Diminishing Derbyshire Estates', *Geographical Magazine*, 53, 980–1, pp. 115–18; on Notts, Robert J. Waller, *The Dukeries Transformed* (Oxford, 1983) pp. 65–73.

4 John K. Walton, *Lancashire. A Social History 1558–1939* (Manchester, 1987) p. 349.

5 C.B. Phillips and J.H. Smith, *Lancashire and Cheshire from AD 1540* (London, 1994) p. 314.

6 Quoted in Mandler, *Fall and Rise*, p. 242.

7 H. Clemenson, *English Country Houses and Landed Estates* (London, 1981) pp. 143–4.

8 Peter Brandon and Brian Short, *The South East from AD 1000* (London, 1990) p. 329.

9 Hardy and Ward, *Arcadia*, p. 234.

10 John Davies, 'The End of the Great Estates and the Rise of Freehold farming in Wales', *The Welsh Historical Review*, Vol. 7, No. 2, Dec. 1974, p. 208. Much of this paragraph is based on this essential article.

11 Clemenson, *English Country Houses*, p. 127.

12 Oxfordshire Federation of Women's Institutes, *Oxfordshire within Living Memory* (Newbury, 1994) p. 19.

13 Ibid. p. 145.

14 Fred Archer, *Farmer's Son. A Cotswold Childhood in the 1920s* (London, 1986).

15 Charles Kightly, *Country Voices. Life and Lore in Farm and Village* (London, 1984) pp. 170–1.

16 Madeleine Beard, *English Landed Society in the Twentieth Century* (London, 1989) p. 67.

17 Quoted in Douet, 'Norfolk', p. 134.

18 Davies, 'Rise of Freehold Farming', p. 197.

19 Beard, *English Landed Society*, p. 67.

20   Ibid.
21   Kightly, *Country Voices*, p. 172.
22   Roy Perrot, *The Aristocrats* (London, 1968) p. 174.
23   Cannadine, *Decline and Fall*, p. 167.
24   Thompson, *Landed Society*, p. 339.
25   Ibid. p. 338.
26   Quoted in Robin Fedden, *Anglesey Abbey, Cambridgeshire. A Guide* (London, 1996) p. 6.
27   Clive Aslet, *The Last Country Houses* (London and Newhaven, 1982) p. 80.
28   Lesley Lewis, *The Private Life of a Country House 1912–39* (London, 1982).
29   Ibid. p. 12.
30   Ibid. p. 157.
31   Thompson, *Landed Society*, p. 337.
32   The following figures are from Sturmey, 'Owner-Farming', p. 296.
33   Douet, 'Norfolk', p. 139.
34   Maxton (ed.), *Regional Types*, p. 83.
35   J.A. Hanley, A.L. Boyd and W. Williamson, *An Agricultural Survey of the Northern Province* (Newcastle upon Tyne, 1936) p. 21.
36   Ibid. p. 31.
37   Brown, *Farming*, pp. 83–4.
38   Whetham, *Agrarian History*, pp. 213, 265.
39   Perren, *Agriculture*, p. 42; Sturmey, 'Owner-Farming', p. 302.
40   J.A. Venn, *The Foundations of Agricultural Economics* (London, 1933) p. 542.
41   Douet, 'Norfolk', p. 139.
42   Ibid. p. 133.
43   Interview, AJH/Harold Hicks, farmer, Trunch, Norfolk.
44   Charles Rawding, *Binbrook, 1900–1939* (Binbrook, 1991) p. 13.
45   Whetham, *Agrarian History*, p. 267.
46   Interview, AJH/Harold Hicks, farmer, Trunch, Norfolk.
47   *FW*, 17 Aug. 1934, p. 21.
48   A.G. Street, *Farmer's Glory* (London, 1932) p. 234. For his return to sugar beet see A.G. Street *A.G. Street's Country Calendar* (Oxford, 1986) original edition 1935.
49   *FW*, 26 Jul. 1935, pp. 28–9.
50   Ibid. 1 Mar. 1935, pp vi–viii.
51   Bensusan, *Latter Day*, pp. 52–4.
52   Street, *Country Calendar*, p. 38.
53   Arthur Amis, *From Dawn to Dusk* (Warwick, 1992) p. 20.
54   Street, *Farmer's Glory*, p. 271.
55   E. Lorraine Smith, *Go East for a Farm. A Study of Rural Migration* (Oxford, 1932) p. 36.
56   Interview, AJH/Harold Hicks, farmer, Trunch, Norfolk.
57   Interview, AJH/Miss Irene Jones, small holder, Alpington. Norfolk.
58   Ashby and Evans, *Agriculture of Wales*, p. 7.
59   Richard Moore-Colyer, *Farming in Depression; Wales 1919–1939*, Welsh Institute of Rural Studies, Working Paper No. 6, Aberystwyth, Oct. 1996, p. 19.
60   Bensusan, *Latter Day*, p. 97.
61   Ashby and Evans, *Agriculture of Wales*, pp. 97–8.
62   Archer, *Farmer's Son*, p. 129.
63   David Jenkins, *The Agricultural Community in South-West Wales at the Turn of the Twentieth Century* (Cardiff, 1971) pp. 259–63; Bouquet, *Family, Servants*, pp. 10–11.
64   Jenkins, *Agricultural Community*, p. 263.
65   Tony Harman, *Seventy Summers. The Story of a Farm* (London, 1986) pp. 143–65.
66   *FW*, 28 Aug. 1935, p. 30.
67   RHC, Minutes of Preston Farmers PFL AD1/3, 27 Nov. 1937.
68   Ibid. PFL AD1/2, 8 Feb. 1930.
69   Ibid. PFL AD1/3, 9 Feb. 1935.
70   Graham Cox, Phillip Lowes and Michael Winter, 'The Origins and Early Development of the National Farmers' Union,' *AHR*, 39 No. 1, 1991, p. 30.
71   Street, *Farmer's Glory*, pp. 272–3.

72   Andrew Flynn, Phillip Lowes and Michael Winter, 'The Political Power of Farmers: An English Perspective', *RH*, 7 No. 1, 1996, p. 25.

73   Douet, 'Norfolk', pp. 144–5.

74   There is no account of the 'Tithe War' but see *FW* throughout the period for its course.

75   *Facts and Incidents in an Unequal Struggle published by the Ashford, Kent and Sussex Tithepayers' Association*, Ashford, n.d. but ?1949, p. 25.

76   For later tithe seizures see *Facts and Incidents*, pp. 32–8; on the NFU attitude see *FW*, 26 Jun. 1936.

77   *FW*, 3 Aug. 1934, p. 6.

5 The traditionalists: farm workers and domestic servants

1   There are discrepancies of a minor kind with the figures in this chapter. Put simply the 'regional' and county breakdowns do not add up to the simplified 'national' figures given within the same census period. I cannot explain this – but the differences are slight. There is a further problem in that some writers use figures from the annual agricultural returns, which are again marginally different. Finally there is the perennial problem of 'whom', especially relating to casual workers and to women workers. Where possible I have dealt with this.

2   A.W. Ashby and I.L. Evans, *The Agriculture of Wales and Monmouthshire* (Cardiff, 1944) p. 86.

3   *FW*, 9 Aug. 1935.

4   Winifred Foley, *The Forest Trilogy* (Oxford, 1992) pp. 146–9.

5   Mr G. Cottingham, South Lincolnshire, in G.K. Nelson, *To be a Farmer's Boy* (Stroud, 1991) p. 129.

6   Nelson, *Farmer's Boy*, Mr L.F. Maw, Selby, Yorkshire, p. 160.

7   Ibid.

8   Ibid. p. 162.

9   NRO 302/27. Woods MSS, Castle Heaton Farm, Wages Book, Oct. 1921.

10   For the bondager system see Howkins, *Reshaping*, Chs 1 and 4. For a more detailed account see Judy Gielguid, 'Nineteeth Century Farm Women in Northumberland and Cumbria. The Neglected Workforce', Unpublished Ph.D. thesis, University of Sussex, 1992.

11   Caunce, 'Twentieth-century', p. 163.

12   Harold Canning, *Follow the Plough. Harold Cannings' Life as a Farm Worker from 1917 to 1970*, edited by Susan Rowland (Lewes, 1992) p. 42.

13   See for example, George Ewart Evans, *Horse Power and Magic* (London, 1979) pp. 3–5.

14   *FW*, 21 Jun. 1935, pp. 28–9.

15   See Arthur Amis, *From Dawn to Dusk* (Warwick, 1992) pp. 20–2.

16   See Bob Copper, *A Song for Every Season. A Hundred Years of a Sussex Farming Family* (London, 1971) pp. 117–25.

17   Derek Heater, *The Remarkable History of Rottingdean* (Brighton, 1993) pp. 84–5.

18   *Census of England and Wales, 1921. General Report* (London, 1927) p. 122.

19   *FW*, 29 May 1942, p. 12.

20   G.K. Nelson, *Countrywomen on the Land. Memories of Rural Life in the 1920s and '30s* (Stroud, 1992) p. 42.

21   Ibid. pp. 51, 59.

22   In Stephen Hussey, 'We Rubbed Along All Right: The Rural Working-Class Household Between the Wars in North Essex and South Buckinghamshire', Unpublished D.Phil. thesis, University of Essex, 1995, p. 99.

23   Doris Hall, *Growing Up In Ditchling* (Brighton, 1985) pp. 16–18.

24   *Census of Population, 1921 Occupation Tables*, p. 13.

25   Nelson, *Countrywomen*, p. 118.

26   Caunce, 'Twentieth-century', p. 165.

27   For a detailed account of the strike see Alun Howkins, *Poor Labouring Men. Rural Radicalism in Norfolk 1870–1923* (London, 1985) Ch. 8.

28   Ibid. p. 168.

29   Interview, AJH/William 'Billa' Dixon, farm worker/publican, Trunch, Norfolk.

30   Howard Newby, *The Deferential Worker* (Harmondsworth, 1977) p. 236.

31   Ashby and Evans, *Agriculture of Wales*, p. 88.

32 Douet, 'Norfolk', p. 131.

33 *LW*, Feb. 1931.

34 Robert C. Richardson, *Some Fell on Stony Ground* (Wymondham, 1978) p. 81.

35 Caunce, 'Twentieth-century', p. 164.

36 Ashby and Evans, *Agriculture of Wales*, pp. 88–9.

37 Quoted in Armstrong, *Farmworkers*, p. 184.

38 John Boyd Orr, *Food, Health and Income* (London, 1936). See also John Pemberton, 'The Boyd Orr Survey', *HWJ 50* (Autumn 2000).

39 Canning, *Follow the Plough*, p. 38.

40 Oxfordshire Federation of Women's Institutes, *Oxfordshire Within Living Memory* (Newbury, 1994) pp. 44–5.

41 ESRO Heathfield Parish Council minute book P372/2/2, 3 Sept 1918.

42 Ibid. 21 Apr. 1926.

43 ESRO P372/2/3, 16 Oct. 1928.

44 Cambridgeshire County Record Office (hereafter CCRO) Cambridgeshire Labour Party Papers 416/0 36.

45 ESRO County Council Minutes. Sub-Committee of General Purposes Committee. Housing Rural Workers and Dwellings Acquisition Sub-Committee, 24 Jul. 1931.

46 Ibid. 14 Mar. 1939; 9 May 1939.

47 Ibid. 18 Jul. 1939.

48 ESRO C/C11/21/3, Circular letter from the Board of Agriculture and Fisheries ... Land Settlement, 18 Dec. 1918.

49 Ibid. Circular letter from Board of Agriculture and Fisheries ... Land Settlement, 14 Jan. 1919.

50 CCRO Cambridgeshire County Council (hereafter CCC) Small Holders Committee Minute Books, Jan. 1918–Oct. 1919.

51 CCRO 424/01 War Agriculture Committee Minutes, 30 Dec. 1919.

52 CCRO CCC Small Holdings, 8 Feb 1918.

53 Ibid. 7 Jun. 1919.

54 Ibid. 19 Jun. 1920.

55 ESRO East Sussex County Council (hereafter ESCC) C/C11/21/3 Small Holders and Allotments Sub-Committee, 4 Feb. 1919.

56 The figures in the following paragraphs are derived from *Census of England and Wales 1921, Occupation Tables* (London, 1924) pp. 3–21.

57 Mary Bouquet, *Family, Servants and Visitors. The Farm Household in Nineteenth and Twentieth Century Devon* (Norwich, 1985) pp. 77–9.

58 Foley, *Forest Trilogy*, p. 140.

59 Quoted in Deirdre Beddoe, *Back to Home and Duty. Women Between the Wars 1918–1939* (London, 1989) pp. 62–3.

60 Ibid. pp. 51–2; Elizabeth Roberts, *A Woman's Place. An Oral History of Working-Class Women, 1890–1940* (Oxford, 1984) pp. 54–6.

61 My thanks to Selina Todd for this point and others relating to this section.

62 Oxfordshire Federation of Women's Institutes, *Oxfordshire*, p. 145.

63 Ibid. p. 143.

64 Alison Light, *Forever England. Feminity, Literature and Conservatism between the Wars* (London, 1991) p. 119.

65 Foley, *Forest Trilogy*, pp. 137–8.

66 For a more detailed discussion see Alun Howkins, 'Types of Rural Community', in E.J.T. Collins (ed.), *The Agrarian History of England and Wales, Vol. VII* (Cambridge, 2000).

67 See Alun Howkins, *Reshaping Rural England* (London, 2nd edn, 1995) pp. 28–31.

68 Derek H. Aldcroft, *The Inter-War Economy: Britain 1919–1939* (London, 1970) p. 231–2.

69 Bridget Williams, *The Best Butter in the World. A History of Sainsbury's* (London, 1994) p. 86.

70 Council for the Preservation of Rural England Papers (hereafter CPRE), RHC; File 37/1 Batch 4.

71 See Sid Hedges (S.G.), *Bicester wuz a little town* (Bicester, 1968) Ch. 6.

6 New countrymen and women: workers and trippers

1 'Classically' see John Stevenson and Chris Cook, *The Slump: Society and Politics in the Depression* (London, 1977) who interestingly leave out the rural areas.
2 Quoted in Peter Hall, Henry Gracey, Roy Dewett and Henry Thomas, *The Containment of Urban England*, Vol. I (London, 1973) p. 82.
3 Peter Hall, 'England circa 1900', in H.C. Darby (ed.), *A New Historical Geography of England and Wales after 1600* (Cambridge, 1976) pp. 436–46.
4 *Census of England and Wales 1921*, p. 21.
5 *Report of the Royal Commission on the Distribution of the Industrial Population*, Cmd 6153 (London, 1940) p. 152.
6 Thomas Sharp, *Town and Country* (London, 1932) pp. 6–7.
7 Robin H. Best and Alan W. Rogers, *The Urban Countryside* (London, 1973) p. 24.
8 Alison Light, *Forever England. Feminity, Literature and Conservatism Between the Wars* (London, 1991) p. 216.
9 Census groups XXIII (770–799); XXIV (800–879); XXVII (900–929) and XXVIII (930–939).
10 Carol Anne Lockwood, 'The Changing Use of Land in the Weald Region of Kent, Surrey and Sussex, 1919–1939', Unpublished Ph.D. thesis, University of Sussex, 1991, p. 32.
11 Alan A. Jackson, *The Railway in Surrey* (Penryn, 1999) p. 109.
12 Ibid. p. 118.
13 *John Betjeman's Collected Poems. Enlarged edition* (London, 1977) p. 23.
14 Jackson, *Railway in Surrey*, p. 139.
15 Ibid. p. 133.
16 Ibid. pp. 148–52.
17 F.E. Green, *The Surrey Hills* (London, 1915).
18 Marie B. Rowlands, *The West Midlands from AD 1000* (Harlow, 1987) pp. 335ff.
19 Geoffrey W. Place (ed.), *Neston, 1840–1940* (Chester, 1996) p. 244. The memories of David Scott.
20 RHC; CPRE File 37/1 Batch 4, Northumberland and Newcastle Society.
21 F.M.L. Thompson, 'Town and City', in F.M.L. Thompson (ed.), *The Cambridge Social History of England. Volume I. Regions and Communities* (Cambridge, 1990) p. 84.
22 Andy Medhurst, 'Negotiating the Gnome Zone', in Roger Silverstone (ed.), *Visions of Suburbia* (London, 1997) pp. 240–1.
23 Ibid. p. 257.
24 George Orwell, *Coming Up for Air* (London, 1948) pp. 146–56.
25 Jackson, *Railway in Surrey*, p. 120.
26 Frank McKenna, *The Railway Workers 1840–1970* (London, 1980) p. 41.
27 Raymond Williams, *Politics and Letters. Interviews with New Left Review* (London, 1981) p. 21.
28 Ibid. p. 24.
29 Griffiths, 'Labour and the Countryside', p. 143.
30 Charles Rawding, *Binbrook 1900–1939* (Binbrook, 1991) p. 33.
31 R.C. Whiting, *The View from Cowley. The Impact of Industrialisation on Oxford 1919–1939* (Oxford, 1983) pp. 38–9.
32 Arthur Exell, 'Morris Motors in the 1930s. Part I', *HWJ*, No. 6 (1978) p. 54.
33 Whiting, *View from Cowley*, p. 39.
34 John Lowerson, 'Battles for the Countryside', in Frank Gloversmith (ed.), *Class, Culture and Social Change. A New View of the 1930s* (Brighton, 1980) p. 263.
35 Quoted in ibid. p. 263–4.
36 *Cyclists' Touring Club Gazette*, Vol. XXXIX, No. 8 (Aug. 1920) p. 132.
37 Lockwood, 'Changing Use of Land', p. 207.
38 C.E.M. Joad, 'The People's Claim', in Clough Williams-Ellis, *Britain and the Beast* (Readers Union Edition, London, 1938) pp. 72–3. See also Catherine Brace, 'A Pleasure Ground for the Noisy Herd? Incompatible Encounters with the Cotswolds and England, 1900–1950', *RH*, Vol. 11, No. 1 (Apr. 2000).
39 RHC, CPRE File 111/3 batch 1. Surrey Anti-Litter League.
40 ESRO P372/2/1–3 (Heathfield PC).
41 ESRO Uckfield RDC. Rights of Way File.

42 David Matless, '"Ordering the Land": The "Preservation" of the English Countryside, 1918–1939', Unpublished D.Phil. thesis, University of Nottingham, 1990, p. 170.

43 John Sheail, *Nature in Trust. The History of Nature Conservation in Britain* (Glasgow, 1976) p. 71.

44 RHC, CPRE 7/1/g batch 2. Isle of Wight holiday camps and caravans.

45 RHC, CPRE 37/1 batch 4. Northumberland and Newcastle Society.

46 See Lockwood, 'Changing Use of Land'. Chs 5 and 7.

47 Lowerson, 'Battles for the Countryside', p. 276.

48 RHC, CPRE File 161/3. Teashop signs.

49 See for example Bouquet, *Family, Servants and Visitors*, pp. 65–7, 121–31.

50 E.D. Mackerness (ed.), *The Journals of George Sturt 1890–1927* (2 vols, Cambridge, 1967) Vol. II, p. 870.

51 Clough Williams-Ellis, *England and the Octopus* (Portmerion, 1928); *Britain and the Beast* (London, 1937).

52 Williams-Ellis, *Britain and the Beast*, facing p. 64.

53 For Eastbourne see ESRO East Sussex CC Planning Committee C/C6/ File 1; for Cuckmere see C/C/ File 5.

54 Robin H. Best and J.T. Coppock, *The Changing Use of Land in Britain* (London, 1962) p. 190.

55 *Report of the Committee on Land Utilisation in Rural Areas* Cmd 6378 (London HMSO, 1942) p. 40.

56 See Peter Mandler, 'Politics and the English Landscape since the First World War', *Huntingdon Library Quarterly*, 55 (1992) 459–76 and 'Against "Englishness": English Culture and the Limits to Rural Nostalgia, 1850–1940', *Transactions of the Royal Historical Society*, Sixth series, VII, p. 174.

57 See Peter Brandon, *The South Downs* (Chichester, 1998) and Ch. 13, *passim*.

58 A.G. Street, 'The Countryman's View' in Williams-Ellis, *Britain and the Beast*, p. 125.

7 War and state agriculture, 1937–45

1 Keith A.H. Murray, *Agriculture. History of the Second World War. United Kingdom Series* (London, 1955) p. 47.

2 See Edith H. Whetham, *The Agrarian History of England and Wales. Volume VIII 1914–39* (Cambridge, 1978) p. 328.

3 The Rt Honble Lord Addison of Stallingborough, *A Policy for British Agriculture*, Left Book Club Edition (London, 1939) p. 204.

4 R.J. Hammond, *Food. Vol. I: The Growth of Policy* (London, 1951) p. 8.

5 See also John Martin, *The Development of Modern Agriculture. British Farming since 1931* (Basingstoke, 2000) pp. 28–35.

6 Murray, *Agriculture*, p. 49.

7 Ibid. p. 59.

8 For the 1937 and 1939 Acts see Murray, *Agriculture*, pp. 51–9 and Jonathan Brown, *Agriculture in England. A Survey of Farming, 1870–1947* (Manchester, 1987) pp. 126–7.

9 Murray's volume provides an excellent account of the administrative and production history.

10 Mass-Observation Archive, University of Sussex (hereafter M-O Archive), Town and District Survey, Box 22, File B. I would like to thank the Trustees of the Mass-Observation Archive at the University of Sussex for their permission to use material from the archive. On potash see Murray, *Agriculture*, pp. 87–8.

11 For the regional revival in fortunes see Martin, *Development*, Ch. 1.

12 Murray, *Agriculture*, p. 64.

13 M-O Archive, Diaries No. A5010, journalist, Chelmsford, 24.8.1939.

14 Ibid. 31.8.1939.

15 M-O Archive, Diaries No. D5054, tea merchant, Essex, 31.8.1939.

16 M-O Archive, Diaries No. M5366, housewife, Little Wilbraham, Cambridgeshire, 28.8.1939.

17 M-O Archive, Diaries No. H5324, garage worker, Snettisham, Norfolk, 24/25.8.1939.

18 Williams-Ellis, *Britain and the Beast*, p. 90.

19 M-O Archive, Diaries No. H5324, garage worker, Snettisham, Norfolk, 27.8.1939.

20 Ibid. 29.8.1939.

21 M-O Archive, Diaries No. P3596, writer/artist, Port Isaac, Cornwall, 17.9.1939.
22 All names are changed, except those of full-time M-O workers. This was guaranteed at the time and remains the case now.
23 M-O Archive, Diaries No. M5366, housewife, Great Wilbraham, Cambridgeshire, 4.9.1939.
24 M-O Archive, Diaries No. F5313, housewife, Hassocks, Sussex.
25 There is a large literature on evacuation, much of it emotional and difficult to work with, but see T.L. Crosby, *The Impact of Civilian Evacuation in the Second World War* (London, 1986). There were also published contemporary studies carried out most notably in Oxford and Cambridge.
26 Thomas Harnett and Tom Harrison (eds), *War Begins at Home* (London, 1940) p. 305.
27 M-O Archive, Diaries No. M5376, school-teacher, Burwash, Sussex, 8.9.1939.
28 Harnett and Harrison, *War Begins at Home*, pp. 315–17.
29 M-O Archive, Diaries No. H5324, garage worker, Snettisham, Norfolk, 24.10.1939.
30 M-O Archive, Diaries No. M5376, school-teacher, Burwash, Sussex, 28.9.1939.
31 M-O Archive, Town and District Survey, Box 24, File A.
32 For an interesting if brief discussion of this see David Matless, *Landscape and Englishness* (London, 1998) pp. 179–84.
33 M-O Archive, Diaries No. P5396, writer/housewife, Port Isaac, Cornwall, 3.9.1939.
34 M-O Archive, Diaries No. M5376, school-teacher, Burwash, Sussex, 3.9.1939.
35 M-O Archive, Diaries No. H5332, school-teacher, Cullercoats, Northumberland, 3.9.1939.
36 M-O Archive, Diaries No. H5324, garage worker, Snettisham, Norfolk, 3.9.1939.
37 M-O Archive, Diaries No. M5366, housewife, Little Wilbraham, Cambridgeshire, 3.9.1939.
38 Harold Howkins, Diary. In author's possession.
39 Murray, *Agriculture*, pp. 82–3.
40 Alan Armstrong, *Farmworkers. A Social and Economic History 1770–1980* (London, 1988) p. 214.
41 Ibid.
42 Murray, *Agriculture*, p. 85.
43 Murray, *Agriculture*, pp. 159, 189, 210.
44 Ibid. p. 274.
45 Brian Short et al., *The National Farm Survey 1941–43. State Surveillance and the Countryside in England and Wales in the Second World War* (Wallingford, 2000) pp. 186–8.
46 M-O Archive, Diaries No. D5054, tea merchant, Walton-on-Naze, Essex, 26.11.1939.
47 M-O Archive, Town and District Survey, Box 19.
48 M-O Archive, Diaries No. H5324, garage worker, Snettisham, Norfolk, 24.10.1939.
49 M-O Archive, Town and District Survey, Box 19.
50 M-O Archive, Town and District Survey, Box 20.
51 M-O Archive, Town and District Survey, Box 19.
52 Ibid.
53 M-O Archive, Diaries No. M5376, school-teacher, Burwash, Sussex, 13.9.1939.
54 M-O Archive, Diaries No. M5366, housewife, Great Wilbraham, Cambridgeshire, 26.11.1939.
55 A.W. Foot, 'The impact of the military on the British farming landscape in the Second World War', Unpublished M.Phil. thesis, University of Sussex, 1999, p. 138.
56 M-O Archive, Diaries No. M5376, school-teacher, Burwash, Sussex, 18.9.1939.
57 Ibid. 9.3.1940.
58 Tony Harman, *Seventy Summers. The Story of a Farm* (London, 1986) p. 175.
59 Murray, *Agriculture*, p. 371.
60 Martin, *Development*, p. 49.
61 Ibid. p. 50.
62 M-O Archive, Diaries No. M5376, school-teacher, Burwash, Sussex, 23.1.1940.
63 *FW*, 29 Mar. 1939, p. 10.
64 RHC, CR VEA, Minutes of the Vale of Evesham Asparagus Growers' Association.
65 M-O Archive, Diaries No. M5376, school-teacher, Burwash, Sussex, 5.10.1942.
66 Ibid. 22.9.1943.
67 M-O Archive, Diaries No. H5324, garage worker, Snettisham, Norfolk, 18.6.1940.
68 M-O Archive, Town and District Survey, Box 19. Letter dtd 7.6.1940.
69 M-O Archive, Diaries No. M5376, school-teacher, Burwash, Sussex, 29.5.1940.

70   Ibid. 24.6.1940.
71   M-O Archive, File Reports, File 170 Suffolk Village Report 6.6.1940.
72   M-O Archive, Town and District Survey, Box 22, File B.
73   M-O Archive, Town and District Survey, Box 22, File G.
74   M-O Archives, 'Air-Raids' Box 10 File K.
75   M-O Archive, Diaries No. M5376, school-teacher, Burwash, Sussex, 14.12.1940.
76   Sadie Ward, *War in the Countryside* (London, 1988) p. 32.
77   Bill Petch quoted in ibid. p. 57.
78   Armstrong, *Farmworkers*, pp. 215–16.
79   *FW*, 17 Nov. 1939, p. 18.
80   Ibid. 29 May 1942, p. 12.
81   Stephen A. Caunce, 'Twentieth-century Farm Servants: the Horselads of the East Riding of Yorkshire', *AHR*, Vol. 39, Pt II (1991) pp. 164–6.
82   Richard Anthony, *Herds and Hinds. Farm Labour in Lowland Scotland, 1900–1939* (East Linton, 1997) pp. 187–8.
83   Nicola Tyrer, *They Fought in the Fields. The Women's Land Army: the story of a forgotten victory* (London, 1996) pp. 4–5.
84   Ward, *War in the Countryside*, p. 18.
85   *FW*, 15 Dec. 1939, p. 10.
86   Quoted in ibid. p. 16.
87   Joan Mant, *All Muck, No Medals. Land Girls by Land Girls* (Lewes, 1995) p. 111.
88   Ward, *War in the Countryside*, p. 40.
89   M-O Archive, Diaries No. H5324, garage worker, then gardener, Snettisham, Norfolk, 21.4.1941.
90   Ibid. 29.10.1941.
91   Ibid. 29.12.1941.
92   Ibid. 13.4.1942.
93   Ibid. 30.1.1943.
94   Ibid. 3.9.1943 and 10.9.1943.
95   M-O Archive, Diaries No. 2957, farm worker, Stoney Stratford, Bucks.
96   Ward, *War in the Countryside*, pp. 49–53.
97   See John Martin Robinson, *The Country House at War* (London, 1989) Ch. 1.
98   M-O Archive, Diaries No. H5337, housewife, Fritwell, Oxon.
99   Ibid. 4.2.1944.
100 Ibid. Oct.–Nov. 1944.
101 Ibid. 1.2.1945.
102 M-O Archive, Town and District Survey, 'Worcestershire Village', Box 22, File G.
103 M-O Archive, Diaries No. C5045, nursery man, Newick, Sussex.
104 M-O Archive Diaries No. M5376, school-teacher, Burwash, Sussex, 12.2.1941.
105 M-O Archive, Diaries No. M5139, farm worker, Stoney Stratford, Buckinghamshire, 1.8.1941.
106 M-O Archive, Diaries No. M5376, school-teacher, Burwash, Sussex, 9.3.1940.
107 Ina Zweiniger-Bargielowska, *Austerity in Britain. Rationing, Controls and Consumption, 1939–1955* (Oxford, 2000) p. 18.
108 Ibid. pp. 20–1.
109 M-O Archive, Town and District Survey, 'Western Village' (Sherridge?Malvern?), Worcestershire, 5.1.1941. Box 24, File F.
110 Ibid. No. 2830, commercial traveller, Wellington, Somerset.
111 Ibid. No. 2431, farmers son/leather worker, Market Harborough, Leicestershire.
112 'Wartime Social Survey' quoted in Zweiniger-Bargielowska, *Austerity*, p. 73.
113 Quoted in R.J. Hammond, *Food Volume II: Studies in Administration and Control* (London, 1956) p. 665.
114 Martin, *Development*, p. 51.
115 Ibid. No. 2924, book illustrator, Wormingford, nr. Colchester, Essex.
116 Ibid. No. 2778, man, unknown occupation, Yealington, S. Devon; No. 2862, unemployed woman, Wood Stanway, Gloucestershire.
117 M-O Archive, Town and District Survey, Box 24, File D.

118 See ibid.; M-O Archive, Directives, Food Situation, Feb. 1942, No. 2856, woman, unknown occupation, Cambridge; and Rationing, 1943, No. 3336, farm worker Macclesfield, Cheshire.

119 The most famous of these were a series of posters of the rural south of England by Frank Newbould, and issued by Army Bureau of Current Affairs (ABCA) with the slogan 'Your Britain. Fight for it now'.

120 M-O Archive, Directives, Post War Problems, Sept. 1942, No. 2954, male, unknown occupation, Preston, Lancs.

121 Ibid. No. 2457, civil servant, Newcastle.

122 Ibid. No. 3095, bank clerk, Swindon, Wiltshire.

123 Ibid. No. 2925, clerk, Oswestry, Shropshire.

124 Ibid. Nos 2737; 2844; 2845 and 3090.

125 See Kenneth O. Morgan, *Labour in Power, 1945–51* (Oxford, 1984) pp. 32–3.

126 M-O Archive, Directives, Post War Problems, Sept. 1942, No. 2830, commercial traveller, Wellington, Somerset.

127 Ibid. No. 2695, Royal Navy rating, Plymouth, Devon.

128 Ibid. No. 2873, housewife, Sherringham, Norfolk.

129 Ministry of Works and Planning, 'Report of the Committee on Land Utilisation in Rural Areas' (hereafter the Scott Report) Cmd 6378 (London, 1942).

130 Ibid. p. iv.

131 Matless, *Landscape*, p. 220.

132 Scott Report, pp. 33–6.

133 Ibid. pp. 55–6.

134 Ibid. p. 90.

135 Ibid. p. v.

136 Ibid. pp. 90–1.

137 M-O Archive, Diaries No. Y5464, poultry worker, Peterborough, Huntingdonshire.

138 M-O Archive, Diaries No. H5337, housewife, Fritwell, Oxfordshire, 1.4.1944.

139 M-O Archive, Diaries No. M5376, school-teacher, Burwash, Sussex, Aug. 1943.

140 M-O Archive, Diaries No. H5337, housewife, Fritwell, Oxfordshire, 3.8.1944.

141 M-O Archive, Diaries No. M5376, school-teacher, Burwash, Sussex, 25.1.1944, for example.

142 M-O Archive, Diaries No. M5139, farm worker/forester, Stony Stratford, Buckinghamshire.

143 M-O Archive, Town and District Survey, Box 10, File F.

144 M-O Archive, Diaries No. M5376, school-teacher, Burwash, Sussex, 13.9.1945.

145 M-O Archive, Town and District Survey, Box 10, File F.

146 M-O Archive, Diaries No. G5089, postman/farm worker, Looe, Cornwall, 18.2.1941.

147 Ibid. 15.4.1941.

148 M-O Archive, Directives Rationing, 1943, No. 3075, market garden worker, Oxford.

149 M-O Archive, Directives Rationing, 1943, No. 3336, farm servant, Macclesfield, Cheshire.

150 M-O Archive, Diaries, No. H5337, house wife, Fritwell, Oxfordshire.

151 Ibid. 18.8.1945.

152 M-O Archive, Diaries, No. M5376, school-teacher, Burwash, Sussex, 21.6.1944.

153 Ibid. 14.7.1944. For the return of children see 5–31.12.1944.

154 Ibid. 4.8.1944.

155 Ibid. 29.7.1944.

156 Ibid. 6.9.1944.

157 Angus Calder, *The People's War: Britain 1939–45* (London, 1969).

158 Morgan, *Labour in Power*, p. 41.

159 M-O Archive, Diaries No. H5337, housewife, Fritwell, Oxfordshire, 27.7.1945.

160 M-O Archive, Diaries No. H5324, garage worker, then gardener, Snettisham, Norfolk, 15.8.1945.

8 'Tractors plus chemicals': agriculture and farming, 1945–90

1 M-O Archive, Directives, Post War Problems, No. 1563, social worker, Chiswick, London.

2 Ibid. No. 3013, housewife, Berkhampstead.

3 Ibid. No. 1645, agricultural worker, Norfolk.

4 Ibid. No. 2957, agricultural worker, Buckinghamshire.

5   *FW*, 13 Oct. 1939, p. 16.

6   Ibid. 2 Jan. 1942, pp. 17–28; 9 Jan. 1942, pp. 28–9.

7   Ibid. 6 Jul. 1945, p. 11.

8   M-O Archive, Political Attitudes and Behaviour, File A, Attitudes of Farmers and Labourers, m, Farmer, Betteshanger, Kent.

9   J.K. Bowers, 'British Agricultural Policy Since the Second World War,' *AHR*, Vol. 33, Pt I (1985) p. 66.

10   John Martin, *The Development of Modern Agriculture. British Farming since 1931* (Basingstoke, 2000) p. 58.

11   Keith A.H. Murray, *Agriculture* (London, 1955) p. 291.

12   For what follows see ibid. pp. 348–54.

13   Ibid. p. 348.

14   Martin, *Development*, pp. 68–9.

15   Quoted in B.A. Holderness, *British Agriculture since 1945* (Manchester, 1985) pp. 13–14.

16   Howard Newby, *Country Life. A Social History of Rural England* (London, 1987) p. 184.

17   Ibid. p. 186.

18   Martin, *Development*, pp. 69–70.

19   Ibid. p. 85.

20   Tony Harman, *Seventy Summers. The Story of a Farm* (London, 1986) pp. 206–7.

21   Murray, *Agriculture*, pp. 352–3.

22   Quoted in David Cannadine, *The Decline and Fall of the British Aristocracy* (New Haven and London, 1990) p. 637.

23   Peter Mandler, *The Fall and Rise of the Stately Home* (London and New Haven, 1997) p. 326.

24   Cannadine, *Decline and Fall*, p. 671.

25   Mandler, *Fall and Rise*, p. 357.

26   Ibid. p. 356.

27   I am grateful to Paul Brassley for this point.

28   Alan Armstrong, *Farmworkers. A Social and Economic History 1770–1980* (London, 1988) p. 222.

29   Department of Employment and Productivity, *British Labour Statistics. Historical Abstract, 1886–1968* (London, 1971) p. 101.

30   Bob Wynn, *Skilled at All Trades. The History of the Farmworkers' Union 1947–1984* (London, 1993) pp. 23–4.

31   Murray, *Agriculture*, p. 85.

32   Ina Zweiniger-Bargielowska, *Austerity in Britain. Rationing, Controls and Consumption 1939–1955* (Oxford, 2000) p. 83.

33   Ibid.

34   Ibid. p. 86.

35   Bridget Williams, *The Best Butter in the World. A History of Sainsbury's* (London, 1994) p. 131.

36   Holderness, *British Agriculture*, p. 52.

37   Martin, *Development*, p. 97; Holderness, *British Agriculture*, pp. 48–9.

38   Holderness, *British Agriculture*, p. 69.

39   Martin, *Development*, p. 98.

40   Holderness, *British Agriculture*, p. 60.

41   I am grateful to Paul Brassley for this point.

42   Ibid. pp. 60–3; Martin, *Development*, pp. 120–5.

43   Howard Newby, *The Countryside in Question* (London, 1986) p. 6.

44   Paul Brassley, 'Output and technical change in twentieth-century British agriculture', *AHR*, Vol. 48, Pt 1, p. 71.

45   Ibid. p. 63.

46   Ibid. pp. 71–2.

47   Ibid. pp. 72–3; Martin, *Development*, pp. 112–13.

48   A detailed discussion of technical and scientific change is outside the scope of the book but see, Martin, *Development*, Ch. 5; Holderness; *British Agriculture*, Ch. 4; Q. Seddon, *The Silent Revolution. Farming and the Countryside into the Twenty-First Century* (London, 1989); K. Blaxter and N. Robertson, *From Dearth to Plenty. The Modern Revolution in Food Production* (London, 1995).

49   Brassley, 'Output and technical change', pp. 68–70. See also Paul Brassley, 'Silage in Britain, 1880–1990: The Delayed Adoption of an Innovation', *AHR*, Vol. 44, Pt 1 (1996) pp. 63–87.

50   Graham Harvey, *The Killing of the Countryside* (London, 1997) pp. 22–3.
51   Brassley, 'Output', pp. 68–9.
52   Ibid. p. 76.
53   Holderness, *British Agriculture*, p. 44–6.
54   Alun Howkins, 'Peasants, Servants and Labourers: The Marginal Workforce in British Agriculture, *c.*1870–1914', *AHR*, Vol. 42, Pt I (1994) p. 53.
55   Howard Newby *et al.*, *Property, Paternalism and Power. Class and Control in Rural England* (London, 1978).
56   Martin, *Development*, pp. 131–2.
57   Newby *et al.*, *Property*, pp. 36–7.
58   W.M. Williams, *A West Country Village. Ashworthy* (London, 1963) p. 27.
59   H. St G. Cramp, *A Yeoman Farmer's Son. A Leicestershire Childhood* (London, 1985) p. 15.
60   RHC, PF-CR PFL, AD1/2–AD1/3, Minutes of Preston Farmers' Trading Society.
61   Interview, AJH/G. and R. Smith (names changed), Axminster, Devon.
62   Quoted in Martin, *Development*, p. 123.
63   John Young, *The Farming of East Anglia* (London, 1967) pp. 22–3.
64   Tristram Beresford, *We Plough the Fields* (Harmondsworth, 1975) p. 46. For a detailed account of the NFU in this context see P. Self and H.J. Storing, *The State and the Farmer* (London, 1962).
65   Newby *et al.*, *Property*, p. 123.
66   Martin, *Development*, p. 75.
67   See J.K. Bowers, 'British Agricultural Policy', pp. 69–74.
68   Martin, *Development*, p. 133.
69   P.W. Brassley, 'The Common Agricultural Policy of the European Union', in R.J. Soffe (ed.), *The Agricultural Notebook* (19th edn, Oxford, 1995) pp. 5–16.
70   Brassley, 'The Common Agricultural Policy', p. 8.
71   Ibid.
72   See Martin, *Development*, pp. 161–6.
73   Brassley, 'The Common Agricultural Policy', p. 16.
74   Ibid. p. 7.
75   Martin, *Development*, pp. 142, 150.
76   Harvey, *The Killing*, p. 38.
77   The *Guardian*, 13 Aug. 1994, p. 19.

9   A place to work and a place to play: incomers and outgoers, 1945–90

1   Ronald F. Jessup, *Sussex* (London, 1949) p. 14.
2   J. Charles Cox, *Surrey* (London, 1952) p. xi.
3   Sussex Rural Community Council, *Tomorrow in East Sussex* (Lewes, 1946) p. 44.
4   H.F. Marks (ed. D.K. Britton), *A Hundred Years of British Food and Farming: A Statistical Survey* (London, 1989) p. 138; *Rural England. A Nation Committed to a Living Countryside* (Government White Paper) Cm 3016 (London, 1995) p. 49.
5   General Register Office, *Census 1951, England and Wales, General Report* (London, 1958) p. 82.
6   These figures are derived from the Census Returns. *Census of England and Wales 1931. Occupation Tables* (London, 1934) Table 16. *Census 1971. England and Wales. Economic Activity County of Surrey* (London, 1974). I recognise these figures are difficult to interpret but they are the only ones available which enable a comparison to be made with non-agricultural occupations.
7   John Martin, *The Development of Modern Agriculture. British Farming since 1931* (Basingstoke, 2000) p. 131.
8   Howard Newby, Colin Bell, David Rose and Peter Saunders, *Property, Paternalism and Power. Class and Control in Rural England* (London, 1978) p. 47.
9   1951 figure from *Census 1951. England and Wales. Occupation Tables* (London, 1956). The figures for 1971 from *Census 1971. Economic Activity County Leaflets* (London, 1977).
10   Alwyn D. Rees, *Life in a Welsh Countryside* (Cardiff, 1950).
11   J.G.S. Donaldson, Frances Donaldson and Derek Baker, *Farming in Britain Today* (Harmondsworth, 1972) p. 140.
12   Rees, *Life*, p. 61.

13   Ibid.
14   Ibid. pp. 142ff.
15   Ibid. pp. 93–4.
16   Ibid. p. 95.
17   Ibid. p. 168.
18   W.M. Williams, *The Sociology of an English Village: Gosforth* (London, 1956) pp. 18–19.
19   Ibid. pp. 39–40.
20   Ibid. p. 149.
21   Graham Paul Crow, 'Agricultural Rationalisation: The Fate of Family Farms in Post-War Britain', Unpublished Ph.D., University of Essex, 1981, p. 4.
22   Ibid. p. 254.
23   W.M. Williams, *A West Country Village. Ashworthy* (London, 1963).
24   Ibid. p. 27.
25   Ibid. pp. 124–37.
26   Ibid. p. 49.
27   Ibid. p. 50.
28   Ibid. p. 222.
29   Ibid. p. 243.
30   James Littlejohn, *Westrigg. The Sociology of a Cheviot Parish* (London, 1963).
31   Ibid.
32   Ibid. p. 1.
33   Ibid. p. 69.
34   Ibid. p. 6.
35   Ibid. p. 32.
36   Ibid. p. 54.
37   Ibid. pp. 32–3.
38   Ibid.
39   Ibid. pp. 28–9.
40   Ibid. pp. 71–2.
41   Newby *et al.*, *Property*.
42   Ibid. p. 213.
43   Ibid. p. 149.
44   Crow, 'Agricultural Rationalisation', p. 237.
45   1951 derived from *Census 1951. England and Wales. Occupation Tables* (London, 1956); 1971 from *Census 1971. Economic Activity Reports* (London, 1974).
46   See Alun Howkins, *Poor Labouring Men. Rural Radicalism in Norfolk 1870–1923* (London, 1985) and Howard Newby, *The Deferential Worker. A Study of the Farm Workers of East Anglia* (Harmondsworth, 1979) pp. 45–56.
47   Bob Wynn, *Skilled at All Trades. The History of the Farmworkers' Union, 1947–1984* (London, 1993) pp. 130–1.
48   Ibid. pp. 122, 130.
49   Newby, *Deferential*, p. 240.
50   *LW*, Apr. 1975.
51   Renée Danzinger, *Political Powerlessness. Agricultural Workers in Post-War England* (Manchester, 1988) p. 162.
52   Wynn, *Skilled*, p. 335.
53   See Danzinger, *Political Powerlessness*, Ch. 6 and Wynn, *Skilled*, pp. 341–55.
54   See Wynn, *Skilled*, pp. 127, 384–7.
55   Danzinger, *Political Powerlessness*, p. 142.
56   Newby, *Deferential*, p. 241.
57   Ibid. p. 310.
58   *LW*, Feb. 1975.
59   Ibid. May 1975.
60   *Census 1971. Economic Activity Reports* (London, 1974–).
61   *Census 1951. England and Wales County Report: Surrey* (London, 1954) p. xiii.
62   J.K. Bowers and Paul Cheshire, *Agriculture, the Countryside and Land Use. An Economic Critique* (London, 1983) p. 47.

63 Jo Little, 'Social class and planning policy: a study of two Wiltshire villages', in Phillip Lowe, Tony Bradley and Susan Wright (eds), *Deprivation and Welfare in Rural Areas* (Norwich, 1986) pp. 139–40.

64 Peter Ambrose, *The Quiet Revolution. Social Change in a Sussex Village 1871–1971* (London, 1974) p. 65.

65 Ralph Fevre, John Borland and David Denney, 'Nation, Community and Conflict: Housing Policy and Immigration in North Wales', in Ralph Fevre and Andrew Thompson (eds), *Nation, Identity and Social Theory. Perspectives from Wales* (Cardiff, 1999) p. 130.

66 Graham Day, 'The Rural Dimension', in David Dunkerly and Andrew Thompson (eds), *Wales Today* (Cardiff, 1999) p. 82.

67 Fevre *et al.*, 'Nation, Community', pp. 130–1.

68 Isabel Emmett, *A North Wales Village. A Social Anthropological Study* (London, 1964) pp. 119–21.

69 See John Aitchison and Harold Carter, 'The Welsh Language Today', in Dunkerly and Thomson, *Wales*.

70 Frances Oxford, 'Epilogue: Elmdon in 1977', in Marilyn Strathern, *Kinship at the Core. An Anthropology of a Village in North-West Essex in the Nineteen-Sixties* (Cambridge, 1981) p. 209.

71 Henley Centre for Forecasting figure. Quoted in the *Guardian* 27 Sept. 1995, p. 7.

72 'Goodbye to all that?', *Observer Review*, 31 Jan. 1999, p. 2.

73 Roger Tredre, 'From late shift to downshift', *Observer Life*, 12 May 1996, p. 19.

74 Ruth M. Crichton, *Commuters' Village. A Study of Community and Commuters in the Berkshire Village of Stratfield Mortimer* (London and Dawlish, 1964) p. 70.

75 Oxford, 'Epilogue', p. 221.

76 Ibid. pp. 221–2.

77 Ibid. p. 220.

78 Ibid. p. 216.

79 Newby *et al.*, *Property*, p. 203.

80 *The Observer*, 21 Jul. 1996, p. 9.

81 See Phillip Lowe, Tony Bradley and Susan Wright (eds), *Deprivation and Welfare in Rural Areas* (Norwich, 1986) pp. 19–24.

82 Figures derived from county reports for 1951 Census.

83 Wynn, *Skilled*, pp. 149–50.

84 Crichton, *Commuter*, p. 62; Strathern, *Kinship*, p. 91.

85 Rees, *Life*, p. 28.

86 The material that follows is based on J. Martin Shaw, 'The social implications of village development', in Malcolm J. Mosely (ed.), *Social Issues in Rural Norfolk* (Norwich, 1976) pp. 77–102.

87 Newby, *Deferential*, p. 343.

88 Shaw, 'Social implications', p. 83.

89 David Evans and Simon Neate, 'Policies for access to health care and the outcome in Leicestershire', in Lowe *et al.*, *Deprivation*, p. 219.

90 Evans and Neate, 'Policies for access', p. 225.

91 *The Observer*, 12 May 1996, p. 18.

92 Newby *et al.*, *Property*, pp. 201–8.

10 Defending the natural order? Environment and conservation, 1945–90

1 A basic introduction to this material can be found in John Blunden and Nigel Curry (eds), *A People's Charter? Forty Years of the National Parks and Access to the Countryside Act* (London, 1990). For a more comprehensive discussion see Gordon Cherry, *National Parks and Recreation in the Countryside* (London, 1975).

2 Quoted in John Sheail, *Nature in Trust. A History of Nature Conservation in Britain* (Glasgow and London, 1976) p. 101.

3 See Sheail, ibid. Chs 5 and 6.

4 See Blunden and Curry, *A People's Charter?*, Ch. 4.

5 Barbara Castle, *Fighting all the Way* (London, 1993) p. 172.

6 *Hansard*, 31 Mar. 1949.

7 Blunden and Curry, *A People's Charter?*, p. 87.

8 Marion Shoard, *This Land is Our Land* (London, 1987) p. 242.

9 David Evans, *A History of Nature Conservation in Britain* (London, 1992) p. 88.

10 Ibid. p. 89.

11 On footpaths and rights of way see Shoard, *This Land*, Chs 7 and 8 and Blunden and Curry, *A People's Charter?*, Ch. 6.

12 Shoard, *This Land*, pp. 333–4.

13 Quoted in Blunden and Curry, *A People's Charter?*, pp. 140–1.

14 Quoted in Shoard, *This Land*, p. 321.

15 The Countryside Agency, *The Economic Impact of Recreation and Tourism in the English Countryside 1998* (Wetherby, 2000) p. 13.

16 Keith A.H. Murray, *Agriculture, History of the Second World War*, United Kingdom Civil Series (London, 1955) p. 340.

17 There is now a considerable literature on the inter-war origins of the organic movement and its associated politics but see especially, Phillip Cornford, 'The Natural Order: Organic Husbandry, Society and Religion in Britain, 1924–53' Unpublished Ph.D. thesis, University of Reading, 2000; Tracey Clunies-Ross, 'Agricultural Change and the Politics of Organic Farming', Unpublished Ph.D. thesis, University of Bath, 1990; older and less scholarly is Anna Bramwell, *Ecology in the Twentieth Century. A History* (Newhaven and London, 1990). For an interesting insight into some of those involved see R.J. Moore-Colyer, 'Back to Basics: Rolf Gardiner, H.J. Massingham and "A Kinship in Husbandry"', *RH*, Vol. 12, No. 1, Apr. 2001.

18 See Georgina Boyes, *The Imagined Villages. Culture, Ideology and the English Folk Revival* (Manchester, 1993) pp. 154–65.

19 See Richard Moore-Colyer, *Sir George Stapledon and the Landscape of Britain (Sefydliad Astudiaethau Gwledig Cymr/Welsh Institute of Rural Studies, Working Paper No. 9)* (Aberystwyth, 1998). This paper also appears in revised form in *Environment and History*, 5 (1999).

20 Cornford, 'The Natural Order', p. 470.

21 Ibid. p. 94.

22 Quoted in Cornford, 'The Natural Order', p. 94.

23 Ibid. p. 45.

24 Clunies-Ross, 'Agricultural Change', p. 209.

25 Cornford, 'The Natural Order', p. 490.

26 Clunies-Ross, 'Agricultural Change', p. 168.

27 John Sheail, *Pesticides and Nature Conservation. The British Experience 1950–1975* (Oxford, 1985) p. 19.

28 *FW*, 11.2.1994, p. 5.

29 Marion Shoard, *The Theft of the Countryside* (London, 1980) pp. 34–41.

30 Mass Observation Archive, University of Sussex, Spring Directive 1995 (hereafter M-O 1995). I would like to thank the Trustees of the Mass Observation Archive for permission to use materials held by them.

31 M-O 1995, A18, m. Addlestone, Surrey, unemployed, b.1944.

32 Ibid. D1606, m. Attleborough, Norfolk, ret. librarian, b.1924.

33 Ibid. H1806, m. Woking, Surrey, factory worker, b.1925.

34 Graham Harvey, *The Killing of the Countryside* (London, 1997) p. 24.

35 Paul Brassley, 'Agricultural Technology and the Ephemeral Landscape', Unpublished paper 1997.

36 M-O 1995, R1452, w. Birmingham, ret. teacher, b.1916.

37 Ibid. B2170, w. Brentwood, Essex, health education officer, b.1945.

38 Ibid. C2053, w. Costessey, Norwich librarian, b.1953.

39 Ibid. F1589, w. Audley, Staffordshire, nurse, b.1932.

40 Ibid. P1282, w. Lichfield, Staffordshire, child-minder, b.1938.

41 Ibid. W2322, m. Stone, teacher, b.1944.

42 Ibid. R470, m. Basildon, lorry driver, b.1934.

43 Ibid. R1468, w. Derby, factory worker, b.1923.

44 Ibid. T540, w. Leeds, clerk, b.1927.

45 Ibid. C2717, m. Nottingham, engineer, b.1966.

46 Ibid. M1498, w. Polegate, Sussex, unemployed, b.1954.

47 Ibid. W2538, w. Cleethorpes, housewife, b.1963.

48   For the nineteenth-century history of animal welfare see Harriet Ritvo, *The Animal Estate. The English and Other Animals in the Victorian Age* (Cambridge, Mass. and London, 1987).

49   See Evans, *History of Nature Conservation*, pp. 43–4.

50   See Sheail, *Nature in Trust*, Ch. 2.

51   See Sheail, *Pesticides*, pp. 146–9.

52   See Robert Garner, *Animals, Politics and Morality* (London, 1993) for a discussion both of the changing arguments about the 'nature' of animals and the battles within the RSPCA.

53   Peter Mandler, *The Fall and Rise of the Stately Home* (New Haven and London, 1997) p. 375.

54   Ibid. p. 381.

55   Ibid. pp. 381–8.

56   Ibid. p. 393. For a (very) critical account of Neptune, and indeed of the Trust as a whole, see Paula Weideger, *Guilding the Acorn. Behind the Façade of the National Trust* (London, 1994).

57   Quoted in Mandler, *Fall and Rise*, p. 394.

58   Merlin Waterson, *The National Trust. The First Hundred Years* (London, 1994) pp. 214–15.

59   See David Pepper, *The Roots of Modern Environmentalism* (London, 1986).

60   Quoted in George McKay, *Senseless Acts of Beauty. Cultures of Resistance since the 1960s* (London, 1996) p. 128.

61   John Lowerson, 'The mystical geography of the English', in Brian Short (ed.), *The English Rural Community. Image and Analysis* (Cambridge, 1992).

62   David Pepper, *Communes and the Green Vision* (London, 1991) p. 33.

63   George McKay, *Senseless Acts of Beauty*, pp. 56–7.

64   Pepper, *Communes*, pp. 78–9.

65   For much of what follows see George McKay, *Senseless Acts of Beauty*.

66   Grant Jordan and William Maloney, *The Protest Business? Mobilizing Campaign Groups* (London, 1997) p. 12.

67   Sheail, *Pesticides*, pp. 230–2.

68   Clunies-Ross, 'Agricultural Change', p. 338.

11   The countryside in crisis, 1990–2001

1   The Countryside Agency, *The State of the Countryside 2001* (Wetherby, 2001) p. 55.

2   Graham Harvey, *The Killing of the Countryside* (London, 1997) p. 38.

3   The farm was that of Oliver Walston who made himself extremely unpopular among his fellow farmers by writing about these payments in the *Sunday Times*.

4   *The Times*, 2 Sept. 1994, p. 5.

5   Ibid. 2 Feb. 1996, p. 5.

6   Ibid. 14 Jun. 1996, p. 5.

7   Ibid. 2 Sept. 1994, p. 5.

8   The *Independent*, 28 Sept. 1991.

9   Ibid. 19 Sept. 1991.

10   *The State of the Countryside, 2001*, p. 49.

11   Department of the Environment/MAFF, *Rural England. A Nation Committed to a Living Countryside*, Cm 3016 (London, 1975) p. 70.

12   The *Guardian*, 6 Sept. 2001, p. 4.

13   *The State of the Countryside, 2001*, pp. 47–9.

14   *FW*, 2 Feb. 1996, p. 5.

15   *The State of the Countryside, 2001*, pp. 61–2.

16   Friends of the Lake District, *Traffic in the Lake District, 1964*, quoted in Garth Christian, *Tomorrow's Countryside. The Road to the Seventies* (London, 1966) p. 141.

17   George McKay, *Senseless Acts of Beauty. Cultures of Resistance since the Sixties* (London, 1996) p. 136.

18   Quoted in ibid. p. 136.

19   The *Guardian*, 7 Dec. 1994, G2 p. 24.

20   Quoted in McKay, *Senseless Acts*, pp. 143–4.

21   Alexandra Plows, 'The Donga Tribe: Practical Paganism Comes Full Circle', *Creative Mind*, No. 27, summer 1995, p. 26.

22   *New Statesman and Society*, 27 Jan. 1995, cover.

23 For a more detailed account of this campaign and the issues it raised see Alun Howkins and Linda Merricks, '"Dewy'eyed veal calves". Live animal exports and middle-class opinion, 1980–1995', *AHR*, Vol. 48, Pt 1, 2000.

24 See a very brief mention in Hilda Kean, 'The "Smooth Cool Men of Science": The Feminist and Socialist Response to Vivisection', *History Workshop Journal*, No. 40, autumn 1995, p. 30.

25 Compassion in World Farming, from Meat and Livestock Commission data.

26 The *Independent*, 20 Aug. 1994.

27 *Agscene*, No. 112, autumn 1993, pp. 4–5.

28 *The Times*, 20 Apr. 1995.

29 Ibid.

30 *Agscene*, No. 116, winter 1994, p. 4.

31 Ibid. 5 Aug. 1994, p. 7.

32 Ibid. 19 Aug. 1994 p. 5; 2 Sept. 1994, p. 7.

33 The *Guardian*, 24 Oct. 1995.

34 See *Evening Argus*, 20 Jan. 1995 for the 'history' of the campaign.

35 *Evening Gazette*, 18 Jan. 1995.

36 The *Sunday Times*, 8 Jan. 1995.

37 *Guardian*, 'Outlook', 7 Jan. 1995.

38 *Evening Argus*, 20 Jan. 1995.

39 *Evening Gazette*, 18 Jan. 1995.

40 *The Times*, 16 Jan. 1995.

41 The *Observer*, 8 Jan. 1995.

42 M-O 1995, R1389, m. 81, Brighton, ret. policeman.

43 M-O 1995, B1512, w. 61, Sheffield, teacher.

44 M-O 1995, B2260, w. 47, Waterford, librarian.

45 M-O 1995, H1263, w. 46, Warwick, secretary.

46 M-O 1995, T2741, m. 74, Peacehaven, Sussex, ret. carpenter.

47 *FW*, 13 Jan. 1995, p. 5.

48 M-O 1995, C1713, w. 46, Preston, receptionist.

49 M-O 1995, H1806, m. 69, Surrey, typesetter ret.

50 Kevin Toolis, 'Epidemic in Waiting', the *Guardian Weekend*, 22 Sept. 2001, p. 22.

51 Quoted in the *Guardian*, 27 Oct. 2000.

52 Ibid.

53 The Royal Society, *Update on BSE* (London, Jul. 1997) p. 2.

54 The *Guardian*, 21 Mar. 2000.

55 The Southwood Report quoted in Vegetarian Society Press Release, 5 Dec. 1994.

56 Toolis in the *Guardian Weekend*, 22 Sept. 2001, p. 22.

57 Ibid. p. 22.

58 See *Times Higher Education Supplement*, 19 Apr. 1996, pp. 16–17.

59 These stories have been widely reported in the press since 1996 and have never been challenged. See the *Guardian*, 24 Mar. 1996, p. 23; John Lloyd, 'The Great Carve-up', *New Statesman and Society*, 17 May 1996, pp. 15–17.

60 The *Guardian*, 21 Mar. 1996, p. 6.

61 Ibid. 6 Dec. 1996, p. 3.

62 The *Observer*, 10 Dec. 1996.

63 Ibid.

64 The *Sun*, 26 Mar. 1996.

65 The *Observer*, 24 Mar. 1996.

66 The *Guardian*, 23 Mar. 1996.

67 Ibid. 28 Mar. 1996.

68 The *Guardian*, 24 Nov. 1998.

69 Ibid. 27 Oct. 2000.

70 Ibid.

71 Christina Hardyment, *Slice of Life. The British Way of Eating since 1945* (London, 1995) p. 162.

72 Ibid. p. 164.

73 The *Observer*, 31 Mar. 1996.

74 John Humphries, *The Great Food Gamble* (London, 2001) p. 237.

75　<http://www.soilassociation.org.uk>

76　*The State of the Countryside 2001*, pp. 22–3.

77　Ibid. p. 55 and Andrew O'Hagan, *The Death of British Farming* (London, 2001) p. 11.

78　*The Times*, 17 Nov. 1995.

79　*FW*, 17 Nov. 1995, p. 8.

80　The *Guardian*, 3 Mar. 1998.

81　The *Observer*, 15 Oct. 2000.

82　The *Guardian*, 9 Jul. 1995; see also Alun Howkins, 'Rurality and English Identity', in David Morley and Kevin Robins (eds), *British Cultural Studies. Geography, Nationality and Identity* (Oxford, 2001).

83　The *Daily Telegraph*, 2 Mar. 1998.

84　Text of speech, Press Association News, 1 Feb. 2000.

85　The *Observer*, 15 Oct. 2000.

86　*Our Countryside: The Future. A Fair Deal for Rural England*, Cm 4909 (London, 2000) p. 140.

87　For a brief history see Paul Brassley, 'Foot-and-Mouth Disease in the Past', in *Rural History Today*, Issue 1, Jul. 2001, pp. 3–4.

88　*Foot-and-Mouth Disease 2001: Lessons to be Learned Inquiry Report*. Chairman Dr Ian Anderson. Presented to the Prime Minister and the Secretary of State for Environment, Food and Rural Affairs, and the devolved administrations of Scotland and Wales, 22 Jul. 2002 (London, 2002) p. 8.

89　The *Guardian*, 22 Feb. 2001.

90　*Lessons to be Learned*, p. 8.

91　Neil M. Ferguson, Christi A. Donnelly and Roy M. Anderson, 'Transmission intensity and impact of control policies on the foot-and-mouth epidemic in Great Britain', *Nature*, 4 Oct. 2001, p. 544.

92　Ibid. p. 544.

93　The *Guardian*, 24 Feb. 2001.

94　Ibid. 26 Feb. 2001.

95　*Lessons to be Learned*, pp. 8–9.

96　The *Guardian*, 24 Mar. 2001.

97　Ferguson *et al.*, 'Transmission intensity', p. 542.

98　Ibid. p. 543.

99　Ibid. p. 545.

100　*Lessons to be Learned*, p. 9.

101　The *Observer*, 4 Mar. 2001.

102　The *Guardian*, 23 Jul. 2002.

103　*Lessons to be Learned*, p. 9.

104　The *Guardian*, 19 Mar. 2001.

105　Ibid. 31 Mar. 2001.

106　Ibid. 23 Jul. 2002.

107　*Lessons to be Learned*, p. 10.

108　The *Guardian*, 7 Mar. 2001.

109　From 'The Editor' section of the *Guardian*, 6 Apr. 2001.

110　From 'The Editor' section of the *Guardian*, 30 Mar. 2001.

111　Speech given at Labour Party Conference, 3 Oct. 2001.
　　　Source: <http://www.labour.org.uk>

112　*Farming and Food: A Sustainable Future. Report of the Policy Committee on the Future of Farming and Food* (London, 2002).

113　<http://www.guardian.co.uk/country> 'Food and farming policy commission report: main points'.

114　From 'The Editor' section of the *Guardian*, 23 Mar. 2001.

Index